Travel with Babies & Young Children

written and researched by

Fawzia Rasheed de Francisco

ROUGH
GUID

www.roughgu

Contents

Chapter 3: BEING THERE 124

Chapter 4: AROUND THE WORLD 174

SMALL PRINT 215

INDEX 220

Introduction

All parents need the break from routine that a holiday offers, but the idea of getting away from it all with your kids in tow can seem anything but relaxing, particularly if you've not done it before. There's a lot to be said for taking the plunge, though. The slower pace that children demand ensures you really get under the skin of the places you visit, and having kids along makes a noticeable difference to how people interact with you. But more than that, travel almost always has positive effects on the whole family: children's natural capacity to stop, be absorbed and play tends to cross over to adults once we're freed from the pressures of daily life, and this paves the way for some truly fantastic moments together. And no matter how young your children are – even if they only remember your trips through the stories you tell them and the photos in the albums – the impact of travel on their view of the world and sense of self-worth becomes ever more tangible as they get older. And for the adults, travel allows you time to pause and reflect – something that's rarely possible when at home.

There's no denying that going away with children isn't always straightforward, but the key to making it work is to be well prepared. You'll need more than the usual dose of common sense, though, as travel with kids demands quite a different approach than for an adults-only jaunt. Finding out what makes for smooth sailing and what doesn't is a matter of trial and error – and my "qualification" for writing this book is that I've travelled extensively with my family: my sons took their first international flights when they were just a few weeks old, and my eldest

REFLECTIONS

"Looking back on my 84 years of life, extensive travels on my own, with my children, and more recently with my grandchildren – I come up with a number of observations: The first is how exceptionally fortunate those of us that can travel are. The second relates to life itself. Some say that you can't possibly relate meaningfully to the present without knowing the future. I've given that a lot of thought; and while I see the logic of having a vision of the future to drive what we do today, I can't entirely agree. There are many moments when we are completely and meaningfully engaged in the present – particularly when travelling, and all the more so when with children, where knowledge of the future just doesn't seem to matter. But even if it does, I suppose being in the midst of children offers precious knowledge of and insights in to the future. Either way, when journeying with children, you feel you are living life to the full. Living right. I derive immense pleasure from such memories."

Dr Halfdan Mahler, Director General Emeritus, World Health Organization

TRAVELLERS' TALES

celebrated his first birthday on his fifth continent. The motivation to write about what I learned was partly to answer repeated requests for advice, but also because I've watched many parents discover that once they began to travel, they wished they'd started earlier or done it differently. So if you're paralyzed with the typical "what if?" questions (will the children adapt to new places, eat the food, get dicky tummies or lost amongst hordes of sightseers), or plagued with images of in-flight tantrums or toppling mounds of luggage, this book should give you the ammunition you need to be able to breeze through the challenges and enjoy the good bits. And to make sure it provides the best possible advice, we've enlisted the help of parents and people in travel-related industries, all of whom lent their experience and expertise; and throughout the book, the text is tailored to the needs of single parents and children with special needs as well as couples travelling with kids.

Once you've made the decision to go away with your children, you'll find that getting organized to leave is always the hardest part. But as soon as you're on your way, travel invariably works its magic, slowing things down, freeing you up to really enjoy yourselves, and throwing light on what's important: fewer and fewer things seem to matter, and those that do matter more. One thing's for sure, though: you and your children will retain the benefits of travel long after you return home.

HOW TO USE THIS BOOK

We've divided this book into four parts to make it easy to find the information you need. **Preparation** covers all the pre-departure steps, from getting your jabs and planning your itinerary to keeping costs down and booking accommodation that suits your needs, as well as what to take, how best to stow it all in your bags, and get it there without slipping a disc. **Making the Journey** has practical tips on how to handle plane, car, bus and train journeys with your kids, as well as general advice on things like motion sickness and keeping the peace. **Being There** tells you how to get the best out of your time away, whether you're going on a beach holiday or a camping trip. As well as basic things like child-proofing your rooms, keeping clean and using public transport, we've also suggested ways to handle the things that go wrong, from insect bites to getting separated or too much attention from the people you meet. Finally, to give you a taster of what to expect in your destination, **Around the World** gives a region-by-region summary of practical insights to make your journey easier, from whether you can get baby formula in Polynesia to the question of breastfeeding in the Middle East.

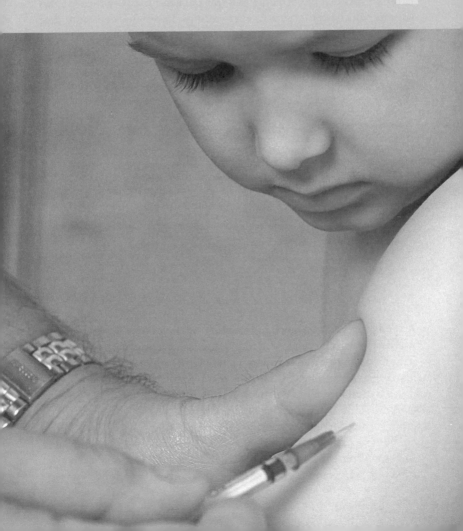

PREPARATION 1

PREPARATION

As everything takes that bit longer with children around, it's best to start **preparations** for your trip as early as possible. If you're planning a long-haul journey to somewhere unfamiliar, allow for a few months to get organized; shorter holidays to places you know or conventional "tourist" destinations are simpler to prepare for, but you should still give yourself plenty of time. This section runs through all of the steps you need to prepare yourselves for leaving, and we've given **checklists** to help you summarize what needs to be done and what to take; the latter are distilled into a single **general packing list** at the end of this section, which you can use to check things off as your departure date draws near.

PUTTING YOURSELF FIRST

When planning a trip with your family, there's a natural tendency to focus all your energies around your children's needs: making sure they remain healthy and safe, and have a good time. While this is natural enough, it's easy to take it too far and end up not giving yourself a second thought – but this is a mistake. Don't let yourself forget that the number one priority is you – and this applies whether the issue is health, safety or general well-being. If you're tired or ill, it's easy to let important things slip, or just not be much fun to be around; if all is well with you, you'll be in a better position to look after others. And if you're positively cheerful, the chances are your children will be, too. As well as considering the kids, reflect on what works for you, both when planning your trip and when you're there. Try not to take on more than you can manage, and make a point of accounting for your needs – after all, it's your trip too!

PLANNING YOUR TRIP

As grabbing your passport and heading off in a burst of spontaneous wanderlust is something you're unlikely to attempt with kids, some **itinerary planning** is both inevitable and worthwhile. If this is your first trip with your children, plan for a slower pace than you might usually attempt. Single-destination trips are the most popular kind of family holiday given the ease of the logistics, but if you want to see more than one place, be realistic about what you can cover with little ones in tow. The less you feel you have to pack in, the more enjoyable and stress-free the holiday – and you'll be better able to take the odd day indoors in your stride if the weather is bad or the kids need to rest.

The pre-departure countdown

Three months before travelling
- ❏ Decide on where and when to go
- ❏ Decide who to go with, and discuss expectations ▶▶ p.10
- ❏ Check health and security information for your destination ▶▶ pp.24, 34
- ❏ Ensure passports (and photos in them) are valid ▶▶ p.41
- ❏ Check visa requirements
- ❏ Research tickets and hold reservations
- ❏ Estimate your budget
- ❏ Book appointments with your doctor, dentist or optician ▶▶ p.34
- ❏ Seek clearance to miss school ▶▶ p.12
- ❏ Apply for international driving licence
- ❏ Prepare papers related to special medical needs ▶▶ p.45
- ❏ Prepare consent to travel papers ▶▶ p.42
- ❏ Purchase and test equipment ▶▶ p.56

Two months before travelling
- ❏ Buy tickets
- ❏ Visit a travel health clinic, and start vaccinations ▶▶ p.34
- ❏ Apply for visas ▶▶ p.41
- ❏ Research travel insurance ▶▶ p.44
- ❏ Research and book accommodation ▶▶ p.24
- ❏ Research logistics/availability of supplies in your destination
- ❏ Check credit card limits ▶▶ p.23

One month before travelling
- ❏ Research healthcare in your destination ▶▶ p.41
- ❏ Take out travel insurance ▶▶ p.44
- ❏ Start planning clothing to take ▶▶ p.49
- ❏ Organize medical kit ▶▶ p.39
- ❏ Advise your bank of travel plans and get numbers for reporting lost/stolen cards
- ❏ Get some local currency
- ❏ Copy essential documents to take and leave with friends ▶▶ p.45
- ❏ Make arrangements for someone to look after or check your home while you're away
- ❏ Pay any bills due whilst you'll be away
- ❏ Decide what toys and games to bring ▶▶ p.69
- ❏ Go over logistics with your hosts (if applicable) ▶▶ p.79

One or two weeks before travelling
- ❏ Start packing ▶▶ p.45
- ❏ Start taking antimalarials ▶▶ p.37
- ❏ Leave copies of documents with friends
- ❏ Organize handover of your home ▶▶ p.81
- ❏ Check and buy toiletries and supplies for the trip ▶▶ p.56

Three days before travelling
- ❏ Buy food for simple no-cook meals ▶▶ p.81
- ❏ Do final laundry
- ❏ Reconfirm flight/taxis
- ❏ Finalize packing

Similarly, be flexible in terms of how you'll spend your days; an adults-only group might walk straight through a market, but kids might discover reams of things to keep them happy and want to linger.

Guidebooks tend to have very little information tailored to travelling with children, so if you want to find out about things like availability of baby supplies or child-friendly activities, or have general questions to help you choose your destination, you might try one of the **online travel discussion forums** listed below, which have designated sections on travel with kids; you can post your own questions, or just browse earlier threads. Just bear in mind that the information can be a bit hit-and-miss, and queries might not be picked up by someone in the know straight away (or at all).

Finally, one general thing to bear in mind when it comes to **buying tickets** is flexibility. The greater the number of people you travel with, the higher the chances that something might prompt a change of plan, so where possible go for tickets that are **re-routable** and **fully refundable**, enabling you to change plans without buying new ones.

TRAVEL DISCUSSION FORUMS

Rough Guides Travel Talk @roughguides.evecommunity.com/eve/forums
Lonely Planet's Thorn Tree @http://thorntree.lonelyplanet.com
Family Travel Board @www.familytravelboards.com
Bootsnall @http://boards.bootsnall.com/eve
PinPointTravel @http://www.pinpointtravel.com/h/chatter/forums/family

WHO TO GO WITH

One of the most important factors in planning a successful holiday with kids is **who you travel with**. If you're going to be the sole adult, bear in mind that you'll probably welcome having someone else with you, particularly if the journey there will be long or the destination is unfamiliar. Sharing tasks and having one person able to stay with the children while the other does something else helps with peace of mind and allows everyone to have some valuable time out.

If you're asking other adults to join you, do remember that keeping everyone happy isn't always easy, and travel can have a make-or-break impact on friendships. Not everyone comes in the Mary Poppins mould, and many people (regardless of whether they're parents themselves) get impatient with the slow pace of travel with children, as well as the limits kids set on what you can do. So before asking someone to come along, think about how they'd fit in with your family – it helps if you've already spent time with the kids together so that they have

PERFECT COMPANY

"Having sailed around the world a few times as a skipper and introduced many youngsters to sailing through my work with the Ahoy Centre, I feel I know a thing or two about choosing the right travel companions. After all, the ultimate test has to be being on a boat together for weeks on end.

While you can never predict how things will turn out, I've come to know this: having someone with a sense of humour – and having a fair dose of the same yourself – is priceless. Fortunately for me, the past six years have been absolutely wonderful – there have been no problems with travel mates whatsoever, as I've found the perfect person to go with: my six year old daughter (and best buddy) Mackenna. She's a great travelling companion because she actually enjoys the process of travel as much as the destination, which makes us very similar. We both prefer trains, buses and ferries to planes, and I think it's because we both enjoy the sense of journeying miles to another place rather than just seeing different airports! However, we do of course spend a lot of time in different airports, but this is no problem, either. Mack is a calm, gentle, sociable little person and even when I'm in a panic she remains serene. She strikes up conversations with anyone and everyone, young, old, male, female, black, white or brown and we often make friends of fellow travellers who find her enthusiasm and confidence an irresistible mixture.

I remember being on a long-distance flight with her once, when there was a screaming child a few seats in front of us. The child was almost apoplectic and the poor mother was becoming increasingly distressed as she sensed the glares and outright hostility of the some of the other passengers.

Mack grabbed a pop-up book and her favourite teddy and without any encouragement from me marched up to the child and gave her the teddy and the book. It was like instantly turning off the volume! She stayed there and entertained both the child and the mother for at least half an hour until the child fell asleep. Then she came back and sat down without a word. Almost every single person on the plane was beaming at her! I was so very proud to be her mum. She's a wonderful little person who enjoys every new experience, and because she's a people-person, it's not only me that sees that. She is the perfect travelling companion."

Tracy Edwards, round-the-world skipper and ambassador for the UK's National Society for the Prevention of Cruelty to Children

an idea of what it means to do things like get the children up and out each morning, and can handle the stop-start pace thereafter. And if you're the kind of person who likes planning every detail or prefer to play things by ear, it helps if your companion is of a similar mindset. **Travelling with other families** has particular advantages. You can take turns looking after the children, which allows everyone some valuable time out, and you have a ready-made set of playmates (perhaps even babysitters) for your children.

But whoever you go with – even if it's your partner – it's important to be frank about **expectations**. Before you go, discuss what each person wants to do, agree how to split chores or take turns minding the children, and talk about the balance of spending time together and apart. If you're going to be together most of the time, it helps if your budgets are similar – difficulties can easily arise if one adult feels they have to watch the purse-strings or spend more than they want to for the other's sake. Equally, come to an agreement about the way you'll split the bills (taking into account the smaller share of expenditures for the children); overlooking this can lead to misunderstandings. Finally, be prepared for the fact that one consequence of friends taking responsibility for your children is that they might dole out the odd bit of criticism – so pass on a hint that this can be a sore point, but be ready to take it in your stride.

HOW MUCH TIME TO TAKE

Holidays never feel long enough, but when you're travelling with young children, it's all the more important to **be realistic about what you can do** – flying halfway around the world for a trip of less than a week clearly isn't a great idea. The less time you have away, the more important it is to book accommodation, plan what you want to do and arrange transport in advance; leave it till you arrive and you'll waste precious holiday time sorting out things you could easily have done from home.

Bear in mind that **arriving** usually takes up half a day, what with finding the place you're staying, getting settled in and taking some time to recharge. **Leaving** can take even longer, from the packing (and trying to fit in all the things you've bought), to paying of bills and saying goodbyes. You may also need to factor in **jetlag**; if you're crossing six or more time zones, you'll need to take things slowly for the first few days, and expect to spend quite a lot of time sleeping at odd hours – which effectively means not planning too much or straying too far from base. Also bear in mind that with kids, hectic days are generally followed by a slow start the next morning, so allow time to take things easy from time to time. Similarly, set aside time for you all to get some exercise after being cooped up in cars or indoors.

TAKING TIME OFF SCHOOL

In most instances, you'll need **permission** to take children out of school during term time. It can be hard to get authorization, but the more you know about the criteria for granting permission, the better you can frame the request. In general, absences are granted in the following **exceptional circumstances**: a short-term post of a parent abroad;

PERMISSION GRANTED

"Getting time off school legitimately got increasingly difficult as the children grew older. And yet, in response to the (second, third, fourth?) request asking that the children be allowed to accompany us on another expedition, the Director of Education for Gwynedd wrote to us conceding once again. In his letter, he said that he had no hesitation whatsoever in granting permission, and that his decision was based on the fact that the children seemed to be managing perfectly well to keep up with schoolwork. He went on to ask if would we consider allowing him to accompany us this time! We still treasure this letter. He understood that there are many facets of education, and that the children were doing just fine travelling with us."

Alan Heason

returning to your country of origin for compelling family reasons (such as a wedding or funeral); the period immediately after an illness or accident; the serious illness of a family member or close friend; or a domestic crisis which causes disruption or the need for temporary relocation. It's highly unlikely that the authorities will accept requests based on the availability of cheaper tickets or accommodation, and the older your child, the more likely it is that rigid procedures will apply.

THINKING THROUGH THE JOURNEY

As far as getting there is concerned, it pays to think through each stage of the journey. Ask yourself these questions:

▶ Will the trip coincide with rush-hour traffic, or mean long periods without toilets or food?

▶ Are you going to be at the airport in the early hours of the morning, and if so, how are the children likely to cope?

▶ If you're making a connection, how will you get from one place to the other in time with the luggage and children? Will you need to get paid assistance with bags, or book a taxi?

▶ What are the conditions likely to be during transit stops, and should you take extra supplies?

▶ Will you need to sleep during stops, and will it be safe to do so?

▶ If you arrive early in the morning, can you check into your room straight away or will you have to wait somewhere with the children until midday?

▶ Will catching an evening flight on your way back mean you have to pay for an extra day in your hotel?

If the answers to any of these questions throw up a problem, start researching alternative routes.

PLANNING ACTIVITIES

It's always worth investing in a good **guide book** before you go. There aren't many that are tailor-made for children, but as long as you have websites, telephone numbers and opening times for the major sights, you can find out in advance about the availability of toilets and food, or whether things like long waits in lines are likely. There's more advice on planning days out on p.134, but in general, it's important to be flexible when you've got young children with you. Try to postpone buying tickets for events or attractions until the last possible moment, when you can be reasonably sure you can use them.

PLANNING CONSIDERATIONS FOR SINGLE PARENTS

The principles of planning time away as a **lone parent** are the same as if you're going with other adults – it all boils down to recognizing your limits and what you want from your holiday. The chances are that you'll appreciate the occasional bit of help with the children, as well as some time out for yourself, preferably not in the context of "couples only" situations where you might feel awkward or excluded if you're on your own. The best start is, of course, to choose a **child-friendly destination** – in Spain, for example, taking your children to restaurants in the evenings is very much the done thing, and this kind of atmosphere makes it much easier for you and the children to have fun together.

To make sure you get time to pursue your own interests, it helps if the **place you stay** takes care of the basics such as food (see p.28 for more on this), and provides supervised recreation for children, and possibly babysitting too. You don't need to book yourself into an all-inclusive *Club Med*-type resort, with every imaginable activity laid on, but when you consider how easy such places make it for parents and children to have a good time, the appeal is obvious. In general, look for accommodation with things like swimming pools, kids' clubs or games rooms, while places with restaurants and in-house bars or clubs make it easier to meet other adults. And if your base happens to coordinate the odd group excursion or activity, all the better; many parents find it easiest to link up with like-minded people if they sign up for a few trips. Group camps or leisure cruises, with entertainment, facilities and supervision for children laid on, are particular favourites for single parents.

Finally, bear in mind that if you're worried that you won't be able to manage certain phases of the trip on your own, you can always get

help – though you may have to pay for it, of course. If you have a lot of luggage, you could have it sent on by a delivery company (see p.45); while asking a friend to come with you, paying a porter or arranging for a pickup can make checking in to flights or arriving at your destination a lot less daunting.

Tailor-made holidays

Increasingly, the holiday industry is recognizing **single parents** as a niche market, and there are lots of packages specifically tailored to what you're likely to want. As well as making sure the basics are taken care of, lots of these enable you to do some pre-trip networking with other parents heading to the same place as you: you subscribe to their web page

HOLIDAY RESOURCES FOR SINGLE PARENTS

Global

ⓦ **www.smallfamilies.co.uk** A wide range of all-inclusive holidays for single parent families to destinations worldwide, mostly departing from the UK. Holidays come with "escorts" – not quite a babysitter, but someone to help with coordination.

ⓦ **www.sptc.org.uk** Low-cost holidays in the UK, the USA and Europe organized by members, as well as facilities for networking and swapping information before you go. You pay a fee to join, and membership is open to non-UK residents.

ⓦ **www.responsibletravel.com** Travel packages for single parent families.

ⓦ **www.mangokids.co.uk** All-inclusive holidays including camping and hostel stays as well as cottages and lodges, with a coordinator to sort out activities for the kids. You can join from anywhere in the world, and purchase your own airline tickets if you want.

UK

ⓦ **www.gingerbread.org.uk** Association for single-parent families with facilities for linking up with others and sharing resources for going on holiday.

ⓦ **www.helphols.co.uk** UK-based charity offering low-cost and subsidized holidays in conjunction with major companies in the UK and Spain for lone parents (including wives of prisoners and with husbands in the forces on active duty abroad) and their children. Membership is £5/$10 a year.

ⓦ **www.oneparentfamilies.org.uk**. Maintains a list of agencies that offer reasonably priced and subsidized holidays for single-parent families, as well as ideas for getting financial help if you need it.

USA and Canada

ⓦ **www.singleparenttravel.net** General advice for single parents, but with a limited number of prearranged holidays on offer too.

Australia, New Zealand and South Africa

ⓦ **www.singleparents.org.nz** Single parent forum, useful for coordinating events and joint holidays.

ⓦ **singletravel.co.za** Specializes in travel for single people (including parents and their children) within South Africa. Some inspiring trips, though few of the options are suitable for young children.

HOLIDAYING AS A SINGLE PARENT

"The mix of excitement and trepidation at embarking upon my first holiday as the newly single mum of a 6- and an 8-year-old were experienced in pretty equal measures. I had been working hard, as Executive Producer of various animation series, such as Bob the Builder, and decided to reward my little family with a Big Adventure. Looking back I can't believe that I chose somewhere as seriously foreign as Kenya for our debut solo destination. A country that needed complicated visas, unwelcome injections, unpalatable malaria pills and a lorry-load of high-strength anti-mozzie sprays. What was I thinking?

But it wasn't like we were going trekking through the African plains with only a couple of hyenas as company. Actually, it was one of those luxurious all-inclusive hotels on a beautiful white sandy beach, with waiters to serve you drinks under the swaying palms. And it didn't disappoint. So many new sights, sounds, smells, just in the hotel – tropical birds, monkeys, and even a family of chameleons – it was all so breathtakingly beautiful and exotic.

There was only one blot on this tropical idyll. A blot that I would never have envisaged (and probably just as well or it might have put me off): loneliness. The kids quickly made friends with other children in the hotel, but I had absolutely no one to talk to. Every evening after dinner the kids would hare off to play whilst I would find somewhere quiet to have a glass of wine and read a book. It's hard sitting reading whilst all around you are groups of cosy couples laughing and chatting. I was a total anomaly in this hotel world and they didn't know what to make of me. I could see the distrust in some women's eyes, convinced I was only there to steal their husbands.

Although I love chatting away to my kids, after a week I was getting desperate for an adult to talk to, and I decided to try harder. I began smiling inanely at fellow diners, swimmers and sunbathers. People may have occasionally smiled back, but one smile does not a stimulating conversation make. I remember pathetically trying to bribe the kids with chocolate to sit and play Uno with me one evening.

Eventually, the ice broke when we joined a dozen or so fellow guests on a two-day safari. The shared excitement at seeing elephants, giraffes and even a lion created a camaraderie. Whilst watching the wildlife, they'd also had a chance to inspect the unusual beast in their midst. When we returned to the hotel, I was soon invited to join those groups of laughing, drinking adults. And whilst some were so tedious that I soon scurried back to my book, others were charming and fun. Soon I was one of the laughing, chatting after-dinner crowd, too. The tom-toms had sent out the message that I wasn't a threat – their husbands were safe.

I have wonderful memories of those holidays in Kenya, and subsequent ones in Mexico and the Caribbean, but each holiday started out in exactly the same lonely way. Now my kids are teenagers, I've decided that next Easter we'll do it again one last time before they refuse to holiday with me anymore. And it'll have to be Kenya again, where it all started. But this time, I won't have the "first week" problem as I'll be bringing two perfectly charming, highly talkative young adults with me."

Kate Fawkes, ambassador for the National Council for One Parent Families and post a suggestion of what you'd like to do, and see who else signs up. Alternatively, you can sign up to someone else's idea or a ready package on offer; everyone can swap profiles, which helps with breaking the ice and meeting people who seem interesting – so avoiding that "if only we'd met earlier" feeling. Internet searches usually throw up loads of companies offering this kind of thing; you can also get in touch with national networks listed on p.15 and see what they recommend – many have links to some of the best tour companies, as well as networking facilities which lend themselves to teaming up for joint holidays, too.

PLANNING CONSIDERATIONS FOR SPECIAL NEEDS

If your children have **special needs**, you might want to start off by talking to other parents whose children have similar conditions, and who may have useful travel tips – try ⊛www.disabledfriends.com or ⊛www.youreable.com. The former specializes in creating friendships around the globe to share views, news and information, while the latter has a "penpal" facility which you can use to the same effect – both potentially very useful for destination research.

When **choosing your destination**, bear in mind that while non-industrialized countries have less in the way of tailor-made facilities, it's often easier to afford help; tickets aside, a bungalow in Tanzania with a cook/cleaner and a nurse as well as a hired car and chauffeur may well cost less than an equivalent period in Europe staying in B&Bs. Do give some thought to the reactions your children will get from people in your destination, though – it might be that people with obvious mental and physical disabilities are likely to get unwelcome attention, which can be unsettling for you all. If this might be an issue, try to limit time in crowds: perhaps arrange for a pickup at the airport, and go for small-scale accommodation rather than busy, sprawling resorts.

Some transport companies – airlines in particular – have guidelines

MEDICALERT BRACELETS

Australia Level 2, 216 Greenhill, Eastwood, SA 5063 ☎1-800/882 222, ⊛www.medicalert.com.au
Canada 2005 Sheppard Avenue East, Suite 800, Toronto, Ontario M2J 5B4 ☎1-800/668 1507, ⊛www.medicalert.ca
South Africa 5th Floor, AON House, Hertzog Boulevard, Foreshore, Cape Town 8001 ☎021/425 7328, ⊛www.medicalert.org
UK 1 Bridge Wharf, 156 Caledonian Road, London N1 9UU ☎020/7833 3034 or ☎0800/581420, ⊛www.medicalert.org.uk
USA 2323 Colorado Avenue, Turlock, CA 95382 ☎1-888/633 4298, ⊛www.medicalert.org

TRAVEL RESOURCES FOR CHILDREN WITH SPECIAL NEEDS

UK

RADAR ☎020/7250 3222, ⊛www. radar.org.uk. The UK-based Royal Association for Disability and Rehabilitation gives advice on holidays and travel with disabilities, and guides to various destinations. Publications include *Children First: A Guide to Services and Holidays in Britain and Ireland: A Guide For Disabled People*, which includes over 1500 listings and details of services and facilities. RADAR also provides keys which unlock over 7000 locked public toilets around the UK as well as a guide to tell you where they are: the key and the book come to less than £15.

Disabled Persons Transport Advisory Committee (DPTAC) ⊛www .dptac.gov.uk/door-to-door. The online version of RADAR's guide for disabled people to holiday accommodation in Britain and Ireland.

Holiday Care ☎0845/124 9971 or ☎020/8760 0072, ⊛www.holidaycare .org.uk. Some information on financial support available for holidays as well as lists of accessible accommodation within Europe, America and other destinations.

Motability ☎0845/456 4566, ⊛www .motability.co.uk. Provides accessible cars, powered wheelchairs and scooters.

National Autistic Society ☎020/7833 2299, ⊛www.nas.org.uk. Maintains a list of places to stay that work with autism and related disabilities, in the UK, USA and elsewhere.

USA

Society for Accessible Travel and Hospitality ☎212/447 7284, ⊛www .sath.org. Information on pre-packaged trips, including cruises – search on "children" to navigate to the right place on the site.

Kids Camps ☎561/443 2924, ⊛www

and restrictions for passengers with disabilities. Ask when booking your tickets; they'll want to be assured that you can look after yourselves, or have the necessary support if you can't. If you'll need to use specialized electrical equipment on planes, airlines might need to check that it won't interfere with the aircraft circuits. Getting a test scheduled and receiving clearance to travel can take months, so start off the process as early as you can; call the airline's head office to locate the right person to talk to, and take it one step at a time. Equally, if anyone in the family has a metal implant, be sure to take along x-rays and a doctor's letter verifying this; these will help get through security checks smoothly and avoid delays.

Finally, getting an **identity bracelet** that has details of your child's medical condition, treatment and their doctor or clinic's name is useful in case of emergencies; some sources are listed in the box on p.17. Similarly if anyone has serious **allergies**, you might want them to travel with a card which specifies, in the language of your destination, what they're allergic to and how serious the condition is – useful both in restaurants and for emergencies. Allergy UK (⊛www.allergyuk.org) produce cards in 27 different languages.

.kidscamps.com. State-by-state directory of children's camps around the USA which suit a broad range of special need.
Centers for Disease Control and Prevention (CDC) ⓦwww.cdc.gov /travel/spec_needs. Basic information on travelling if you have special needs, and useful lists of resources.

Australia and New Zealand
Australian Council for Rehabilitation of the Disabled (ACROD) PO Box 60, Curtin ACT 2605 ⓣ02/6282 4333, ⓦwww.acrod.org.au. Lists travel agencies and other operators that manage tours for people with disabilities.
Disabled Persons Assembly 4/173–175 Victoria St, Wellington, New Zealand ⓣ04/801 9100, ⓦwww.dpa. org.nz. Lists travel agencies and tour operators.

Tour companies
Access-Able ⓦwww.access-able .com. Information on contacts, worldwide tours and other resources for people with special needs.
Disability Travel ⓦwww .disabilitytravel.com. Specializes in wheelchair travel and group tours.
Flamingo Tours and Disabled Ventures ⓣ027/215 574 496, ⓦwww .flamingotours.co.za. Specializes in accessible tours to nature reserves in South Africa.
Moss Rehab Hospital ⓦwww .mossresourcenet.org. An excellent resource for finding travel agents around the world that specialize in holidays for the physically and mentally challenged.
Trips Special Adventures ⓦwww .tripsinc.com. Trips in the USA and Europe for people with physical and mental disabilities.

Getting help at airports

If you need to arrange **special assistance** from either airline or airport staff, whether it's help with carrying things or organizing a wheelchair, be prepared to spend some time on the phone; while the websites of major airlines usually have designated contacts for this kind of thing (usually within a children/special needs section), many don't – which is often reason enough to choose a major commercial airline.

If you're having difficulties arranging what you need or your situation is particularly complex (you'll need help using toilets during the flight, say, or your child is touch-sensitive and will react badly to being frisked), call the airline's head office, or the airport if appropriate. Confirm that the person you speak to has the authority to help, and say you'd like to get **written responses** to your queries; if anything goes wrong or doesn't materialize during the journey, having written confirmation makes it easier for staff to put things right. If making all these arrangements feels like too much of a challenge, you could get a travel agent to handle it all on your behalf; they have access to people within airlines that the general public don't, so it's easier for them to pursue special requests and formalize agreements.

Most airports are **wheelchair accessible** throughout, and can provide assistance with access to toilets. For detailed information on airport layout and toilet locations, visit the airport's website; ⓦwww .worldtravelguide.net has links to airport sites worldwide.

PLANNING CONSIDERATIONS IN PREGNANCY

Bear in mind that **each pregnancy is different**. While avoiding carrying too much or sitting for too long is pretty obvious, you'll also need to factor in that you might have to eat frequently to prevent morning sickness as well as because you're hungry, and that you'll need to be near to toilets either because of nausea or the fact that your bladder can't wait. And if you're heading somewhere hot, the climate might tire you more than usual, and high humidity can make you unwilling to move at all. So, apart from being sure you have reasonable access to food and toilets, and air-conditioned transport and accommodation in hot or polluted places, opt for shorter trips and break journeys with plenty of rest stops.

Regardless of how well you feel and how you've fared during previous pregnancies, you can never be certain that this one will be free of **complications**; the fact is that women are more likely to need healthcare when pregnant than at any other time in their lives, so it makes sense only to visit places where you can easily get to a hospital. And if you're thinking of going to a malarial country, be mindful that pregnant women are especially susceptible to contracting **malaria**, and its effects can be serious both for mother and foetus. As the recommendations for pregnancy keep changing, it's critical to seek specialist advice regarding antimalarials (see p.37), complete the course fully and follow all the usual bite avoidance precautions (see p.152).

As the risk of complications is lowest during the second trimester, this is the **best time to travel**. Morning sickness – which isn't easy to handle while travelling – is most frequent in the first trimester; the third trimester has most women needing to urinate frequently and feeling heavier and less energetic than usual. In general, though, flying presents little or no risk to the mother or foetus. It's crucial to check on your **airline's regulations** before you book: most insist that you carry a medical certificate if you want to fly after your 28th week; this amounts to a doctor's letter specifying the delivery date and confirming that you're fit to travel. Flying after the 36th week is generally not allowed, and if you're expecting twins or complications during birth, this limit will usually go down to 32 weeks.

SAVING MONEY

When you're travelling with children and having a good time, it's particularly easy to let the cash flow, but there are many ways to make your **budget** go further without having to keep saying "no" to the children and yourselves. You don't need to keep heading off to theme parks and the like to keep the kids entertained; stopping to watch craftsmen at work or spending some time by swings or a stream can be just as much fun; see p.137 for more ideas, and p.135 for suggestions on how to bargain when travelling with kids.

Your **destination** is crucial to your travel budget: if you choose wisely, you might find it costs less to go abroad than stay at home. But wherever you head for, staying in small towns or rural areas always works out to be less expensive than big cities. If you can **travel off-season** or during the school term when other families can't, you'll find reduced prices for everything from tickets to accommodation, while travelling during the week rather than on weekends, and at times not used by business travellers, usually brings the price down further still. Early booking tends to mean lower prices, but you can also get cut-price **late bookings** from travel agents and via the Internet. However, bear in mind that "last-minute" means what it says – being able to drop everything and go rarely works when you've got young children.

Good-value accommodation for families

The main advantage of all-inclusive **package deals** that include flight, transfers, accommodation, food and drink is that you've pre-paid for all the basics and only need to shell out for extras once you're there. You can often get better deals on these packages than you would by booking similar flights and accommodation yourself, as large tour operators negotiate discounts with airlines and hotels, but it's worth doing a few comparisons to check. Bear in mind, though, that while packages with tours included may well be excellent, they do tie you in to whatever is offered. So, think twice about getting roped into arrangements with rigid timetables and large groups of people, however good a deal they seem – it's unrealistic to expect young children to fall in line.

Camping (see p.141) is the ultimate money-saver when it comes to family holidays, and children often prefer sleeping out to staying in hotel rooms, but other ways to cut costs include **home exchanges**. If you swap with another family (rather than a childless art fan with Persian rugs and a priceless porcelain collection), you can end up with a child-proofed home, toys to play with and insider's information on things to do and healthcare services. Home-swaps are simple to arrange, and we've given a couple of websites that coordinate them below; of these, Matching Houses facilitates exchanges between parents of children with similar special needs, which opens up the possibility of sharing equipment, including adapted vehicles.

Other possibilities include **farm stays** and **university accommodation**, which have potential pluses such as animals to look at, sports facilities and wide open spaces; we've given a few booking sites below. **Hostels** are generally inexpensive, and are particularly good if you need little more than a bed for the night as facilities tend to be basic. While there are exceptions, most hostels cater for single travellers and provide dorm rooms (often single-sex) and shared bathrooms. If splitting up won't work for you, check to see if you can all sleep together, or whether the hostel has private or family rooms as well as dorms – many do these days. If you're going down the **hotel** route, always check for special family deals, from discounted rates to free meals for children; many international chains offer these, so have a look on their websites to see what's on offer.

One thing to note is that with the exception of youth hostels, people travelling as a lone adult with children tend to get a raw deal; **single supplements** are often charged if there's only one adult in the room,

LOW COST ACCOMMODATION

Home-swaps

⊛**www.homelink.org** Long-established house swap organization with over 13,000 homes in 69 countries.

⊛**www.matchinghouses.com** House-swaps for families with special needs; you swap with a family who have similar needs (and equipment) to your own. They also have details of accommodation adapted for people with special needs. Free service, with about 500 homes in 36 countries.

Accommodation adapted for special needs

⊛**www.accessatlast.com** Self-catering holidays in twenty countries, with purpose-built or adapted accessible accommodation, and carers if required.

⊛**www.chooseusa.com/wheelchair.php** Adapted and purpose-built homes around the USA.

University and college accommodation

British Universities Accommodation Consortium ☎0114/249 3090, ⊛www.venuemasters.co.uk.

Farm holidays

Scottish Farm Holidays ☎&℻01890/751830, ⊛www.scotfarmhols.co.uk.
Welsh Farm Holidays ☎029/2047 5226, ⊛www.visitwales.com.
European Federation for Farm and Village Tourism ⊛www.eurogites.com.
True New Zealand ⊛www.truenz.co.nz/farmstays.
Farm Stays Western Australia ⊛www.farmstaywa.com.au.

CREDIT CARDS

If you're going to be using **credit cards** whilst away, check that the monthly and daily limits fit comfortably with your spending plan – they might not be enough to cover travel with the entire family, especially if you're using cards for big expenses such as hotel bills. If you're travelling with another adult, try and avoid the scenario of one cardholder paying all the bills, as this dynamic can end up placing subtle pressures on the relationship as well las imiting independence and flexibility – the one not paying bills will likely be left out of some decision-making, and will always be left minding the children.

and children's rates might not be available if you don't fit into the two-parent-two-children mould. There's not much you can do about this other than to look for slightly more enlightened places that have made a point of doing away with unfavourable rates specifically to attract single-parent families – fortunately, they're on the increase.

Eating well on a budget

If you're going to stay in a hotel or guesthouse with a restaurant, don't assume that you will have all your meals there – it's almost always cheaper to eat somewhere else. It's also worthwhile stocking up on some basic drinks and snacks (see p.127) for when you just want to stay in your room.

Most hotels, guesthouses and the like provide **breakfast**, but unless it's included in the room rate, it's often a waste of money for children, particularly if they only eat a piece of bread or a bowl of cereal. If breakfast isn't included, try asking for "complimentary" ones for the children – not as far-fetched a request as it might sound given that managers know how little children eat. Alternatively, you could take along something to snack on for the first day, and buy in simple breakfast to eat in your room thereafter – two days' worth of food bought in local shops and delicatessens is usually equivalent to the cost of a single meal in a restaurant.

We've given some more tips on eating out on p.128.

Assistance with travel costs

If money is tight when you're planning a family holiday, it's worth checking out whether any **support** is available. We've listed some organizations which help families take well-deserved breaks on p.24, but it's worth looking around to see if you qualify for any state or charity support. While direct financial assistance is hard to come by, you might be able to get subsidized accommodation, or borrow equipment to make things more affordable. Start by asking at your local library or community centre; alternatively, the organizations listed on p.24 provide subsidized holidays and/or grants to families in financial need or who have other special needs. Most listed sites are UK-based (there are few options out of the US, Canada and other parts of the world), but some are open to applicants from other countries.

ACCOMMODATION

One of the most important ingredients of a successful family holiday is well-chosen **accommodation**. As your mobility tends to be reduced, it's best to avoid isolated places where you might not have easy access to places to eat, get cash or make arrangements for the next leg of the trip. Children take a while to get going, and also tire quickly; on some days, you might well find yourselves back in your room just a few hours after leaving, or not going out at all. Ideally, your base should be a pleasure to stay in – a home away from home – so make sure you research the possibilities thoroughly.

   Finding accommodation when you arrive can be challenging with children in tow; it's hard not to feel pressured to take the first place you find or the first rate you're offered – besides, it's practically impossible to bargain with tired or enthusiastic ("let's stay here!") children around. So even if you do want to keep things flexible, it's worth pre-booking for your first few nights, which allows you to look for other places in a more leisurely way.

Choosing accommodation

The first thing to consider is **location**: if you're planning a beach holiday, you'll want a room that's close to the sea; if you'll be going on a lot of day-trips, somewhere with easy access to transport connections is best. Whatever your plans, you'll find logistics much simpler if you're

A ROOF OVER YOUR HEAD

"We expected a beach hut and that's what we got. The wooden shack was on stilts with a little stairway and porch, nestled under some palm trees, just fifty metres from the sea. The inside was just the one room with a double bed and a single for the four of us. While clean, the slats on the wooden floor and walls all had gaps, and the glass on one of the windows was broken. It was clear we were going to need the mosquito nets which were provided. The bathroom was curious – a cordoned-off area in the middle of the room. The only thing that separated the toilet, sink and shower from the rest of the bedroom was a bit of tiled floor on which they stood, surrounded by a low wall to retain water from the shower. The electricity supplied just the one fan and light bulb, and came on for a few hours each night. This was basic, but despite the faces pulled, we all got used to it quickly enough.

These were the Perhentian Islands, off the northeastern coast of Malaysia; we were on the smaller of the two, and were there for the wildlife. The beach and snorkelling were spectacular. We spent most of the time outdoors, living in our swimming costumes. Whenever we got back to the hut, we washed our feet and costumes at a tap by the hut. The little wooden porch turned out to be very comfortable – we spent a lot of time there reading in the shade whenever we'd had too much sun. The tin shower, which hung precariously from the ceiling, actually worked just fine – all in all, we started to appreciate that we had all we needed.

We set the children all sorts of tasks to keep them busy, from washing their clothes to sweeping the floor free of sand each day. Everyone was happy. It was idyllic – we got immersed into the rhythm of beachlife: snorkelling, diving, watching the palms, nursing huge appetites in time to sample the many beach-shack restaurants, followed by siestas, lots of reading and admiring the shell collection of the day. We ended up being really sorry when it came to leaving, and looked back on our beach hut stay with affection.

Getting back to Kuala Lumpur was like arriving on a different planet: the hotel had doormen with brass buttons, air-conditioning and a lobby with fountains, glorious flower arrangements and marble floors. The kids yelped when we got to our rooms, throwing themselves on the beds with "ooos" and "aaahs" as they touched the sheets and discovered the minibar. The contrasts of the two types of accommodation were a total accident, but I really think this kind of comparison helps kids to appreciate luxury when they have it, but also learn to do without. Since then, we've always looked for a combination of basic as well as more comfortable places to stay."

Alicia Cogollos

not far from places where you can eat out, buy groceries and pharmacy supplies, wash clothes, do your banking, get onto the Internet and so forth. Obviously, you also need to consider your family's individual requirements: if your child has special needs, having a doctor on call or everything under one roof might be reassuring, so consider aiming for larger hotels or resorts. Small-scale or family-run establishments have different advantages – they might be better in terms of personalized attention, for example.

When your kids are with you, another main concern is **recreation**: games rooms, swimming pools (preferably fenced off, with a separate baby pool), playgrounds or even resident animals can keep children absorbed for hours. And if there's space for them to run around outdoors, all the better, particularly if the layout of the place allows you to keep watch on them from your room or porch or a chair by the poolside. Don't forget your own wish list, though, be it a cocktail bar, live music or a spa – facilities for adults are all the more important when it's likely you'll have to stay in most nights.

It's hard to gauge in advance, but a place with an **informal atmosphere** is a great help when it comes to letting the children be their usual

A BUG-PROOF ROOM

Your choice of accommodation can make a big difference to how much you'll get bitten, something that's all the more crucial if there's **malaria** in your destination. You'll obviously want to be well away from standing or stagnant water, so don't go booking a place at the edge of a mangrove swamp, but extras such as air-conditioning, screens on the windows and nets on the beds go a long way to reducing the number of bites you'll all get.

inquisitive and noisy selves, and let off steam when they need to. Decor is a good indication of whether children will be welcomed or merely tolerated: places slathered with crystal vases and cream carpets might not bode well. If a hotel makes a big deal of its children's menus, kids' club or babysitting services, you're probably on to a good thing. Finally, size also matters: resort complexes can be enormous, with facilities spread out over several acres, and the smaller your children, the more you'll appreciate a compact layout.

Details to check in advance

Before finalizing room bookings, make sure you go over the basics, such as whether windows, doors and balcony railings are **childproof**. If you need more than one room, ask for **adjoining** ones, or rooms on the same floor at the very least. If you're all going to be in the same room, find out what the options are in terms of **adding beds or cots** for free or at minimal cost. And if there's a choice between shared or private bathrooms, always go for the latter, so that you can have the usual bath playtime and everyone can use the toilet without having to wait.

Entertainment is also worth checking out in advance. TVs are usually standard in hotel rooms, but ask if there's cable or satellite, and whether there are any children's channels available. A DVD and/or CD player is a terrific extra, and if you know your room has either, you can come prepared with music or movies – a great standby for rainy days or if someone's laid up with the sniffles.

If you're **self-catering**, get detailed information on the kitchen: number of rings on the

Child-friendly accommodation

- ❑ Comfy, clean rooms
- ❑ Frequently changed linen, extra towels and pillows
- ❑ En-suite bathrooms
- ❑ Good food with lots of options and flexible meal times
- ❑ Children's TV channels
- ❑ Babysitting and childcare
- ❑ Swimming pool
- ❑ Indoor and outdoor play areas
- ❑ Informal atmosphere and friendly staff
- ❑ Games rooms and toys
- ❑ Cots and high chairs

TO COOK OR NOT TO COOK

Going the **self-catering** route can work out a lot cheaper than eating out all the time, and it doesn't have to mean getting lumbered with the very chores you're trying to escape by taking a break. You don't need to cook every meal, but you might find it useful to be able to prepare the odd snack – particularly if you'd rather have a quiet day in. Children also enjoy having the odd home-made dish that suits their finicky preferences, even if it's just a salad or pasta with a knob of butter. So rather than planning three-meal-a-day menus, use the kitchen to store picnic food, drinks and snacks. Lay in some ingredients that are easy to prepare, and remember that you can always eat out, order in the odd takeaway, and get your favourite bakery items for breakfasts which – best of all – you can eat without having to get dressed.

stove, whether there's a dishwasher, microwave and toaster – whatever matters to you – and check on facilities for washing and drying clothes.

Services to look for

Ask about **room cleaning**, and whether rooms are serviced daily. If your children still wet their beds, find out if you can get sheets changed at will. In terms of **meals**, check when food is available, and whether it can be delivered to your room. If you're jet-lagged, breastfeeding or ill, you'll probably want to eat at odd times, and if the kitchen hours are limited, you'll probably want to stock up with some snacks. It's worth asking what **laundry** services cost before relying on using in-house facilities, as they can be prohibitively expensive.

If you're banking on using hotel **babysitting** services, get as much information as you can in advance: find out who the sitter is, how long they've worked for the hotel and whether or not they have any qualifications. Arrange to meet the babysitter before booking them, perhaps arranging tea and a chat in your rooms with your children; this way you can get a feel for them and how your kids will take to them. If you're not satisfied with the sitters your hotel offers, it might (depending on your destination) be worth doing some independent research into childcare where you're staying – there may be a registered childminder or a local agency you could use.

Supervised childcare such as a **kids' club** sounds good, but can mean little more than a bunch of children lumped together in front of a TV while an attendant keeps an eye on them. Ask how many children are cared for, whether groups are split according to age, and what specific activities might be – and be prepared to check it out yourself when you arrive. With both babysitting and supervised childcare, you can't afford to take chances – if anything seems amiss, be prepared to cancel your plans and start looking for alternatives.

Privacy and disturbing your neighbours

Babies and young children can be responsible for a fair few **decibels**, and whether you're staying with friends or family or in a hotel or guesthouse, it's hard to relax if you feel your crying baby or bed-bouncing toddler is disturbing everyone. If you're paying for your accommodation, ask to be put in a room at the end of a corridor to minimize the chance of disrupting others – many hotels do this automatically for families. If you're staying in someone's home and don't have a choice in terms of where your rooms are, it's a little trickier. If you can't avoid being on top of one another, do what you can to plan regular periods away from base – it's likely that both you and your hosts will appreciate the breaks.

STAYING SAFE

There are no particular **security risks** attached to travelling with children – except, perhaps, that they can be an added distraction which makes you more vulnerable to petty theft, itself the most common risk when on the road. Travelling with other adults who can share supervision is one of the best means of keeping yourselves and your belongings safe, but it's important to keep things in perspective – families are far less likely to experience problems than, say, groups of single men. And before going further, it's worth noting that **kidnapping** – which many parents understandably fear – is not something you need be overly concerned about unless you go against all security advice and travel in countries with poor security reputations, or leave your children unattended. In the very few instances where children have been abducted, the responsible party almost always turns out to be an

CULTURAL SENSITIVITY

An awareness of **local etiquette** impacts on safety in lots of subtle ways when travelling. If you respect the local lores and customs, you're less prone to provoke hostility and more likely to get help should problems arise. Researching your destination's culture and traditions, dress codes, religions and politics is always a good start (we've given some country-specific tips in Chapter 4), as is giving some thought as to what it means to be your sex, colour, nationality and religion in your destination. **Women** travelling without male company can attract unwelcome attention in some places, especially male-dominated parts of the world, and having children in tow doesn't necessarily diminish it. It can help to seek out female company when choosing seating on trains or buses etc, and employ age-old strategies such as wearing a fake wedding ring and a pair of sunglasses to avoid eye contact, or inventing stories of a phantom husband who's just around the corner or at the next stop.

estranged parent. A disappearance such as the tragic events concerning Madeleine McCann in 2007 will always make international headlines, but it's important to remember that awful though such cases are, the vast majority of families travel without incident, and the risk of anything happening to your child is extremely low.

Choosing your destination

When planning a family break, most parents instinctively opt for a relatively **safe destination** – clearly you'd avoid places in the midst of conflict or with high levels of crime. That said, most countries have some "no-go" areas even if they're generally considered safe; and others have undeservedly poor security reputations on account of problems in just a few regions. Furthermore, women travellers often face different issues to men. This is the tricky aspect of **security advice** – appraising the risks is an inexact science, with a host of different considerations to bear in mind. The best start is to consult the government travel advisory websites listed see below. If you remain uncertain, find out

---

TRAVEL ADVISORY WEBSITES

@travel.state.gov
The US Department of State's Bureau of Consular Affairs site is generally up-to-date on the latest security flare-ups across the globe, and is worth consulting even if you're not from the US. Bear in mind, though, that the advice is intended for American citizens, and factors in USA-relations worldwide.

@www.fco.gov.uk/travel
The UK Foreign and Commonwealth Office site, with a wealth of country-specific information as part of the "know before you go" campaign. Apart from security advice, you'll find tips on insurance, local customs and health, and you can sign up for email updates on the security situation in your destination.

@www.voyage.gc.ca
Canada's Consular Affairs department provide an extensive online resource (in English and French) which – depending on the country – goes quite a bit beyond traditional security alerts, providing information on the nature of flare-ups, local customs and do's and don'ts.

@www.smartraveller.gov.au
The Australian Government's Department of Foreign Affairs and Trade comprehensive country-by-country advice is particularly detailed for places in the Asian Pacific. Australians can register on the site before travelling, so that in the event of a security issue, they can be reached and helped.

@www.safetravel.govt.nz
Security advice from the New Zealand Ministry of Foreign Affairs and Trade, though the list of countries isn't complete or regularly updated. Citizens of New Zealand can register to get alerts on emergencies and obtain the contact details for those responsible for handling their affairs at each destination.

if your country has an embassy in or near to the place you plan to visit (check ⓦwww.embassyworld.com for details), then call and ask the consular section for advice, mentioning that you're travelling with children. If your embassy gives you the go-ahead, you can assume that as destinations go, this one's fine – most officials overplay the risks to be on the safe side.

If you know someone in your destination – even friends of friends – do seek them out for first-hand advice on what's happening on the ground. You might also try the online travel discussion forums detailed on p.10; these can link you up to others that have visited – or better still, to residents.

A safe place to stay

Asking the following basic questions before you book a room will go a long way to ensuring you're as safe as possible in the place you to stay. For tips on checking safety in your room once you arrive, see p.124.

▶ What facilities are there for storing valuables – is there a safe in the room or at the reception desk?

▶ Where will your room be? The ground floor is the easiest prospect for thieves, though a lot more convenient if you're going to be using a stroller. Higher floors are harder to evacuate in the event of an emergency (and if there are no lifts, you'll have to get up and down stairs with your things) but are less easy to break in to.

▶ Will the windows in your room have locks?

▶ Are there general security measures in place, from surveillance cameras to designated guards on duty? Is a receptionist manning the entrance good enough for you?

Looking after your valuables

While you may not have used a **pouch** to hold valuables in your young, free and single days, you might want to now. Losing your cash, credit cars or passport is bad enough at any time, but it's a lot more serious a deal when travelling with your children. Pouches are available in all shapes, sizes and styles, but the important thing is to wear them under your clothing so that they can't be seen by anyone else – go for one designed to go under your shirt, carried in socks, strapped to the lower leg or worn on the inside of trousers attached to your belt (the latter two are best if you're breastfeeding). Money belts are another alternative; they look like normal trouser belts, but have a zip running flat against the inside surface which opens up a cavity into which you can fold high-value notes or travellers' cheques. To get an idea of what's on offer in terms of pouches and belts, visit ⓦwww.saddler.co.uk/acatalog, ⓦwww.letravelstore. com/security.htm or ⓦwww.westernbelt.co.uk.

Keeping track of the kids and the bags

Travel inevitably involves spending time in crowded places, where it's not always simple to keep your hands – let alone your eyes – on your children as well as your bags. The most obvious way to make things easier on yourself is to **minimize your luggage**, or consider using a delivery company (see p.45) that will send on bags ahead of you – not as expensive a prospect as it might sound. Alternatively, ask a friend to come and see you off, or look into getting paid assistance along the way. Taxi drivers can usually be persuaded to carry your bags through to check-in for a fee, and most airports and stations have porters on standby to help with luggage. If your trip involves long transit stops, find out whether trolleys, lockers or **left-luggage** facilities exist – most guidebooks have this type of information. When you arrive at your

PASSPORT TO TRAVEL

"When you travel for years and without incident, you begin to feel you know it all – until something happens to prove otherwise. The last such lesson I learnt resulted from a break to Thailand that my wife and I took with our then 9-month-old son.

While waiting in the bus station to go from Bangkok to Hua Hin, my bag was snatched. It happened just after we boarded the bus and were sorting out where our son would sit; the bag was on the ground by my feet for just a few seconds, but what I hadn't realized was that there were two doors, front and back – and whoever took the bag left by the back exit.

My (British) wife and our son got new passports within hours of finding the embassy. But I had no such luck; I'm Colombian. There wasn't a Colombian embassy in Bangkok – just a consul, and she didn't have powers to issue a passport. In the first instance, we had to spend hours with the police, as all of us needed their report to proceed further. But because of my situation, I had to go from one ministry to the next for a series of papers and official translations, and fax and call Colombia to convince the authorities there that I was who I said I was. All the tickets had to be changed, and this also involved countless steps.

Once through the bureaucracy in Bangkok, I had to go to Hong Kong on temporary travel papers to get a new passport, and of course I was drilled by the officials there on arrival. There always seemed to be yet another hurdle: when I finally got my new passport, I discovered that I had to get a completely new set of visas. The whole thing took about two weeks, during which we managed one decent weekend on the beach where we did our best to forget it all; but otherwise, my wife was stuck minding our son in a hotel while I did the rounds. All in all, we did well to manage a few laughs and resist fighting or blaming one another. After the event, I felt pretty idiotic buying one of those pouches to carry passports under your shirt, but the main lesson is, of course, hang on to your passports at all times.

Andres de Francisco

STAYING TOGETHER

If you're concerned about getting separated from your children, try **practising staying together** before you go. First off, drum it into your children that they should never lose sight of you in crowded places, and devise a plan so that they'll know what to do should the group get split up; best options are that they either wait where they are, or go to a pre-agreed meeting point. If the children never leave your side while practising, give them lots of positive feedback and maybe even a prize. You can also deliberately slip out of sight while continuing to keep an eye on them to watch what they do; if they make mistakes, give them pointers for the next time. Funnily enough, these kinds of drills don't make children paranoid; instead (pretty much like Brownies' or Scouts' training), they usually enjoy mastering the skills.

destination, it's well worth paying for someone to come and meet you, particularly if it's been a long journey; after all, this is when you're most likely to be tired and disoriented. **Pick-up services** are usually simple to arrange through travel agents or the place you're staying, and won't cost much more than a taxi.

Minding the children when travelling mostly requires no more than the usual precautions you'd take on a day out. But for long journeys, and in preparation for busy places, dressing them in bright, easily identifiable clothing helps them stand out from the crowd. In terms of keeping **young children** at close range, there are additional options, from the low-tech tactics of using a leash all the way up to a child tracking device (see p.62); these signal an alarm if you get separated, and set off a bleeper worn by your child to help you find them fast. Clearly, the more children you have, the more inclined you'd be to buy one; they're also useful if your children have special needs that make them prone to go walkabout or get disoriented. A further precaution is to have younger children carry your contact details in a pouch around their neck or in a pocket. However, don't display your child's name in full view – if someone tries to be friendly and calls their name, they could get confused and wander off.

"Because of their size, parents may be difficult to discipline properly."

P.J. O'Rourke

Whistles can be a good way for **older children** to find you should they get separated. Get one for everyone, and thread them on cords around the neck. Older kids also need help with remembering where you're staying as you travel – make sure they have the phone number and address somewhere on them.

HEALTH MATTERS

Looking after sick children and being poorly yourself is always unsettling – perhaps more so when you're away from home – and as healthcare abroad can be expensive, it's worth doing what you can to avoid getting ill in the first place. The information in this section outlines the main **travel health preparations**, from getting a pre-trip checkup to having the right jabs.

Note that there's more holiday health information, and some background on how to stay well while you're there, in "Being there", p.151–166. For tailor-made travel health advice, it's crucial to visit a specialized clinic; you might also want to get hold of one of the books detailed on p.40.

GETTING HEALTH RISKS IN PERSPECTIVE

Contrary to what you might believe, you're only fractionally more likely to get common illnesses such as coughs and colds when travelling than you are at home. The risk of contracting more **serious conditions** – cholera, typhoid, tuberculosis etc – is actually quite low for travellers as long as you get the right vaccinations, take malaria prophylaxis if appropriate, avoid potentially dodgy food and water and don't take unnecessary risks. And while it's true that travellers do have a higher risk of contracting the various forms of **diarrhoea**, it's important to remember that "traveller's tummy" is easy to prevent and generally gets better on its own, while antibiotics are readily available to treat the more serious gastro conditions such as dysentery and giardiasis.

Pre-trip health essentials

The first step in ensuring that you and your family are fit to travel is to get everyone checked over. Visit the **dentist**, and if anyone wears **glasses**, get a spare set to travel with, as well as details of the prescription in case you need to find replacements whilst away.

If you're going overseas or might be doing anything physically challenging, see your **doctor** at least two months before you leave to discuss your plans and review any ongoing health issues; this is especially important if you or your children have special medical needs. When making the appointment, mention the ages of your children and ask if they need to come to the appointment; when you go, bring everyone's vaccination records, and ask the doctor to note down their blood groups for you. If any of your children have a **pre-existing medical condition**, ask for help in identifying a doctor in your destination who specializes in the same condition. If your child might need to see someone while away, ask for a statement of the diagnosis, the latest test results and details of your treatment regimen. If you're **pregnant**, tell your doctor that you'll be travelling and discuss the trip with them. If you've previously had a miscarriage or a Caesarean section, you might need advice on how to keep up antenatal care while on the move.

Regular and just-in-case medication

Make sure that you have supplies of **regular medications** to last the whole trip, as well as just-in-case remedies for common ailments. If you plan to take **prescription medicines** and **syringes** across borders, you might need what's known as a medical attestation from your doctor confirming that they're for personal use. Some countries require attestations to be certified by the national health administration – your doctor should be able to advise. If you need to carry prescriptions with you, ask for them to be made out with generic rather than brand names of medicines to ensure that you get what you need easily (and probably more cheaply) when away.

Vaccinations

Before you leave, check with your doctor that everyone is up to date with regular **vaccinations**, including tetanus shots, and get them to advise on what to do if you'll be away when boosters of childhood jabs are due. While some doctors are well-versed in travel vaccinations and health risks around the world, others aren't, and might advise you to

MEDICAL CONSULTATIONS

"Parents come to our travel clinic with a variety of concerns before travelling – you get all types. In the first instance, and for parents who are worried about a particular destination or trip, I can almost always find a solution. This is usually a matter of providing information, putting things in proportion, suggesting preventative measures, and offering prophylactics and just-in-case treatments for the most common risks. But on occasion, I get parents who outline travel plans that are not only extreme, but also unlikely to be of interest to, or enjoyable for, their children. This presents dilemmas; but in general, I take them through the medical reflections, but also ask them whether this trip is really a good idea. I might outline the conditions, reminding them of the hardship that the trip will involve and pointing out why the children might find it difficult or uninteresting. But I feel particularly strongly when parents decide to go to areas far removed from healthcare. It's one thing for them to take calculated risks for themselves – we all do – but there's something perverse about doing this on behalf of children who can't make such judgements for themselves. Since starting my own family, I have toned down my own ambitions quite a bit – I used to be much more gung-ho about travel, but you can't expect to push the limits with children in the same way you can when on your own."

Dr Richard Dawood, Director, Fleet Street Travel Clinic, and editor of *Travellers' Health*.

visit a **travel health clinic** (see below). Staff at these are specialists, keep abreast of changing regulations and the availability of medicines around the world, and should be able to provide useful printed information to take away with you. Some travel jabs need time to become effective, and others are administered in more than one dose, so you need to **start thinking about vaccinations two months before you to plan leave**. Equally, as some vaccines have side-effects, you'll want to avoid having grumpy children, sore arms and jab-related fevers just before you depart, so get them done early.

Children under 18 months won't be given any travel-related jabs. Yellow fever vaccination, even if normally obligatory, isn't given to children below 9 months, but may be to those aged 1 and over. If you have **children over 18 months**, they'll usually be given the same travel jabs as adults, unless there are specific contraindications. Fortunately, clinicians are usually pretty good at dealing with kids, and may well provide little bribes during injections, and fancy plasters afterwards.

TRAVEL HEALTH CLINICS

Australia and New Zealand
Travel Clinics Australia ☎1300/369 359, ⊛www.travelclinic.com.au. Lists of travel health clinics around Australia.
Travel Medical and Vaccine Centres ☎1300/658 844, ⊛www.tmvc.com.au. Over twenty health clinics in Australia, New Zealand and Thailand.

Canada
Public Health Agency of Canada ☎1300/369 359, ⊛www.phac-aspc.gc.ca. Listings of travel clinics around Canada, with both French- and English-language versions.

UK
MASTA ⊛www.masta.org/travel-clinics. Details of 25 travel health clinics around the UK.
Hospital for Tropical Diseases Travel Clinic Mortimer Market, Capper Street, London WC1E 6AU ☎020/7388 9600. Travel clinic within the UK's main facility for treating tropical infections.
Fleet Street Clinic 29 Fleet Street, London EC4Y 1AA ☎020/7353 5678, ⊛www.fleetstreetclinic.com. Travel clinic run by Dr Richard Dawood, author of *Travellers' Health*, which arranges home visits (for a fee) to save you a trip. The website has useful links to travel health resources worldwide.

USA
Centers for Disease Control ⊛http://wwwn.cdc.gov/travel/ contentTravelClinics.aspx. The CDC website lists clinics around the USA.

Worldwide
The International Society for Travel Medicine ⊛www.istm.org. A list of clinics worldwide which specialize in international travel health; details include clinicians' names, contacts and email addresses – useful if you want to make contact before arriving and to check provisions for special needs.

Live vaccines such as yellow fever are generally not recommended for **pregnant women**, so if your doctor advises against a live vaccine and your destination country insists upon it as a prerequisite for entry, ask for a medical exemption certificate to present to the authorities. Equally, bring all vaccination records with you – some countries require proof of the jabs you've had before allowing you entry.

WE'RE PROTECTED!

Doctors and travel clinicians don't tend to emphasize the fact that **travel vaccines are not 100 percent effective**. If you aren't careful with food and water, for example, you can still get typhoid and cholera despite being vaccinated, so don't assume that just because you've all had the jabs, it's OK for you and your family to throw caution to the wind. Take the time to find out about infectious diseases and ways to avoid them in your destination – ask at a travel clinic, or visit the WHO website (see p.40).

Antimalarials

If you're travelling to a country in which **malaria** is endemic (check the list of affected countries at ⓦwww.who.int/ith/en), you need specialist advice on the appropriate antimalarial prophylaxis, as strains and recommended drugs change all the time. You'll also need to make sure you take ample supplies of insect repellent, clothes to cover everyone up in the evenings and, if the place you're staying in doesn't have them, bed-nets impregnated with insecticide. For more on bed-nets, repellents and other methods to avoid mosquito bites, see p.63 and p.152.

A course of **antimalarials** is usually started up to two and a half weeks before departure, both to allow protective levels to build in the blood and to check for side-effects, so don't be tempted to get them once you arrive; in any case, antimalarials sold in countries with poor drug regulatory systems might be fakes, with little or no protective effect. If

TRAVELLERS' TALES

TAKING THE TABLETS

"Getting antimalarials down kids is a bit of a challenge ("yeuch! yeuch!"), and I found my smaller kids were better at it than the older two. I explained why and quoted the family story of my uncle dying of malaria in India back in the mists of time, then got them to open their mouths, put the pills on the backs of their tongues and gave them a cup of water. After a couple of weeks, three of the four were very good at it. Things would be a lot simpler if drug companies made kid-sized tablets so you didn't spend ages trying to cut them in half, ending up with a pile of shards from which you have to try to estimate the dose."

Rebecca Blackmore

you're **pregnant**, it's a good idea to bring extra doses of antimalarials, as they can make you nauseous and you might need to take an additional pill now and again if you can't keep one down. Also bear in mind that antimalarials don't pass through breast milk in sufficient quantities to protect babies, so they will need a separate course.

You can get antimalarials in **syrup** form, though **tablets** are much more common. As children are usually prescribed smaller amounts of the same antimalarials as adults, this means breaking tablets into pieces. Manipulating crumbs of broken pills makes accurate dosage difficult (and crushed tablets taste foul), so it's a good idea to buy a ready-made pill-cutter; these are widely available and cost next to nothing. You can try and mask the taste of tablets by wedging bits of them into a soft sweet, or crushing them into jam, syrup or a sugary drink (but make sure your child gets all of the tablet, as they don't dissolve well). For babies, use a plastic disposable syringe to squirt solutions into their mouths; but as their tastebuds aren't fully developed, they're unlikely to protest if given crushed tablets. Finally, take particular care to keep antimalarials out of children's reach – overdosing is dangerous.

What to pack in your medical kit

Most people travel with some form of **medical kit**, from a box of painkillers and a few plasters to an entire pharmacy. How far you go is up to you, but having things on hand when you need them can be a real bonus when travelling with kids. Basic items will probably be readily available at your destination, but the hassle of buying something as simple as a plaster can cost you a lot in time and tears. Also bear in mind that while pre-prepared medical kits look attractive, there will always be items you don't need, or extras you might want to carry – it's better (and cheaper) to prepare your own. Nonetheless, it's important for the finished result to look like a medical kit: unidentified tablets packed into an unlabelled plastic bag can be a recipe for trouble when you get to customs, so pack it all together into a waterproof, airtight box.

To help you assemble your own kit, we've provided an exhaustive **list** of suggested items on opposite. Don't assume you need to take everything; instead, use the list to identify what might apply to your family and the possible pitfalls of your trip. The one indispensable thing is a good **thermometer**. It's unwise to leave judging temperatures to a hand test – with young children, the difference in a couple of degrees matters a lot. Digital thermometers are the most accurate and are better able to withstand the rigours of travel; mercury versions are no longer allowed on planes in any case.

If healthcare tends to be poor in your destination, consider carrying

Medical kit – things to consider

General
- ❏ Regular medication
- ❏ Contraceptives
- ❏ Vitamins and fluoride
- ❏ Antifungals eg clotrimazole cream
- ❏ Plastic spoons (5ml and 2.5ml) for measuring doses
- ❏ Plastic syringes (5ml or 10ml) for giving liquid medicines orally

Allergies
- ❏ Antihistamine pills/syrup
- ❏ Hydrocortisone cream
- ❏ Nasal sprays/eye drops

Breastfeeding
- ❏ Antibiotics for mastitis
- ❏ Breast packs – hot/cold compresses for swelling
- ❏ Breast pump

Bruises and stiff limbs
- ❏ Arnica gel
- ❏ Heat balm

Colds, fevers, headaches and pain
- ❏ Painkillers for adults and children
- ❏ Teething gel
- ❏ Digital thermometer
- ❏ Cold remedies and/or Echinacea tincture
- ❏ Nasal decongestant
- ❏ Vitamin C

Common infections
- ❏ Antibiotic drops for ears and eyes
- ❏ Medicines for urinary tract infections and thrush

Constipation
- ❏ Laxatives
- ❏ Vaseline

Diarrhoea
- ❏ Oral rehydration salts
- ❏ Antidiarrhoeal medication
- ❏ Acidophilus pills

First aid: blisters, cuts and scrapes
- ❏ Antiseptic spray or liquid
- ❏ Antiseptic wipes
- ❏ Plasters
- ❏ Surgical tape
- ❏ Bandages
- ❏ Sterile dressings
- ❏ Scissors and safety pins
- ❏ Cotton wool
- ❏ Disposable gloves
- ❏ Sterile syringes and needles

Malaria, insect bites and stings
- ❏ DEET-based insect repellent
- ❏ Insecticide-impregnated mosquito nets
- ❏ Insecticide room spray
- ❏ Antimalarials
- ❏ Tweezers
- ❏ Antihistamine cream

Motion sickness
- ❏ Antisickness tablets
- ❏ Sea-bands
- ❏ Ginger capsules

Pregnancy
- ❏ Antacids
- ❏ Iron/folate, calcium, vitamins
- ❏ Heartburn and nausea remedies
- ❏ Compression stockings

Sun and heat
- ❏ High-factor sunblock
- ❏ Lipscreen
- ❏ Medicated talcum powder
- ❏ Aftersun cream
- ❏ Calamine lotion
- ❏ Aloe vera gel

a supply of **disposable syringes**, **needles** and **alcohol wipes**; you'll be sure that they're sterile, and it's good practice for travellers not to deplete precious local stocks. Note that while syringes and needles are

ADDITIONAL RESOURCES

Travel health websites

Ⓦ **www.who.int** While not particularly simple to navigate, the World Health Organization's website contains definitive reference information used by health practitioners worldwide, from country-by-country lists of vaccination recommendations to advice on disease prevention and updates on epidemics and health emergencies. Note that information on children is rarely listed separately (searching on "children" is unlikely to help), but is integrated under more general headings such as "vaccines" or "diarrhoea". For an overview of travel health risks and prevention advice, download the excellent International Travel and Health pamphlet.

Ⓦ **www.cdc.gov.travel** The US government's Centers for Disease Control's site is well laid out and simple to use. The disease factsheets and travel advice for individual countries are particularly useful, as are sections concerning children, pregnancy, breastfeeding and women in general. You can customize and print out your own book of health information and advice for your trip, and buy their Health Information for International Travel publication.

Ⓦ **www.masta.org** The MASTA travel health website is simple to use, with information on individual diseases, health risks by country and advice for travelling with children and when pregnant. For a small fee, you can get personalized health briefs for your journey. The advice is based on a database maintained for 250 countries and takes seasons, and types of travel and accommodation into account.

Ⓦ **www.fitfortravel.scot.nhs.uk** Maintained by Health Protection Scotland, the most useful resource within the reams of information are the maps of the world – you click on your destination and get a list of the health risks and basic information on prevention as well.

Ⓦ **www.iata.org** The International Air Transport Association site has information on rules, regulations and provisions for air travel, as well as safety and health in the air. It's also useful to those wanting general information on health and safety, and standards for the aircraft industry – deep vein thrombosis and air quality are covered in detail.

Books

Richard Dawood *Travellers' Health*. Now in its fourth edition, this has been the standard travellers' reference tool for some years and has a chapter dedicated to paediatric health.

Nick Jones *The Rough Guide to Travel Health*. A comprehensive book on what to expect and how to prevent and deal with health challenges, covering allopathic, homeopathic and "alternative" treatments. Children are covered within the "special needs" section. Dosages for treatments such as antimalarials are particularly useful, and it's compact enough to be travel-friendly.

David Werner *Where There is No Doctor: A Village Healthcare Handbook*. If you have to tackle health problems on your own and particularly in developing countries, this is an essential book to take with you. It offers clear and illustrated information, covering ways to keep your child healthy, recognize warning signs and deal with symptoms.

Jane Wilson-Howarth and Matthew Ellis *Your Child's Health Abroad*. Specifically geared to children's health, this is a good resource for travelling parents, inspiring confidence rather than fear. Informed and balanced with insights of parents.

often included in pre-prepared medical kits, they're unlikely to be the smaller needle-bore sizes required for children; they're available from most good pharmacies.

Healthcare in your destination

There are lots of good reasons for doing some pre-trip research into doctors and hospitals in your destination, from needing continued care for a pre-existing condition to just reassurance that reliable care is available. It's particularly important to check if you're going somewhere with weak infrastructure or where tropical infections are present. If healthcare facilities are poor, you might want to reconsider your plan – the smaller your child, the more important it is to be able to get a quick and accurate diagnosis should they get ill. It's also important to consider **language barriers**, and look for doctors who you'll be able to communicate with. This isn't as difficult as it sounds: if your country has an embassy in your destination, staff there will have a list of practitioners who speak your language, so get in touch and ask. For more on finding embassies, see p.31.

If you're **pregnant**, check out what's available in terms of facilities for premature babies and management of birth complications and Caesarean sections. It's also useful to identify someone to turn to should you want to discuss niggling worries.

THE PAPERWORK

The basic **documents** you need to take with you – passport, any visas, insurance papers etc – are pretty obvious, but there can be a lot of bits of paper to keep track of, so it's well worth buying a travel wallet to store them in. If your kids already have **passports**, check the validity of the photographs. Most countries require a change of picture between ages one and three, and then at regular intervals thereafter, but regardless of the guidelines, get passports updated if the picture no longer bears a reasonable likeness. In any case, it's good to travel with extra passport-type **photographs** (particularly of the children) in case you need to replace lost passports, get a new visa or something similar – another reason to get new pictures done.

If you're going to need visas for your destination, don't be surprised if they're a requirement for children as well as adults, and that their fee is the same as yours. As many countries require visas to be collected in person by applicants (including children), you may have to make a trip to the main embassy in your country, although it's often possible to apply in writing first to avoid two trips. It's worth getting visas that last a bit longer than your expected journey in case you want to stay longer or get held up by missing a flight.

PERMISSION FOR YOUR CHILDREN TO TRAVEL

Though you might assume that passports are all you need to travel with your children, there are a number of instances where you might need extra legal documentation. If you have an adopted child, you must take their **adoption** papers; and if you're the only parent travelling – regardless of your marital status – you might be asked for **proof of consent** from the other parent for your child to travel. This is pretty rare, but it is a possibility if you're going to countries where overseas adoption and/or child trafficking is common – and if you're asked for proof of consent and you don't have it, you might be refused entry. But regardless of your destination, if the name on your child's passport is not the same as yours, or if your child bears little resemblance to you, the chances of this being an issue increase; conversely, the older your child, the less likely officials are to ask.

TRAVELLERS' TALES

STOPPED AT EMIGRATION

"My husband is Indian, and the children are all skin tones. Last year, I was travelling with my daughter Caroline who is autistic as well as much darker than me. My husband wasn't travelling with us. When we reached emigration, the official started asking Caroline questions. As you know, autistic children look much the same as any other, which in this case didn't help. Caroline was confused. To questions such as 'Does your father know you are travelling?' she said, 'I don't know.' The official started looking suspicious and moved to detain us as the questioning progressed, until that is, she started drooling. He then took me for my word that she had a disability. Next time, I'll be sure to take a letter of consent along."

Suzanne Maheu

A STANDARD PARENTAL CONSENT LETTER

Address of absent parent
Date

To whom it may concern

Re: Consent for my daughter/son to travel to (country)

I, (absent parent's name), the mother/father of (child/ren's names, nationality and passport number/s) hereby give my consent for my child/ren to travel with their mother/father (your name, nationality and passport number) to (x country). They will be travelling by (plane/train/car – give details such as airlines or vehicle licence plate numbers if you have them) on (give dates or state "during the months x to x").

Signed

(absent parent's name)
Co-signed and stamped by a solicitor or notary

The standard requirements for authorization to travel are your child's birth certificate, your marriage certificate (if applicable) and a signed and attested **parental consent letter** (see above) from the other parent confirming you can travel with your child. If the other parent is no longer alive, you may need proof. If you're **divorced** or **separated** from the child's other parent, it's best to broach the proposed trip with lots of time to spare; and note that although you might assume that it's fine to travel with your children if you're their legal **guardian** or have sole guardianship, this isn't always the case, and you might need to get consent. Present the idea to your ex alongside a detailed travel plan that spells out your itinerary and includes contact numbers. The nearer the destination and the shorter the trip, the more likely you are to get consent. If they do agree, travel with a copy of the divorce certificate as well as a parental custody document (although some countries don't need signed consent letters if the absent parent isn't mentioned on the birth certificate). Whether you're separated from the other parent or not, it's also useful to have copies of their ID papers (driving licence, or the photo page of their passport); the more documents you have, the less likely you are to be questioned.

If you have no idea where the other parent is – really no idea, rather than just haven't spoken to him or her in a while – get a statement prepared and attested to that effect by a solicitor or notary. Fortunately, in this instance, the one letter should be all you need for years to come. If you might have problems getting the other parent to go to a notary, it's best to take your chances with an unattested letter than to go with nothing at all.

Note that for authorisation to **travel with other people's children**, you will need a similar letter signed by both parents.

TRAVEL INSURANCE

Travel insurance providers consider families to be a relatively safe bet as they tend to make fewer claims than adults-only groups, and many policies provide free coverage for children. The main thing to check when buying family travel insurance is whether there's a generous **cancellation** clause to cover the costs of delayed or changed travel plans. Most travel companies will refund part of a ticket if you can't use it, but the amount refunded often comes with caveats and depends on the type of ticket (how much you paid in the first place) and how close cancellation comes to the date of travel. Travel with children demands some flexibility – you might not be able to fly when you planned to because your toddler has a bad cold, for example – and if you don't get cancellation cover, you might end up having to buy new tickets from scratch. It's also worth checking that your cancellation cover includes missing your departure.

It's also crucial to check the **hospitalization** and **medical care** small print, as travel policies don't necessarily include a stay in hospital or prolonged medical care beyond initial consultations and the costs of medication. Also make sure that the insurance extends to **repatriation** should someone fall ill, and covers the costs of keeping all family members together

"An active 2 year old can cause as much damage as an inebriated 18 year old."

Paul Dittmer, father and spokesman for Columbus Direct

during health emergencies as well as getting paid help to look after the children should you get sick. **Personal liability cover** is also critical for travel with children, and isn't always automatically included; this covers damage to another person or their property, be it from spilt juice on someone's laptop to inadvertently tripping someone up.

Getting insured in pregnancy

Insurers will want to know how many weeks pregnant you'll be when you travel, and how long you're going to be away. In most instances, you won't qualify for standard travel health cover if you're planning to start your trip less than nine weeks before your **delivery date**. But even if there will be fewer than nine weeks to go, make sure the policy covers delivery costs even if you don't think there is the slightest chance that your travel plans will coincide with this event. Also check that it covers all the care you might need before, during and after delivery (antenatal, delivery and post-partum care), as well as repatriation fees and care for you and the baby, even if it's delivered prematurely.

Insurance for special medical needs

If your child has a **pre-existing medical condition**, they probably won't be covered by standard travel insurance, and will need a tailor-made policy. Once you have a detailed travel plan, go over it with the insurance provider – in most instances you ought to be able to make minor adjust-

Travel documents

- ❏ Passports and visas
- ❏ Summary card of passport and visa details
- ❏ Tickets
- ❏ Insurance papers
- ❏ Itinerary
- ❏ Medical and vaccination records, medical certificates, x-rays of metal implants, blood group details, prescriptions, medical attestations for carrying medicines, vaccination exemption letters.
- ❏ Adoption papers
- ❏ Authorization to travel with your child
- ❏ Driving licence
- ❏ Reservation records and receipts
- ❏ Extra photographs

ments to extend a standard travel policy to cover what you need.

WHAT TO TAKE

You'll always need a fair bit of luggage when travelling with children, but it pays to be realistic about what you can do without for a couple of weeks, whether it's a favourite dress or a steam sterilizer. **Involving your children** in packing decisions helps avoid infuriating "you didn't bring!" sulks. Ask them what they want to take, help them draw up

BAGGAGE DELIVERY COMPANIES

If your best efforts fail and it looks like you're going to be weighed down with mountains of bags, you might want to send on suitcases and bulky items such as prams via a **baggage delivery company**. It's not a budget option – you'll pay around £70/US$145 to send up to 30kg of luggage one way between European countries, and £110/US$230 between the UK and US, but prices per kilo come down the more you send, and you'll get better rates if you send things a few weeks rather than a few days before you travel. Try ⊛www.firstluggage.com or ⊛www.carrymyluggage.com for a quotation. There are also companies which specialize in **delivering baby products** such as formula, baby food and nappies/diapers – try ⊛www.babiestravellite.com.

their own packing lists, and set aside time to step in and rationalize what they eventually put in the bags. And once you're away, leave it to them (within reason) to decide which toys to carry on a particular leg of the trip. If they're carrying their own backpack, they'll soon get the list down to something manageable.

WHAT TO TAKE IT ALL IN – CHOOSING YOUR LUGGAGE

As a general rule, aim for bags that are small, light and have a soft casing – these are easier to lift, less likely to hurt the children should they fall on or bash into them, and can also serve as makeshift beds or something to sit on. Small pieces also pack well into irregular spaces such as car boots/ trunks or luggage racks. Whatever you choose, it should be **lockable**; if you use combination locks rather than padlocks, set them all to the same number to cut out unnecessary hassle. And finally, don't forget to check the latest **security restrictions** (see p.98) and the **dimensions** allowed for unchecked bags (56cm by 45cm by 25cm at the time of writing).

The all-purpose day-bag

Whether boarding a plane or heading off on a day-trip, you'll need a roomy bag to hold the bits and pieces you need on hand, from snacks and toys to extra clothing, nappies/diapers, medicines and toiletries. A bag with a wide opening allows you to reach into all the corners without unpacking the contents, and it should also be simple to open and shut, preferably with one hand. Bear in mind that pop buttons are easy to open, but fiddly to close; zips are more secure, but make sure it's a robust one with chunky teeth less likely to break under pressure.

If you've got a baby, look for a bag with several **stretch pockets** that you can use to keep bottles upright or stow small items such as pins or dummies/pacifiers. Also – and particularly if you'll be carrying dirty diapers – look for a bag that's **easy to clean**: wipeable plastic linings might seem good, but they have a tendency to rip, whereas a cloth bag can be thrown into a washing machine. Bags with detachable, cushioned changing mats aren't always practical, as these take up a lot of space; a simple roll of plastic sheeting is a more compact and practical alternative to a mat in any case. All this considered, though, you might find you end up with a **backpack**; while you won't be able to dip in and out without taking it off, and it's unlikely to have pockets suitable for holding bottles, the upside is that you have both hands free.

In general, choose the lightest bag you can find, with straps that won't cut into you or slip off your shoulder. Your day-bag will be in constant use and will probably find its way into many photographs – and if you plan on sharing the carrying and nappy/diaper changing with your partner, you'll both need to feel comfortable carrying it around.

Backpacks for the children

If you're children are old enough to carry a bag themselves, get them their own **backpack**. They won't be carrying much (their load shouldn't exceed 10 percent of their body weight), so as long as they like the bag and the zips work, anything will do. Mini-suitcases on wheels are best avoided unless you're travelling mostly by car, as small children often get themselves and others into tangles with their inexpert "driving" skills, and find them cumbersome to open and close.

PACKING – WHAT GOES WHERE

Once you've decided what bags you're bringing, give some thought to how you're going to use what you take before you start packing. Things that will be used rarely, are needed only later in the trip or are fragile and need special packing are best packed separately to what you'll need every day.

Ideally, **hand-luggage** ought to be limited to valuables and things that you need for the journey: nappies/diapers and changing paraphernalia, wet-wipes, snacks and whatever you've chosen in the way of entertainment. If you're flying, be sure to check the security regulations and pack accordingly (see p.98). Organize **documents** according to destinations or stages of the trip – putting each set into its own see-through plastic bag or folder prevents damage from spills and snags, and helps you spot what you need without too much rummaging around.

As far as **general luggage** is concerned, there's no perfect formula, although you might want separate bags for the children to prevent them mucking up your things if they root through looking for something, or use mini mesh bags to keep each person's things separate within cases. Swimming and sports gear are best packed into their own bag, ready to grab and go; similarly, it makes sense to pack everyone's jumpers and shoes together: they don't need careful folding, and can be thrown into any bag regardless of its shape. It's a good idea to put small items like children's socks and underwear into separate bags within your cases. This way, you won't lose them amongst everything else – if you don't physically set them aside, an emergency search for something like a bib will quickly destroy careful packing. Plastic bags, drawstring cloth bags and pillowcases are all useful for separating small things.

PACKING STRATEGIES

"I came across these little mesh bags which come in various shapes and sizes. Some are perfect for shirts, others for underwear – you choose according to what you have. The bags are made of plastic mesh, so it's easy to keep things organized as you can see what's inside, and the semi-rigid frame means clothes keep their shape. They also come in different colours, so everyone in my family has their own colour – my youngest daughter has pink, of course. Packing, unpacking and repacking when moving from place to place is simple – you arrive, sling the mini-bags into a drawer, and when it's time to go, just throw them back into the suitcase. Everything stays organized, and nothing gets crushed or mixed up. When travelling with the family, it's inevitable that you'll start mixing up everyone's stuff at some point, but even if one suitcase gets full and you place your mini-bags elsewhere, it's easy to find and reorganize them later on."

M.M.

CLOTHING

Deciding what **clothing** to take for yourself can cause a bit of angst, but for children, decisions should be pretty straightforward. Besides considering the weather and everyone's needs from head to toe, think about the phases of your trip: you might need to buy special gear to equip the kids for the beach, for walks or for dressy evenings out. There may be cultural issues to factor in, too: if etiquette demands that you need to cover up arms and legs, it's likely that there will be dress codes for children, too – shorts may need to be below the knee, for example. Also consider taking some old clothes, socks and underwear to use as rough wear; throw them out before you return and you'll save on washing, as well as creating space for things collected on your travels. In general, though, go for low-maintenance clothing which is easy to wash and dry, doesn't crumple easily, and which requires little or no ironing. And wherever you have a choice, go for darker colours and patterned fabrics, which take longer to show up dirt than whites. Travel might seem like a good opportunity for breaking your children's peculiar dress habits, but there's no point taking along clothes that they won't wear. You might not want to give in to all-pink wardrobes and the like, but make some allowances for their favourites: if your child prefers wearing the same two T-shirts, be sure to bring them.

How much to take

It's easy to **overpack** – kids' clothes seem to take up very little room until, of course, you discover that you're short of space when all the other bits and bobs they need are factored in. It's better to pick up the odd item when travelling than carry around clothes you never need; if you overdo things, you end up creating work for yourself, as it's difficult to keep bags organized and find what you want. A useful starting point for deciding **how much to take** is to go on the longest period during which you won't be able to wash and dry clothes. Generally, children will go through more changes on holiday than they do at home – they get particularly dirty when out and about and whenever it's hot – so take one and a half times the normal ration; if it's going to be particularly hot and humid, you'll need double the norm. For a four-day stretch without the ability to wash clothes, take enough to last six or eight – bearing in mind that many things can be worn several times before needing a wash.

Keeping cool

If you're heading for the **heat**, choose clothes made from natural fibres, as it's better for children to sweat into cloth than be naked – sweat irritates delicate skins and can lead to prickly heat and/or sweat rash (see p.163). And as heat is often accompanied by mosquitoes, take along long-sleeved tops, trousers and socks to cover up with in the evenings. Expect to change your **baby** up to three times a day – particularly if they're not used to the heat and will sweat a lot. The easiest way to protect babies from insect bites (apart from mosquito nets), is to put them in a light cotton fabric sleeping bag, with a long-sleeved top, and slather a healthy dose of insect repellent on the fabric. For more on avoiding mosquito bites, see p.152. Hats are useful sun protection for all ages, but it's better to keep babies out of strong sunshine altogether.

Children will need two sets of clothes per day, and sunhats with wide brims and neck flaps are worthwhile for extended periods playing outdoors. Equally, don't overlook the fact that children's eyes are more vulnerable to glare than yours; get them sunglasses, or goggles with elasticated straps which stay on better.

Swimwear

Swim nappies/diapers are a brilliant idea for **babies,** as they allow you to use public pools without fear. It's also a good idea to get UV-protective swimwear which covers necks as well as shoulders. **Swimsuits with in-built floats** or buoyancy jackets relieve you of having to fuss with arm bands and rings, are safer if there's any chance of your child jumping in without your noticing, and you can reduce the number of floats as their swimming gets stronger. You might also want to get rubber shoe-socks to protect their feet. See p.139 for more on beach gear.

Keeping warm

If you're heading for **cold weather**, bring lots of layers rather than bulky woollens for everyone. **Babies** are mostly sedentary and don't create as much internal heat as larger folk, so they need more insulation than everyone else, including plenty of blankets as well as mittens and booties for going outdoors. Cotton vests will keep chests covered when changing nappies/diapers on the move; all-in-one cotton or flannel jumpsuits with fitted socks and pop-buttons down the front and legs also make things easier. Front-opening fleece or pile cardigans and warmer trousers are great as another layer over undergarments, and only need washing if they get soiled, so you don't need to bring too many.

If your **children** still wet themselves and will be playing outdoors, bear in mind that wool and cotton soak up water, and being wet in low temperatures is a hazard as well as uncomfortable – choose trousers in hi-tech fabrics such as fleece or pile. Similarly ski/snow jackets are always better than down jackets, as the latter take ages to dry. Tops and jackets with zip-fronts are best, as you can undo the front for a bit of ventilation rather than taking them off (and possibly losing them) altogether. For really cold conditions, long-johns and long-sleeved vests made from synthetic insulating fabrics that don't absorb moisture such as Capilene, polypropylene or Thermax are great; apart from keeping the children warm, they can double up for pyjamas as well. Children will also need their own gloves (take extra sets), hats and warm footwear; connect each pair of gloves (and baby mittens) with elastic or ribbon threaded through their clothing to make sure they don't get lost. Balaclavas are warmer than hats, and if it's very cold, opt for full snow suits – these come in all sizes.

If you're travelling **from a hot to a cold climate**, how much you invest in new clothes is a dilemma – it can be ridiculously expensive to buy coats and the like for just a few weeks away. One way around this is to get most of what you need from a secondhand store once you arrive. Most big cities have such shops, though you might have to hunt around or ask locals in order to find them.

Keeping dry

For light wet spells, you'll usually have something on hand to wrap your baby in, but if you might encounter lots of inclement weather, particularly if you're hiking and are planning to carry your baby on your front or back, bring rain ponchos and wraps with openings and a hood, or all-in-one waterproof jumpsuits or jacket-and-trouser combos. Children will need the same sort of gear, but for heavy rain and blustery conditions, take PVC-coated nylon jackets or oilskins;

look for Velcro or elasticated fastenings for collars, sleeves and trouser bottoms, flaps over jacket openings, and draw strings around the neck. Waterproofs can prove expensive, so if you're buying these new, aim for larger sizes, and get separates for older children to get the most out of the purchases.

Shoes and socks

Babies' socks and bootees have a habit of getting kicked off and lost, so attach them to each other as per gloves (see p.51). For **children**, the easier shoes are to slip on and off the better, although flip-flops fall off when children are asleep, and can prompt blisters; it's better to go for sandals with straps at the back and Velcro bindings, which can be worn with socks to prevent blisters, cold toes and mosquito bites.

If you're going to do some walking, don't bother with **hiking boots** for young children. Kids under eight won't cover much in the way of real distances, and they don't weigh enough to make shock absorption a serious issue, but good tread and ankle support for uneven ground is important – a quality pair of high-top sneakers will be fine, and they don't need synthetic walking socks, either. Regardless of what you take, always break shoes in well before the trip; you'll avoid blisters and have time to change them if you need to. Finally, bring lots of identical **socks** to avoid wasting time trying to match up pairs – and if you're going somewhere where it's usual to take off shoes before entering homes and places of worship, make sure socks are in reasonably good condition.

Walking, biking and camping

Besides bringing good footwear and rain gear, choose **colourful clothing** which stands out, and take retro-reflective sashes and belts with Velcro attachments in case you get delayed and are still out after dark. Aim for **layers**, and be prepared to slip these off and on in rapid succession according to the weather. Spending most of your time outdoors also means being a bit more circumspect than usual when choosing things like sunhats, sunglasses or waterproof jackets and trousers; you'll want quality, durable ones. Also factor in the need to protect legs from cuts and scratches: long socks and trousers made out of strong fabric (with bicycle clips if biking) will do. If you're **camping**, take flip-flops to slip on and off when around the tents; they're also useful for wearing in showers and keeping dirt off wet feet. Wellington boots make wading through dewy grass less of a trial, and also allow for wonderful play in puddles and streams. And even if it's unlikely to rain, take along waterproof jackets for damp and cold evenings, as well as warm hats and sweatshirts with hoods.

Whatever you take, time outdoors means that everything will get seriously dirty and probably damaged – leave treasured clothing behind. Everyone will probably end up wearing the same clothes day after day, and sleeping in them occasionally, too – for children, this can be a big part of the no fuss, liberating aspect of the experience. You'll probably need much less clothing than you think: children can easily get by with one outfit for every two days.

Dressing up

Even if you're planning a very laid-back and casual trip, it's surprising how often the unexpected makes you wish you'd brought something more **formal**. Fortunately, all children need is the odd accessory – something for the hair, or a particularly smart top. Taking something that you can throw on to look presentable is a good idea if you're interested in getting free upgrades on flights and hotel rooms, which are usually given to those that look like they might be able to afford the higher rates anyway. Looking presentable can seem quite a challenge under normal circumstances, and all the more so with babies, who have a way of getting you crumpled and smelly in no time, but all it takes is a jacket, shawl or silk scarf to cover up the worst.

Clothes for the journey

Choose comfortable clothing for everyone, and avoid belts or anything too close-fitting. Natural fibres help skin breathe but often crease easily, whereas synthetic fibres do the reverse; combination fibres give you the best of both worlds. Either way, consider what the clothing will feel like to sleep in (if that's what lies in store) and how everyone might end up looking at the end of the trip, especially if you're going to have your child on your lap for long stretches. Accidents do happen, so it's worth carrying **changes** of clothes for the children as well as tops for yourself. If the trip will entail swings in temperature, take layers, and dress children that still crawl on floors in trousers or leggings to keep dirt off their legs. Do give a thought to using **toilets**. Stretch-top trousers with elastic or zips to open the bottom of the legs are best for toilet stops – you can pull them down or take them off altogether without removing your children's shoes. Skirts can be simplest for girls, particularly if they might need to squat in the open or use toilets with wet floors.

If you're **breastfeeding**, you won't need reminding to take front-opening tops and bras, and to choose fabrics which are comfortable, easy to clean and in colours that don't make it obvious if you get wet. But also take a shawl or poncho for warmth and privacy – in windy conditions, you might need something to ward off dust and keep your baby snug, and shawls can double up as excellent blankets, pillows and screens to help shy children dress in public. If it's going to be a long trip, you'll probably want a change of bras and tops as well. If you're **pregnant**, be particularly sure not to wear restrictive clothing, and to take along support stockings and stretch-fabric or lace-up shoes to improve circulation in your legs.

✓ Basic clothing

BABIES

The standards	Dressing for the cold	Dressing for the heat/sun	Wet weather extras
Cotton bodysuits	All-in-one jumpsuits	Cotton clothes	Plastic poncho or rain gear
Bibs	Front-opening sweaters	Cotton sleeping bag	
Swim nappies/ diapers	Long-sleeved tops	Sunhat, UV-protective swimwear	
Something dressy for special occasions	Warm trousers	Front-opening sweaters, long-sleeved tops and trousers	
Bedding, shawl, cloths	Mitts, hats, booties, socks	Socks	
	Warm sleeping bags		
	Snow suit		

CHILDREN

Underwear	Long-sleeved vests or thermal vests and leggings	T-shirts and cotton tops	Waterproof anorak and trousers
Socks	T-shirts	Shorts, skirts or dresses	Water-resistant or quick-dry footwear
Swimwear	Fleece or pile sweaters	Lightweight sweater or cardigan	
Walking shoes	Tracksuit pants	Sunhats with brims and neck-flaps	
Sandals	Warm, waterproof jacket	Socks	
Pyjamas	Hats, scarves, gloves	Long sleeved tops and trousers	
Formal clothes		Sunglasses	
Hair accessories		UV-protective swimwear	

A **baby**'s first trip often involves being introduced to relatives. If you're planning to dress your baby up for the big moment, play it safe and change him or her into the special outfit just before arrival. It's also wise to protect their clothing with ample-sized bibs, and to keep these on at all times to catch wet burps.

TRAVEL TOILETRIES

Toiletries are heavy, so if your bathroom is stocked like a pharmacy, prepare to make some hard decisions – but most things will be available in your destination. One way of minimizing toiletries is to take baby shampoo and soap for everyone – though if you'll be using more than one bathroom, having two sets of things avoids having to go to and fro with toothpaste and the like. It's also wise to take lots of smaller packs of tooth-

✓ Travel toiletries

❏ Toothbrush/toothpaste/dental floss
❏ Deodorant
❏ Baby soap and shampoo
❏ Moisturizers
❏ Nailbrush
❏ Nail clippers
❏ Prickly heat powder
❏ Sun block
❏ Washcloth/wet wipes
❏ Tissues/toilet paper
❏ Detergent for washing clothes
❏ Travel towels
❏ Shaving gear
❏ Scissors

paste, shampoo and so forth rather than big family sizes; you can then throw each one away when it's finished rather than carting around large but ever-emptier containers. Collecting small free samples of things like shampoo, moisturizer and perfume can be useful to keep you going until you can buy more in your destination; perfume samples should be enough for the whole trip, and means you don't need to cart around fancy glass bottles.

If you've a long journey ahead, you'll want some toiletries in your hand luggage to freshen up during the trip – use plastic bags to separate items which will get wet such as toothbrushes or flannels, and check the latest security regulations (see p.98) concerning amounts of creams and liquids you can carry.

EQUIPMENT

From buggies to car seats, nappies/diapers to sterilizers, the paraphernalia you need to take with you when travelling with children can mount up. The less you take, the more freely you can get around, so if you aren't convinced that every single piece of equipment justifies itself and

THE BARE NECESSITIES

"My husband and I travelled in the States when he was doing his medical residency; this was when our first daughter, Gloria Chiquita, was born. It was the hottest summer I have ever lived through. My brother gave us a gift of a large and beautiful baby carriage; but it was too hot to use. We were staying in a tiny apartment-studio, and as we couldn't afford to buy a crib (and there was no room for it anyway), we lined a drawer with bedding and other soft things for our baby to sleep in. It worked fine, and when we weren't using it, we could just put it back out of the way. All of my five children know this story. When they became parents themselves, I made a point of reminding them to look for ways to make do with less."

Gloria Serpa-Kolbe

will make life easier then **leave it behind**. Think about substituting bulky or heavy things for more travel-friendly alternatives, and work out what you might be able to buy when you get there.

Carrying children

If you're thinking of taking something along to help with **carrying the children**, weigh up how much mileage you'll get out of each piece before finalizing what to take. Buggies, baby-carrier backpacks and the like make for awkward luggage, and if you don't end up using them much, you'll kick yourself for bringing them in the first place.

For **babies** unable to support their own weight, the most you'll need is a flat-backed, fully reclining pram or carrycot, a baby sling and a car seat. Older babies and **toddlers** can generally get by with a pram or stroller with a reclining seat, a backpack-style carrier and a child's car or booster seat. All-in-one prams/buggies for babies under six months old, with detachable seats that double up as a car seat and carrycot, are heavy, expensive and difficult to manoeuvre on your own. Unless you have help and/or are mostly travelling by car, they're not worth taking.

Carrycots, travel cots and baby bedding

Hand-held **carrycots** are superb for babies small enough to carry when on the move, and can double up as a bed, too. Although some hotels offer beds for babies, they're often pretty poor, with saggy mattresses and no shields to prevent babies from falling out, or have a frame so deep that the thought of lifting your child out in the middle of the night might put you off using it altogether. It's better to play safe and bring your own. If you're buying a carrycot for the first time, make sure that it's solid enough to take the odd bash and protect your baby. Other features to look for are plenty of stretch pockets on the outside of the frame, and a design that's easy to clean. Most carrycots come with a detachable cover for the body and a shade for the head, and some have a built-in net screen as well; apart from the obvious protection against the sun and bugs, these are useful for blocking out glaring ceiling lights – such as in airports – which tend to bother babies. If you are planning to use the cot on a flight, check with the airline that the dimensions fit their specifications.

Travel cots that break down into several pieces and pack away into their own bag are useful for babies and toddlers too large for carrycots; as well as a place to sleep, they provide a contained and clean play area, and simplify the process of sorting out a bed for your child each time you move. Four-poster travel cots with mesh-screened sides and a base off the ground are particularly good for camping.

As **bedding** suitable for babies won't be supplied by the place you stay in, you'll need to travel with a couple of cotton sheets, two blankets if appropriate to the climate, and a plastic under-sheet or waterproof mat. You can always cover them with your own shawl or jumper on top for extra warmth, and it's a good idea to bring **cloths** to place under your child's head to keep the area fresh – this way, wet burps and sweaty heads won't mean changing all the bedding. Zip-up **baby sleeping bags**, with openings for the head and arms and with a long zip down the front, are particularly useful for keeping limbs warm or protected from bugs; they're widely available, and come in warm or cool fabrics.

Baby slings

Carrying babies in a **sling** strapped to the body is understandably popular; both hands remain free and you can detect changes immediately, sensing the moment your child wakes, sneezes, or has a stomach cramp – it's also easy to keep their arms and legs out of harm's way. As carried babies tend to cry less, suffer fewer bouts of indigestion and are said to be more attentive (as they can easily engage in their surroundings), slings are the perfect travel aid: they're comfortable, practical, and fold away into no space at all. They're suitable for babies over one week old, measuring at least 53cm tall and weighing more than 3.5kg, and the best ones have wide straps that distribute weight, are machine-washable and have a back or neck support for the baby.

Child-carriers

If your baby is too heavy for a sling but you still want to carry them, consider a **child-carrier**. These backpack-like contraptions are particularly good if you're going to be doing a lot of walking, as they significantly extend the time that you can comfortably carry children. The upper weight limit obviously depends on your own build and, to a certain extent, your height; the typical weight range for child-carriers is 16–27kg, but always check that the specifications match the weight of your child before buying. Sturdy frames offer better protection to your child should you fall over, while padded, wide shoulder straps, a hip belt and sternum strap help with weight distribution. If you and your partner plan on taking turns using the carrier, the straps should also be easily adjustable, while versions with frames that sit on the ground without toppling over allow you to feed your child without having to take them out of the carrier. Last but not least, look for a model with restraining straps – you won't be able to stop your child wriggling, but you do want to keep them in.

Prams and buggies

A **pram** or **buggy** can be useful on holiday even if your child is walking, serving as a place for them to rest during day-trips, a makeshift bed when out in restaurants and something to help with carrying the bags. And even if you don't get a huge amount of use from it, a single transit stop in an airport can make it worth taking a pram or buggy along – it all depends on your trip.

If your destination is unlikely to have paved sidewalks/paths, it might be worth investing in an all-terrain version. They can be bulky when folded, though, so if there's any chance you'll be driving, make sure yours will fit into an average car along with everything else you have to take. If you might run into a lot of rain or sun, get a rain guard and/or a sun/insect screen; these can cut UV light by 70 percent, as well as keeping out bugs and gusts of wind. For colder climes, a snug inner lining is worth having; they also make a perfect underlay for a makeshift bed.

Portable high chairs

If it's likely that most restaurants in your destination won't have **high chairs**, you could take a portable version with you, essentially a fabric sleeve with an in-built seat that you can slip over the back of regular straight-backed chairs. Apart from being light, they're easy to fold away into a day bag, and simple to wash as well.

Child car seats and other restraints

Regardless of the regulations in your destination, always use **children's car seats** whenever driving with your kids. If you're buying one for the first time, take your time to choose the right one. Long journeys demand a heavy, comfortable seat with reclining options (you might even want a play table), and it's sensible to think about the seat lining in terms of what the weather will be like – you'll want cushioned fabric for the cold, and cool, easy-to-wash linings for hot and humid conditions. If you're planning to use the seat on planes within the USA or Europe, airlines may insist on models bearing the approved safety signs recognized by their region. But the main thing to check is that the seat matches the weight and size of your child – the box below lists the guidelines. If you're going to use the seat in several different cars – taxis, say – go for a universal model which works with all kinds of seatbelts; and if you aren't confident that you can install the seat safely, take the instructions with you. For general guidelines and information on some of the common errors when fitting child's car and booster seats, go to ⓦ www.childcarseats.org.uk.

The Internet has reams of useful information concerning regulations on child car seats around the world: try ⓦ www.isic.org for destinations worldwide and ⓦ www.actsinc.org/childpassengersafety.cfm for more detailed specifications within the USA.

GUIDELINES FOR CHILD CAR SEATS

Type	Weight	Approximate age
Rear-facing baby seat	0–10kg (22lb)	0 to 6 or 9 months
Rear-facing baby seat	Up to 13kg (29lb)	0 to 12 or 15 months
Forward-facing child seat	9–18kg (20–40lb)	9 months to 4 years
Booster seat	15–25kg (33–55lb)	4 to 6 years
Booster cushion	22–36kg (48–79lb)	6 to 11 years

Electronic monitors

A **baby monitor** is worth considering if you'll want to leave your child sleeping nearby. Obviously, they're not substitute childminders, but they do save you the hassle of having to get up and check on your child every five minutes. Of the three basic types, **audio monitors** are the most common. These transmit sounds to a monitor which you carry, or use a relay system which calls your mobile phone, so that you're alerted the moment your baby wakes and cries. You get to hear your child, and the better systems work both ways so that you can talk to and reassure them until you get back. **Video monitors** work on similar principles, with the extra feature of being able to see your child. You train a webcam-sized camera onto them and carry a monitor which displays their image – some have night-vision to help you see in the dark. Other kinds of monitor are designed to signal alarms if your child's **temperature** drops, but whatever type you get, make sure that an alarm will sound when batteries get low; and that you properly test whichever one you buy to make sure it works and that you know how to use it correctly.

Child monitors can be a real help to keep an eye on young children and those with special needs in crowded places such as airports and shopping malls. The parent carries a tracking device – about the size of a TV remote control – while the child wears a watch-like contraption. Should the distance between the child and the tracker exceed the user-defined range, or if the bracelets are removed, an alarm sounds. Furthermore, once the tracker sounds the alarm, you can push a button to set off a bleeper on your child's bracelet to help track them down. If you get one of these, be sure to test it at home before you go and carry ample supplies of batteries.

A **car-seat monitor** is a worthwhile investment if you plan to drive for long periods and are the only adult in the group. You fix the camera to the back of a front seat, train it on your child, and the image is beamed to a monitor in the front so you can see what's going on without having to turn around. These can be powered from a regular cigarette lighter. If you consider getting one, look for night vision capacity as well. They're not cheap, however – an additional rear-view mirror (see p.108) is a less expensive alternative.

Mobile phones

Even if you're not ordinarily a **mobile phone** user, it's worth taking one with you when you travel. You'll always be able to seek help quickly if you need it, and if there's more than one adult in the party and you're likely to want to split up, things are a lot easier if each person has a phone. If you plan on using your existing phone abroad, check with your service provider as to whether it will work in your destination, and that you're able to "roam" (make and receive calls overseas); it's a good idea to check costs for this, as they can be exorbitant. One way to get around roaming charges is to buy a **SIM card** at your destination, and use this in your own phone to make calls at local rates. Note that if your own mobile is locked into its home network, you'll need to get it **unlocked** before using another SIM; mobile phone shops will usually do this for you, or you can follow the steps on Ⓦwww.unlockme.com.

Photographic equipment

Many parents feel compelled to upgrade **cameras** or buy fancy new underwater models just before travelling, but whatever you get, keep it relatively compact, and make sure it's simple to use. If you buy a fairly basic camera, you won't be paranoid every time your child makes a grab for it.

Mosquito nets

Irrespective of whether there's malaria, yellow fever or dengue in your destination, it's sensible to buy a **bed-net** for your baby if there are likely to be any mosquitoes – it's usually simple enough to find nets for children and adults when you get there, but most hotels won't have ones you can use on cots. The best nets are impregnated with insecticide, and it's important to make sure the one you buy has enough fabric to tuck in the cot on all sides. It should also be generous enough to afford plenty of ventilation when you hang it. Baby-sized bed nets are available online and in travel-gear shops.

Washing equipment

Children get grimy at the best of times, but travel has a way of getting them really filthy. If your children still crawl around on the floor, one way of keeping them reasonably clean is to take a **plastic sheet** that you can put down anywhere for them to play on.

In most destinations, the water is usually fine for bathing even if it's not safe to drink, and as long as you can rely on being able to dunk your child into water now and again, you won't need to cart along a baby bath. You should bring a universal **plug** for sinks and baths, though, as these are often missing or ill-fitted. If you're going somewhere where hygiene and sanitation standards are poor, get your children to practise washing hands before eating, not touching things in public spaces, and using bottled instead of tap water to brush teeth and drink. As with activities designed around practising staying together, you can present these tasks as a game to be mastered.

MEALTIME EQUIPMENT AND FOOD

Wherever local standards for **food and drinking water** are high, you won't have a lot to think about in terms of equipment. However, in places where tap water is unfit for drinking and the chance of a bout of traveller's tummy is high, you'll need to make sure that everything that goes near mouths is clean. Making water safe to drink is simple (if your destination demands it, your guidebook will explain how to do this), but as bottled water is so widely available these days, it's a lot easier to stick to this when travelling with kids than carry around purifying equipment. Otherwise, all you'll need is a knife to peel fruit and veg, and if your children are using bottles or in the process of weaning, you'll need to take along the **bottle paraphernalia**, feeding bowls and spoons that you use at home. Other useful extras include a Thermos flask, which you can fill with boiling water to

STICKY RICE

"When my daughter Piper was 10 months old, I had a break in my filming schedule and decided it would be a fabulous idea to mix work and pleasure, and do publicity during my time off – which is how, between "meet and greets", we ended up in a community of mini trailer homes in St Tropez. We had Grandpa Volkers' two-room, yellow-curtained cubicle all to ourselves for seven days, and we couldn't have been happier.

Just outside our box was our patch 'lawn – of not so much grass as dirt, sand and twigs. It wasn't really an ideal environment for a 10-month-old to be crawling around in, so we laid down an old woollen army blanket from God knows where, and strung her jolly jumper up on a tree so she could while away the hours bouncing up and down in the shade while we did whatever we did when we weren't on the beach. On this particular day, I made some white rice, and was intermittently feeding clumps of it to Piper as she flew up and down beside me. At some stage, Piper got tired and wanted out of the situation, and so I hoisted her and her sticky fingers out of the contraption only to discover that her pudgy and pink feet were also sticky, and covered from toe to heel in a fine layer of dark grey wool. Little did I know it, but when pounded over and over again, white rice doubles as a particularly effective glue – my daughter had two foot-shaped wool carpets glued to the base of her feet. It took one entire week to scrape and scrub this extra epidermis off, and let me tell you, she was not happy about it. I think a scrubbing brush found under the sink was our final saviour. She came clean in the end, and despite the agony it was an event in a glorious patch of time none of us will ever forget."

Gillian Anderson

warm bottles and jars of food on the move, and possibly a portable electric kettle, too. For toddlers, non-spill drinking cups also come in very handy. In terms of **supplies of food and formula**, your choice of destination will determine whether you need to take everything you'll need from home, or whether you can bring enough for the first few days and then buy more when you get there. Infant rice and jars of baby food are particularly useful for simplifying feeding on outgoing and return trips.

Sterilizing on the move

When travelling, you need to be more fastidious than you would at home when it comes to cleaning items related to feeding babies. If you have to **sterilize** things regularly, consider taking a steam sterilizer; while these are bulky, portable versions weigh very little, and they work so well and with minimum fuss that they really are worth it. If you're self-catering, the alternative is to use a pressure cooker or a large saucepan; a rolling boil for 30 minutes, or 15 minutes in a regular pressure cooker is more than sufficient. If you don't have facilities to boil water, bring a plastic bowl (with a lid) that's large enough to submerge two bottles, and enough sterilizing tablets to cover twenty litres of water a day – you'll be able to sterilize the odd batch of fruit and vegetables as well as your bottles. If you'd prefer something ready made, look for coldwater sterilizers in baby shops or online. For **sterilizing small items** on the move – dummies/pacifiers, teething toys etc – you can use a sterilizing tablets in a watertight screw-top container; a non-spill drinks beaker is perfect.

 Feeding and sterilizing equipment

- ❏ Bottles, teats, disposable plastic bottle liners
- ❏ Feeding bowls and spoons
- ❏ Bibs, cloths and wipes
- ❏ Sieve/tea-strainer, fork, spoon and mixing bowl
- ❏ Self-sealing tupperware boxes
- ❏ Thermos flask
- ❏ Portable kettle
- ❏ Non-spill drinking cups
- ❏ Breast-pump
- ❏ Bottle brush, soap, small wedge of sponge, tongs
- ❏ Pressure cooker or an electric steam sterilizer
- ❏ Bowl for chemically sterilizing bottles
- ❏ Sterilizing tablets
- ❏ Screw-top container and drinking water for sterilizing on the move

For general **washing up**, you can use shampoo in place of dishwashing liquid, your toothbrush instead of a bottle brush. This isn't as grim as it may sound; so long as you cold-sterilize your toothbrush when you're done, you get the added bonus of a totally clean toothbrush as well as spotless implements. Alternatively, cut a wedge from a normal dish sponge.

"Even when freshly washed and relieved of all the obvious confection, children tend to be sticky."

Ann Lebowitz

FOOD FOR THE JOURNEY

For reasons of convenience as well as economy, it's sensible to take along some **food for the journey**. Pack a combination of fresh food such as sandwiches, vegetable sticks and fruit as well as long-life snacks like nuts and raisins, biscuits or processed cheese and crackers – these help stave off the odd hunger attack until you find local supplies. But whatever you take, bring things in portions that can be polished off in one sitting, as half-consumed food can be a real hassle to deal with. Also anticipate spills: water is a better choice than juice, dates are better than chocolate.

As food and used packaging often need to be carried in the same bag,

✓ Food for the journey

- ❏ Infant formula
- ❏ Infant rice
- ❏ Jars of baby food
- ❏ Fresh snacks: vegetable sticks, sandwiches, fruit etc
- ❏ Long-life snacks: nuts and raisins, cereal bars, individually wrapped crackers, cheese wedges, easy-open tins, sweets and biscuits, dried soup
- ❏ Sachets of coffee, tea, sugar, hot chocolate
- ❏ Water bottles

take strong self-sealing plastic bags to keep things clean and separate. If your child is on **bottles**, bring what you need to make up fresh ones along the way; to save space, fill spare bottles with water, then add milk powder and top up with boiling water when you need them. Otherwise, put **sterilized dummies/pacifiers and spoons** into small resealable boxes – one for clean sets, and another for dirties (and make sure you can tell which is which). And if you're going to carry baby food in glass jars, slip each one into a thick sock to prevent them from breaking.

WASHING CLOTHES

Washing clothes usually features pretty high on the agenda of travelling parents; if you have leaky babies and toddlers, you're probably in for some hand-washing every day. While you can get clothes-washing detergent everywhere, sensitive or allergic skins might warrant taking your usual brands. Boxes of soap powder don't travel well, so either decant into a series of self-sealing plastic bags, layering one inside another, or bring concentrated travellers' washing soap.

NAPPIES/DIAPERS

Dealing with **nappies/diapers** is always a chore, and all the more so when away from home. **Disposable nappies/diapers** mean less mess and stench, and increased space in your luggage as you use your supplies, but in poor regions of the world with weak infrastructure, it's almost irresponsible to use them – in fact, "disposable" becomes a bit of a misnomer in places where facilities for getting rid of them are nonexistent. Furthermore, if you travel for extended periods of time, you will eventually have to find local supplies; wherever disposable nappies/diapers are imported, they can be expensive, and it can prove difficult to find sizes which fit.

Nonetheless, if you usually use **cloth nappies/diapers**, you might want to think twice whilst travelling, as soiled ones inevitably present problems on the road. At the very least, consider making an exception and taking a small supply of disposables for the outgoing and return journeys. Otherwise, you'll need to bring large self-sealing plastic bags to store dirties on journeys, and perhaps a bucket with an airtight lid for washing them in when you get there. If this sounds too grim, you could try making a **do-it-yourself disposable nappy/diaper**. Sandwich swathes of cotton wool roll between two sheets of gauze/muslin-like fabric; hold this in place – as you would a cloth nappy/diaper – with safety-pins

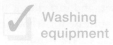

✓ Washing equipment

Keeping clean while out and about
- ❑ Wet wipes
- ❑ Washcloth, bottled water and soap
- ❑ Plastic floor mat for playing

Nappies/diapers
- ❑ Cloth nappies/diapers, safety pins and plastic pants
- ❑ Disposable nappies/diapers
- ❑ Barrier cream
- ❑ Plastic changing sheet

Nappy/diaper washing
- ❑ Bucket with lid
- ❑ Washing bowl
- ❑ Bleach/antiseptic
- ❑ Detergent

Toilet training
- ❑ Portable potty
- ❑ Potty liners
- ❑ Toilet seat covers
- ❑ Plastic mattress mat

before covering up with plastic pants. When soiled, discard the cotton wool (which is biodegradable) and hang on to the material; being lightweight, the gauze is easy to carry and wash, and quick to dry.

But whichever nappies/diapers you choose, there's the question of **how many to take** – the minimum is enough for the outbound journey and your first few days, as you'll probably be able to buy more when you get there. Before you leave, keep track of how many nappies/diapers your child uses on an average day, and take treble the normal count for the journey there to cover more frequent changes as well as possible delays. If you're using cloth nappies/diapers, take enough to last three days – even if you could go for longer without washing them, you wouldn't want to. Bear in mind, though, that the process of deciding how many nappies/diapers to take ultimately takes care of itself: once you know where you stand with your packing, you'll probably fill all the remaining space with them.

When **packing nappies/diapers**, remember that cloth versions can double up as wipe-cloths and towels, making it unnecessary to take the latter. And if your child uses disposables, consider getting a suitably sized box (choose a carton rather than plastic wrapping) straight from the supermarket, and carrying it unopened so that you don't have to take a separate suitcase for what's going to be a fast-dwindling supply. If the box doesn't have handles, make some yourself out of tape or string.

TOILET TRAINING

If your child uses a **potty**, consider taking a portable version – these consist of a frame to sit on, which you line with a disposable plastic bag. Some parents swear by them, but you need to have a certain attitude to use them in urban and crowded settings. If your child is frightened of sitting on toilets (and having to hold tight to avoid falling in), you can take a plastic toilet cover designed for children to place over regular seats. Either way, take wet-wipes to clean seats before and after use, and don't forget **plastic underlay** to keep mattresses dry.

ENTERTAINMENT

Children can and do play anywhere, and the excitement of travel and new places is usually enough to keep them engrossed – even public toilets can provide instant entertainment, what with toilets to be flushed, buttons which eject hot air and reams of paper to be pulled. But at some junctures – and maybe to get them away from places such as toilets – you'll need your own portable supply of things to keep them **entertained**.

Everything you take should be **dispensable** – if your child is attached to a particular teddy bear or blanket, think carefully before bringing it, and imagine the scenes en route if you can't find whatever the must-have toy is. It might be better to "lose" it some weeks before you leave, and then enjoy a reunion on return – unless, of course, as with autistic children, your child depends on having familiar things around. Also factor in that toys can get dirty, dragged across airport floors, dropped in the middle of roads and hugged again seconds later – the easier they are to clean the better.

Don't forget your children will meet others when away, and though travel tends to increase their facility for **playing with others**, kids can still do with a bit of help. It's a good idea to bring toys that more than one person can play with to help bridge gaps, from marbles or tiddlywinks to board and card games. But bear in mind that tears can start when it comes to parting and packing the toys away. For such "emergencies" and for times when you feel like leaving a gift, take extras like packets of balloons to give away.

Toys which stimulate **exercise** are also worthwhile; consider balls made from sponge or perforated plastic as well as bean bags (hacky sacks); these are light and can be used indoors, even in busy places such as airports. And for stretching legs elsewhere, frisbees and tennis balls also pack well, and can be used to play lots of different games.

Lastly, don't overlook the fact that you can just **talk** or **read** to the children and play any number of games that don't require accessories, from memory, counting and clapping games to incy wincy spider or patta-cake, as well as paper games like noughts and crosses or hangman. The real secret to keeping children entertained when on the road is to view travel as time for spending together.

PLAYTHINGS FOR BABIES

Travel toys for **babies** won't differ much from those you'd use at home – they need to be impossible to swallow, easy to keep clean and with no sharp or hard edges. Look for a selection of teething toys that are fun to hold and rattle as well as interesting to look at, while anything that plays lullabies or music can be a real help in distracting them from a crying session, or getting them relaxed and to sleep. You might also

HOLIDAY READING FOR CHILDREN

Exploring nature

Bug Hunter David Burnie. A very creative book for those interested in creepy crawlies, with information to get them started as students of biology and habitats.

A Child's Guide to Wild Flowers Charlotte Voake. A unique and beautiful book, with high-quality, immediately recognizable illustrations. The layout helps children get started with classifying plants and find what they're looking at, but the text is particularly skilful, capturing the character of each plant – the way it feels, smells etc – to help them recall what they see.

Nature Ranger Richard Walker. Ingenious and simple-to-follow activities (including identifying what's in the dirt in your shoes) to make observing nature and walking more fun for children.

Camping

Campfire Cuisine Robin Donovan. One for the adults, with lots of recipes that show campfire cooking can be healthy and rather delicious.

Cooking on a Stick Linda White. Sensible and safe ways to cook on a stick, in pouches or on a grill.

Kids camp! Laurie Carlson. Activities for the backyard or wilderness. Illustrated with line drawings, themes that make good discussion points, projects (such as making an insect viewer), and simple recipes.

The Kids Campfire Book Jane Drake. Covers helpful themes such as preparing and putting out campfires or how to identify night sounds, as well as some silly songs.

Travel by plane

Busy Airports Rebecca Finn. A board book with pictures and pull-outs, covering landing, runways, luggage carousels and the like.

Topsy and Tim go on an Aeroplane Jean and Gareth Anderson. This airport bestseller covers each stage of the trip, and helps parents talk through and explain what's in store.

consider a mobile to hang above their cot, or to place in view when in cars. Do consider ways to secure toys with ribbons or string so that they don't get lost or keep ending up on the floor.

PLAYTHINGS FOR TODDLERS

Despite being a handful, **toddlers** are reasonably simple to entertain. Take books made out of cloth with different fabrics, flaps to open and interesting textures or surfaces to touch and look at, as well as toys that squeak when pressed or play music (although you might want to reserve the latter for moments when you aren't hemmed in on all sides by fellow travellers). Gather a supply of things that you wouldn't mind losing or discarding: paper cups, plastic spoons, yoghurt pots, jam jar lids and beer mats are all good examples. Once you arrive at your

Travel by car

Busy Garage Ladybird Books. A classic, with pictures and lots of detail to spark off conversations and questions, as well as build vocabulary around cars.

Busy Garage Rebecca Finn. Board book with pop-ups and pictures of different scenes in a garage.

My Car Trip Sindy McKay. Takes you through a car trip from packing, being on the road to arriving; this is a helpful starting point for discussing the phases of car travel with your child – including the need to behave well on the way.

Travel by train

Busy Railway Rebecca Finn. This board book has great pictures and pull-outs that allow you to change the scenes.

The Railway Cat Phyllis Arkle. Lovely tales of Alfie the cat and his escapades in and around his train station home, as well as trips to London and escaping hair-raising accidents.

That's not my Train Fiona Watts and Rachel Wells. Pictures with textures to explore for sensory development.

Trains Jo Litchfield. Scenes of railway life, with very simple jigsaw puzzles for little hands to help with coordination as well as vocabulary.

Activity books

Are We There Yet Backseat Books. Intended for children to use on their own, this colourful book is stuffed with puzzles, mazes, connect-the-dots games and colour-by-number drawings.

The Big Book of Car Games Frederic Houssin and Cedric Ramadier. A spiral-bound collection of activities, from simple things like colouring and drawing pages, puzzles, songs and games (including the King of Silence – the winner is the one that stays quiet for the longest!), to more involved pursuits like making your own postcards, puppets and masks.

Fifty Things to do on a Journey Usborne Activity Cards. A pack of robust and durable cards, each outlining a fun activity to break up the time on long journeys; includes puzzles and quizzes, some of which are based on things you might see from a car.

destination, add a few extras to the stash: water, spoons, clean stones (too large to swallow), even veg such as carrots or potatoes; the mix should keep toddlers absorbed for hours.

PLAYTHINGS FOR UNDER-FIVES

For **children under five**, the staples are colouring materials (avoid felt tips and crayons – pencils make the least mess), a hard-backed blank notebook for drawing and to use as a diary, paper, sticks of glue, sticky tape and blunt scissors as well as a pack of cards for simple games. Small toys that invoke the imagination, such as cars and farm animals, are great for long trips. And while things like building blocks or Lego are not terribly practical when on the move, they are worth taking for use at your destination – there will be periods when you want to stay put in your room and need something more involved for the children to play with. While figuring out what to take, don't overlook the fact that travel provides plenty of opportunities for **learning** – so take some reading and skills development books to work on together.

If you're going to be stuck in seats for hours, there's nothing that beats movies; think of taking a **portable DVD player** or a similar device. **Audiobooks** and **music** are also well worth having, and there's no need bring many given that most kids will watch the same material over and over again – perhaps for this very reason, consider taking headphones to give yourselves and your neighbours a break.

Bear in mind that while it's always worth getting some new things,

secondhand and borrowed toys will do – all that matters is the novelty. Keep new things hidden and introduce them one at a time whenever your child needs help with getting engaged – and as you add new playthings, remove others and re-introduce them later.

OLDER CHILDREN

The toys mentioned above will still interest children **over five**, but kids of this age will also be ready to entertain themselves. Even if they aren't great readers yet, travel and long periods with little else to focus on can end up being just the thing to jumpstart progress in their reading. You might also consider puzzles, quiz books and word games. Another simple way to keep children absorbed for hours – albeit with some start-up help – is an unlined **notebook** (see p.76). Otherwise, the over-5s are also ready for **board games** – there are plenty of travel versions with magnetic or pegging systems to keep pieces in place. Even if you don't imagine getting all that much use out of a board game, they make good gifts, particularly in countries where they might be a novelty. And if you've forgotten just how versatile a pack of cards can be, try getting a book such as *Card Games for Kids* by Adam Ward, which has more than fifty ideas, from very simple versions of snap to more involved memory games.

KEEPING CHILDREN HAPPY

"I have travelled a lot on my own with the girls by plane, and more recently with our baby son as well – my husband doesn't have much in the way of free time and can't always come with us. Whenever we travel, I allow a lot of extra time for logistics – my brain seems to be in so many places at the same time. It's not easy travelling with small children on your own; but the kids are always fine. The standards I carry are pencils and paper (the source of lots of games and drawings), plus one book each, one or two treats; a pack of sweets (if all hell breaks loose or if they have been remarkably good), and a lollipop – very good for blocked ears as planes descend.

We read stories together which they always love. I also find things about the places we're going to visit beforehand, and weave these into tales. Bits of history get turned into fairy stories. I don't aim for accuracy – I just try to keep them entertained. We also go over a few words of the language together. They're pretty quick to learn, and the response of strangers to their few new words gets them really excited and ready for more when we arrive. Long-haul flights can be tough, but a DVD player works like magic. I bought one for a long trip a couple of years back and I've never regretted the investment. However, if you do take one along, make sure you decide on which film to watch beforehand to avoid fights between the children. Otherwise, I also make a point of looking out for other families with kids. You quickly get a feel for people if you watch them interacting with their kids, and it doesn't take much to steer children together. Once they start playing with each other, it all gets much, much easier."

Alexandra Jefford

ENTERTAINING AND PAMPERING YOURSELF

"A child is a plaything for an hour."

Mary Lamb 1775–1834

Whatever you do, don't neglect entertainment for yourself; there are likely to be long stretches ahead when the children are asleep or happy playing for hours without wanting to move. Rather than feeling stuck and frustrated, cash in on the fact that you've got time to yourself. A good supply of reading materials and music is an obvious start, Even if you don't usually write a diary, you might want to consider taking something along to jot down thoughts or plans, or take materials to start a new hobby such as painting. And providing you're prepared to look after it, a laptop is an entertainment system in itself. Finally, all things for the mind and body, from exercises and relaxation techniques to beauty treatments, are rare treats for parents who otherwise rarely get time to themselves.

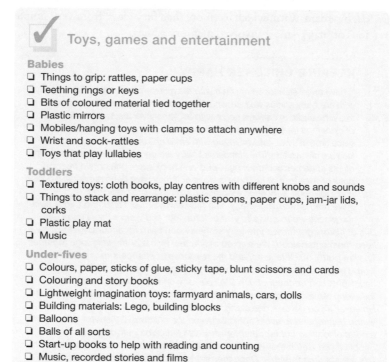

✓ Toys, games and entertainment

Babies
- ❑ Things to grip: rattles, paper cups
- ❑ Teething rings or keys
- ❑ Bits of coloured material tied together
- ❑ Plastic mirrors
- ❑ Mobiles/hanging toys with clamps to attach anywhere
- ❑ Wrist and sock-rattles
- ❑ Toys that play lullabies

Toddlers
- ❑ Textured toys: cloth books, play centres with different knobs and sounds
- ❑ Things to stack and rearrange: plastic spoons, paper cups, jam-jar lids, corks
- ❑ Plastic play mat
- ❑ Music

Under-fives
- ❑ Colours, paper, sticks of glue, sticky tape, blunt scissors and cards
- ❑ Colouring and story books
- ❑ Lightweight imagination toys: farmyard animals, cars, dolls
- ❑ Building materials: Lego, building blocks
- ❑ Balloons
- ❑ Balls of all sorts
- ❑ Start-up books to help with reading and counting
- ❑ Music, recorded stories and films

THE RIGHT STATE OF MIND

One of the inevitabilities of travel is that few things turn out as you imagined. Expectations and fears are debunked, and after a while, your mind has a chance to rest and fully inhabit the moment. Before you set off, though, this serene state can seem a far-off thing, and while you don't want to waste time fussing over pre-trip anxieties, it is a good idea to mentally prepare yourself and your children for what's ahead.

PREPARING THE CHILDREN

Getting your children started on a few holiday-related **projects** before you leave is a great way to prepare them for what's to come. Depending on their ages, you could explore maps, or the history, geography, animal- and plant-life of your destination, or read books or watch a film that's set there. If you anticipate seeing a lot of completely unfamiliar

---

TRAVELLERS' TALES

RAMESES' NAPPY/DIAPER

"We've been on the road with our son since he was born, which makes it nearly five years now. We've been all around northern Africa, and we're currently working our way from the southern tip of Latin America to the north. We'll have to stop sometime soon for school – and are not really sure how he'll cope with staying put – but the travel has been just wonderful.

We've had a few hiccups. There's one time in particular that I remember: I found myself in a spot where I just didn't know what to do. We were in Egypt, deep within a pyramid, making our way to Rameses' tomb on a guided tour. We had a long queue of people behind us – this was a revered site with people praying in corners with candles along the walk. And of course, this was when Amos chose to have the most almighty poo. There was no way of getting out – we were hemmed in with people front and back, and stuck in these narrow, dark tunnels. Besides, either I changed the nappy/diaper then and there, or risked dealing with worse and soon.

I was embarrassed and, frankly, a bit scared of what the locals would think – we might be desecrating holy ground. As it happened, the troupe I was with, including the guide, all quickly twigged (smelt?) what was happening – the guide led us to the chamber which held Rameses' tombs so that I could have a bit more room to manoeuvre. I placed Amos on the ground and got going. People ended up chipping in – candles were brought to help us see better, and the awkwardness soon transformed into hoots of laughter. By the time we got the clean nappy/diaper strapped into place, we were surrounded by a much larger crowd than at the beginning. The guard ceremoniously declared Amos to be the sacred guest of the pharaoh – the first (known) baby to have his nappy/diaper changed under Rameses' direct supervision. Whenever you're worried about something, it often turns out that your fears are unfounded."

Anonymous

AUTISM AND STORYTELLING

"Our trip to San Diego was a disaster; Isaac was really unhappy and cried a lot. However, when we went to Kansas, I tried the storytelling method which I learnt about at a conference. I prepared a story with the kind of detail Isaac has to have. I was careful to be precise with language. For instance, I made the story definite where I knew certain things would happen – for example, "You will see lots of cars" – but was otherwise non-committal, but nevertheless mentioned things that might happen that he would generally enjoy, such as: "We might go to McDonald's". I also put in a few suggestions to make our lives a bit easier, such as: "You will enjoy watching your DVDs". The story had lists of his favourite things we were taking, which meant we had to be really sure we took all of these with us for him to check over. I then told the story each day for over a week, and it made a lot of difference. In the first instance, he was much less anxious when it came to setting off. And there were no meltdowns apart from the one time where my sister-in-law made him a peanut butter and jam sandwich which was different to what he usually gets at home – the kind of thing you can't do much about."

Anna Rankin

things or famous sights, you can build these into a game: cut out picture equivalents and stick them into the first pages of a notebook or their diary (see p.73) to make a sort of **traveller's bingo**. Your child can then keep tallies of each sighting, or cross each picture off until you've seen them all.

Storytelling is also a marvellous way to get children excited and inspired about your destination, particularly if you can come up with a fairytale set in the place you plan to visit – each time you see something that invokes the atmosphere of the story, even if it's a frog that turned into a prince, it's likely to spark off lively conversation. If disruptions to routine bother your child, stories are also a good way of reducing their anxieties. You could dream up a tale centred on the trip with your child as the main character, and include details from what you expect to see to the people they're likely to meet and, in particular, things they can expect to enjoy. Similarly, if you're off to see friends or relatives, tell the children about the lives of your hosts and why these people are special to you and to them, perhaps getting out some photos, too. This helps with breaking the ice when you arrive, and with getting your children to accept that their parents might need time with others besides themselves.

New languages and food

In preparation for new **languages**, teach your children a few basic words; most will enjoy it, and when they get to practise for real, the reactions boost their confidence no end – it's amazing how disarming a simple "hello" or "thank you" can be when uttered by a child. You might also consider copying out a list of basic words for them, adding new ones later on as they pick them up.

If the **food** is likely to be radically different, research dishes that they might enjoy, and try rustling up something similar before you go. This will help to avoid awkward moments when eating out; instead of a "yeuch, what is that?!", you might hope for a "look, they have Mien Hoen noodle soup!" Either way, so long as you're experimental with food, the children will be encouraged to be too – and there's nothing quite like being hungry to get children to eat.

Manners and customs

Think through the **cultural do's and don'ts** before you go – there may be new customs to learn, such as avoiding touching food with the left hand, or walking indoors with shoes – we given a rough idea of what to expect in the "Around the World" section, but it's a good idea to do some research yourself, either by reading guidebooks or checking out online travellers' forums (see p.10). If local people bow or use special greetings with their hands, start practising these with the children; and a bit of reinforcement of universal manners is also a good idea. In particular, remind them not to say that the food or anything else is disgusting out loud, and make them aware that there are people who understand English everywhere.

"Children are natural mimics who act like their parents despite every effort to teach them good manners."

Anon

Anticipating the unpleasant

If you know that your choice of destination will mean coming face to face with people living in **poverty**, aggressive beggars or staring crowds and the like, some preparation will help your children to deal with it all and go some way to prevent them from becoming overwhelmed. Start off by looking at pictures of the kind of scenes you might encounter, and discuss them with your children. Explain what to expect, and be prepared to suggest some reasons for why the world is the way it is. It's likely that this will prompt a series of the "why?" questions that children are famous for: "why are they poor?", "why are they dirty?", "why do they stare?" and so on. It's probably best to avoid being explicit about some of the world's tragedies or telling them anything that might frighten them – just stick to whatever you feel they are ready for. In particular, remind them that they may meet children who

CHARITIES FOR CHILDREN

If what you see on your travels upsets you or your children, you might want to consider ways to put something back or make things better, perhaps by approaching one of the organizations listed below.

General

International Save the Children Alliance @ www.savethechildren.net/alliance. Via a network of country-based NGOs, the ISCA's mission is to "fight for children in the UK and around the world who suffer from poverty, disease, injustice and violence, working with them to find lifelong answers to the problems they face".

Terre des Hommes @ www.terredeshommes.org. An international organization that develops and implements projects designed to improve the living conditions of disadvantaged children all over the world.

UNICEF @ unicef.org. Works towards giving children the best possible start in life, focussing on health, education and other initiatives and through various local partnerships.

HIV/AIDS

The Global Campaign on Children and HIV/AIDS @ unicef.org. UNICEF's global campaign supports various initiatives including HIV/AIDS orphans and interventions to prevent babies getting infected in the first place.

Child Trafficking

End Child Trafficking Campaign @ unicef.org. UNICEF campaign to end child trafficking and support other initiatives to uphold child's rights.

are very poor – this can come as a shock, and might not cross their minds if you don't mention it or specifically seek out pictures to show them. Equally, don't forget how you might react yourself; regardless of how well you prepare your children, your reactions are very likely to affect them more than anything they see. If you aren't sure of how you will respond, consider keeping the children away from anything potentially unpleasant until you can venture out alone and test your own reactions.

Wherever you go, there are likely to be some instances where your child gets **unwanted attention** (for more on which, see p.166). People might stare at them, or total strangers might want to touch or even cuddle them. Certainly, if your child looks very different to the locals, expect some attention and discuss it in advance. You might explain that this happens because their features are different, thereby getting them to perceive the interest as a bit of a compliment – a bit like being a film star. However, assure them that you will watch closely to see how they are, and that if they feel uncomfortable, you'll find ways to get them away without seeming rude.

If your child has an obvious physical or mental **disability**, people in some parts of the world may be less sensitive than others. This is a tough issue to face, and while it may be inappropriate to prepare your child for this kind of thing in advance, you can and should prepare yourself and your other children to keep calm and support your child. Some parents write out and photocopy cards of what they want others to know about the condition; they then give these out to those they end up being seated next to, or hang onto them until a situation arises that prompts handing them out. For example, one parent distributed cards at a restaurant when her child started to have a fit. Such cards may say something to the effect of: "You may have noticed that our daughter/son is different. S/he has a condition called "x" which means . . .". You might also include: "It would help us if you would/would not . . ." And to raise awareness still further, you might want to end with: "If you want to learn more about this condition, check ⓦwww . . .".

YOUR HOSTS

If you're going to be staying in someone else's home, it's always worth putting yourself in the shoes of your hosts before you go. Get in touch and ask if they have any concerns, discuss how you might share tasks such as shopping and cooking, and clarify when you might be able to rely on their help, such as the odd lift from a nearby station when you get back from day-trips. If they can't help, it's best to know in advance rather than assume they can or will. And if you have particular requirements or a special wishlist of things you'd like to do, let your hosts know and perhaps invite them along. Mention whatever it is that's on your mind, and invite them to do the same. If your child has **special needs**, consider sending your hosts the best literature you have on the condition – the more everyone knows, the more relaxed everyone can hope to be.

Even if this isn't the first time you're visiting with the children, expect some adjustments on both sides. With each absence, your children will grow and change fundamentally in terms of their needs; hosts often forget this and spend a lot of time preparing things based on the children's favourites the last time they visited – which, of course, are likely to have since changed. Some people – the elderly in particular – go to great lengths in making preparations, so it's considerate to provide them with direction and help with getting things right. Be specific about food the children like to eat, as a refusal to eat a meal can be hurtful to the cook. And to help break the ice, give your hosts a few insights into whatever's happening in the worlds of your children: things they're into, issues they may be facing at school and so on.

LEAVING HOME

The last days before you **leave home** can be a little draining. As you don't want to start a trip feeling completely exhausted, try aiming to be completely ready to leave on the day before you actually depart. If all goes to plan, you can use the final day to relax, get some exercise or extra sleep. The things that do have to be done last-minute are actually quite minimal; the problem is that many of them take a lot longer than you might anticipate, and come at a time when you're probably not at your best in terms of brainpower. Everyone, including the kids, tends to be a bit agitated as leaving day draws near.

Distractions are common. Children can take up a lot of time you'd rather spend on preparations, and can also create extra work by pulling things out of packed bags and the like. Interruptions also tend to be more frequent: as people learn you're leaving, they may call to make last-minute requests or offer help, and you'll often find yourself trying to do far too many things at once and forgetting what you were supposed to be doing in the first place. It's easy to spend the last day struggling to finalize preparations, but only find the peace to get things done in the small hours of the night. There are ways to avoid this scenario, though, and it's all about being organized in the way you get ready.

AVOIDING CLASSIC TIME-WASTERS

Many of the things that typically consume your time just before leaving can be dealt with much earlier on, so we've suggested ways to avoid the most common time-wasters. In general, though, try to respond to last-minute "must have" thoughts with a "too late!"; there's very little that is really necessary.

▶ Despite efforts to the contrary, you might still find yourself doing **last-minute shopping** for things you need before you go or during the journey, and what's intended to be just a quick dash to the shops frequently takes a lot longer and demands more energy than you might think – but in the majority of cases, the trip is unnecessary in the first place. It's far better to **plan what you need in advance**. Long-life or powdered milk and crackers can serve as backups should you run out of fresh supplies; and a stock of pasta, frozen pizzas and a few tins are all you need to make basic meals. If you want fresh bread for the trip, freeze a loaf and thaw it out the day before you go. Similarly, if you want to carry fruit for the journey, get some apples or oranges ahead of time, as these keep and travel well.

▶ Household chores can be hard when coupled with the extra effort of trying to leave the place clean and cleared for your absence. The key is to **break the regular routine**. While you might be able to cook a meal quickly, it'll always mean cleaning up afterwards – so for the last couple of days before setting off, consider stopping cooking altogether and opting for sandwiches, cold cuts, salads and fruit, or getting takeaways. You might also relax traditions of getting everyone to eat together if this seems hard to do, and leave food out so adults can help themselves.

▶ In terms of **household cleaning**, tackle the big jobs early rather than leaving them till the last minute. Clean out the fridge a few days before you go, then just before you leave, review what's in it and throw whatever might spoil away. If someone is looking after your home while you're away, consider excusing yourself in advance for not leaving the place picture perfect, and asking if they wouldn't mind taking the rubbish out. For most people, this is not too much to ask; taking out rubbish seems to be doomed to be ill-timed – as soon as you do, there's always something else to throw away, particularly if you have a child in nappies/diapers. On that note, if someone is staying at your house while you're away, don't leave the **handover** until the last minute, and arrange a briefing session for at least a week before you go.

▶ You might also spend a lot of time **washing clothes** right until the last minute. It's obviously far better to wear only clothes you don't want to bring in the final few days before departing, but if this isn't possible, then consider taking some dirty things with you, and washing when you next can.

▶ **Minding the children** is always a challenge. Obviously, it's best to block a period to leave them with someone else while you organize the bulk of the packing. Alternatively, arrange a film to keep them entertained, or resign yourself to interruptions, and allow for the extra time that this calls for.

▶ If you keep getting interrupted by **the phone**, unplug it or switch on the answerphone until things are under control; and when you do take calls, start off by announcing that you only have a couple of minutes at the most, and do your best to stick to this.

▶ If you have trouble tearing yourself away from **email**, you aren't alone, but don't leave it all till the eleventh hour. Set up a web-based email address well in advance, and send yourself backups of scanned tickets, reservation details and identity papers, as well as phone numbers and addresses for the trip.

THE DAY BEFORE YOU GO

By **the day before you leave**, you should have sets of clothes organized for the journey – particularly if leaving in the small hours of the morning. Try to envisage all the details, down to the socks, belts and earrings, as indecision or trying to find things when getting dressed can be surprisingly unsettling. You should also aim to have all bags packed and closed on the day before travelling, with space reserved to accommodate toiletries and snacks, which are generally the last things to go in. Nonetheless, it's inevitable that you'll still want to make some changes to what you have in your bags. To avoid leaving something crucial behind, get in the habit of placing anything intended for your bags physically on top of them, and if your children might tinker with your things, keep the open bags out of reach. For obvious reasons, be particularly careful when it comes to documents such as ID, as well as credit cards and cash etc – keep these well out of the children's reach.

Some try to **anticipate jetlag** and set their routine to the time of their destination by staying up late or trying to sleep early. With children, this is unlikely to work, and the results are variable in any case. That said, it certainly helps to get a decent night's sleep on your final night. If you're setting off in the morning, give the children a particularly thorough bath before bedtime rather than bothering with this in the morning; and if setting off in the middle of the night, you might even consider partially dressing them for the trip to avoid disturbing them when it is time to go.

THE LAST DAY

Thankfully, things that have to be left to the **last day** are pretty minimal. As you get dressed, put your housekeys into your pocket; there's a lot of opening and closing doors to come, and with kids and other distractions, it's easy to get locked out. Besides, as soon as you've shut the door, you'll inevitably remember something you forgot, or will want to check that you've switched off the stove. Whatever you do, don't slip your only set of keys through the letterbox for someone

else to use after you go – always plan to take a set of keys with you.

After the final teeth-brushing session, the toilet bag needs to be packed. Once this is in your luggage, the very last thing that needs to go in are fresh snacks (including clean bottles and hot water for babies' bottles); once these are in, you're ready to finally zip up and lock your luggage. But before leaving, get everyone to use the toilet, and do a last tour to see if anything's been forgotten, preferably with the children outside the door and being looked after by someone else. Do a final check that you have the basics: identity papers, tickets and reservation documents, credit cards and cash, prescription medications, insurance papers, food, nappies/diapers and your keys. Count your bags both inside, and on the other side of your front door – and if all is well, you're set!

✓ Packing

Hand luggage

- ❏ Passports and visas ▶▶ p.41
- ❏ Tickets
- ❏ Insurance papers ▶▶ p.44
- ❏ Medical and vaccination records ▶▶ p.34
- ❏ Attestations for carrying medicines ▶▶ p.42
- ❏ Vaccination exemption letters ▶▶ p.34
- ❏ Adoption papers ▶▶ p.42
- ❏ Authorization to travel as single parent ▶▶ p.42
- ❏ Driving licence
- ❏ Itinerary
- ❏ Reservation records and receipts
- ❏ Guidebooks, maps, addresses and phone numbers
- ❏ Photographs ▶▶ p.41
- ❏ Cash, travellers' cheques, credit cards and account details
- ❏ Medication and medical kit ▶▶ p.39
- ❏ Mobile phone ▶▶ p.62
- ❏ Photographic equipment ▶▶ p.62
- ❏ Bottle paraphernalia, dummies/pacifiers, feeding and cleaning items ▶▶ p.65
- ❏ Breastfeeding paraphernalia ▶▶ p.133
- ❏ Nappies/diapers and changing/cleaning accessories ▶▶ p.65
- ❏ Basic toiletries including toilet paper
- ❏ Food and drink ▶▶ p.66
- ❏ Reading and entertainment material
- ❏ Pen

- ❏ Watch
- ❏ Ear plugs, eye shades, neck cushions
- ❏ Spare clothes, shawl or poncho if breastfeeding
- ❏ Tissues and wet-wipes
- ❏ Whistles

Children's backpacks

- ❏ Toys, snacks, drinks
- ❏ Travel socks, warmer clothing
- ❏ Pencil case with crayons, pencils, round-edged scissors, glue stick
- ❏ Diary
- ❏ Reading material

Elsewhere in regular bags

- ❏ Bedding for baby ▶▶ p.57
- ❏ Child carriers – carrycot, baby slings, backpack, pram/buggy, car or booster seats ▶▶ p.57
- ❏ Mosquito nets ▶▶ p.63
- ❏ Toiletries ▶▶ p.56
- ❏ Portable potty ▶▶ p.68
- ❏ Clothing and shoes ▶▶ p.49
- ❏ Swimsuits (and swim nappies/diapers) ▶▶ p.50
- ❏ Entertainment for you and the children ▶▶ p.69
- ❏ Resealable plastic bags
- ❏ Manila envelopes
- ❏ Insulating tape
- ❏ Ball of string
- ❏ Alarm clock
- ❏ Baby bath (if space is not a problem)
- ❏ Sterilizer, plastic bowl for chemically sterilizing bottles ▶▶ p.65

The are more specialized packing lists in "Making the Journey"; see p.105 for travel by plane, p.116 for cars, p.122 for trains and buses, and p.146 for camping trips.

MAKING THE JOURNEY 2

MAKING THE JOURNEY

Journeys can be draining, so it's good sense to make getting there as stress-free as you can. Arriving tired and frazzled isn't an auspicious start to a family holiday, and probably means a couple of days wasted just to get over it. We've suggested some general travel tips in this section, as well as some specifics on how to handle plane, car, bus and train trips with the kids.

WATCHING THE BAGS AND THE KIDS

The added distraction of children when travelling means it's harder than usual to **keep an eye on your things**. The first rule of thumb is to make it difficult for anyone to touch your bags without you noticing, by stacking the pieces one on top of the other and leaning some part of your body against the pile. Also bear in mind that loud noises or scenes and, in particular, people bumping into you, are classic **distraction scams** and might mean that pickpockets or thieves are about — always check your belongings before looking around to see what the fuss is.

Besides being particularly beady eyed in terms of watching the kids each time you change direction and speed, journeys are a key time to employ the techniques suggested on p.33 for keeping track of children in crowds — and in each new place, don't forget to designate a meeting point in case anyone gets separated from the group. If it's likely you'll be in really dense crowds, promising a reward for staying together works as a good incentive.

COPING WITH QUEUES

Travel almost always involves a bit of **queuing**, and the likelihood of children getting restless increases with the time you have to stay put. But there are ways of making it less painful: if there are two adults, the obvious option is for one to hold your place in the line while the other looks after the children. If you're the only adult, try getting in line then asking those in front and behind to save your place, explaining that you have children to look after — most will instinctively understand. You can then look after the kids nearby until your turn comes up.

The best way to deal with **luggage** when queuing is to place bags a few metres ahead of you (but in full view), rather than keeping them by your side and inching them along each time your line moves; when you draw alongside, move them ahead another few metres. (Just make sure you stay near enough to be identified as the owner of your luggage, so that no one could mistake your things as having been abandoned). Lastly, you don't lose anything by asking officials if you can be excused from having to wait; the smaller the children, the more likely the request will be met.

GETTING THROUGH IMMIGRATION

Getting through passport control is always a bit stressful. If you have a summary card (see p.42) that lists passport details and visa numbers, you'll save yourself the trouble of rummaging through your bags looking for all the relevant documents when you have to fill in forms. It's also a good idea to store all your documents together in your hand luggage so that you can get at them easily; custom-designed travel wallets (see p.31) that hold passports, tickets and other travel-related papers are a useful investment.

SECURITY CHECKS

Clearing **security** can take a while, especially when you're carrying extras like a buggy or carrycot, so make sure you get to the airport early and give yourself plenty of time to go through. Security checks can involve x-raying everything from your shoes to your jackets, as well as having to walk through a metal detector, so make sure you're ready. As well as emptying your pockets of small change and removing jackets, don't overload your buggy with bits and pieces, as you'll only have to take everything out at security and it's easy to leave things behind.

Before you get in the queue for security, do a final check on the amount of **liquids** in your hand luggage, making sure they're within the accepted limits (see p.98 for more on this) and placed in a self-sealing plastic bag. You need to be ready to fold buggies for x-rays, and even take off nappies/diapers, but don't actually do this until asked – you might just get away without. Always take your time, allow others to go ahead of you if necessary, and ask for help if you need it – security staff are usually more than willing to assist.

HANDLING DELAYS

Delays are part of travelling, so try and get into the frame of mind of expecting them, and then being pleasantly surprised when they don't happen. You can also go a step further and embrace holdups as opportunities to do other things, from swapping information with fellow passengers headed the same way to getting some exercise, a rest or a good wash.

Some quick strategic thinking is required when delays occur. If you're held up, others will be too, and as space in waiting areas can disappear fast, try to bag a group of seats for your party as soon as a delay is announced, bearing in mind that if it turns out to be long, you might need to lay out the children to sleep, get some food, and use the toilets – in other words, find the best position you can. If you can't find seats to accommodate everyone, get as many as possible – some are better than none, as you can at least take turns and leave those sitting to mind the bags. Also factor in that delays can quickly exhaust your supply of entertainment materials and snacks. You'll probably need to ration what you have, but it's worth asking staff from the company you're travelling with for **food vouchers** and the like to keep you comfortable. If you do buy things to tide you over, keep the receipts, as you may be able to claim for them on your insurance policy. It's not unheard of to be reimbursed for things like toys bought to keep the kids busy, though this is likely only for really protracted delays.

If you're presented with a long delay, you can also ask about being put up in a **hotel**. Airlines vary in terms of what they offer, but six hours is usually long enough to warrant requesting a bed. If you're not in a hurry to leave and the flight is overbooked, you could offer to go on a later service if the airline puts you up in a hotel while you wait. It may well be in their interest to agree, as it's more economic for airlines to accommodate families who'll share rooms than several individuals. Providing you have the time to enjoy it, an unexpected stop in an airport hotel which may well have posh rooms and facilities such as a swimming pool, might end up being the highlight of your child's trip.

KEEPING THE PEACE

When travelling with children, balancing everyone's energies is a necessity, as moods not only transfer but amplify within families. No parent likes playing umpire when upsets arise, least of all when surrounded by an audience of fellow travellers, and anxieties concerning your **children's behaviour** and how it affects others can be really draining. There are things you can do to try and pre-empt problems, though. Being tired or hungry is a sure precursor for irritable moods, so always have some food on hand to stave off hunger attacks, and do what you can to rest along the way. If you're travelling on a plane that offers round-the-clock entertainment, or if you have your own portable DVD player, set limits to the amount of screen time and enforce a bit of shut-eye or just "time-out" quiet time.

You can't expect perfectly still and silent children all through your journey, but you do have to be able to set some boundaries when they're needed. An indirect tactic is to build in periods where children can **let off steam**, so that when you need them to sit (reasonably) still, you can expect more compliance. Whenever you find some space where other people are unlikely to be disturbed (a roomy, out-of-the-way airport corridor, perhaps), encourage the children to play. Certainly, don't expect them to respond well to constant requests to "behave" all the way through a trip, and if your child does have a crying fit or a tantrum, remind yourself to forget about everyone else. It's a waste of both time and emotional energy to try and double-guess what everyone else thinks – particularly as fellow passengers or transport staff are unlikely to be much help; just concentrate on your child and addressing whatever they need to get over what's wrong.

If you're travelling with more than one child, a bit of **squabbling** is pretty inevitable, but it's a good idea to do what you can to pre-empt it. You could start by explaining that problems can arise if the adults lose concentration because of bad behaviour – particularly, of course, if you're going to be driving – but also say that it's rude to fight in public. Be firm about the fact that if an argument starts when you're on the move, you will stop it immediately rather than try to find out what happened or who started it, and that everyone involved will be penalized in some way. This way, if your children tend to provoke each other, they might think twice before lapsing into old habits. One way of tackling upsets is to immediately tell the children to close their eyes and keep quiet, which usually has an instant calming effect. Alternatively, "punishments" could include anything from less time watching movies to foregoing treats.

KEEPING CLEAN ON THE MOVE

Children tend to act like dirt-magnets at the best of times, but the concern when you're travelling is **hygiene** rather than grime. When moving through areas shared by thousands of people, you need to be scrupulous about cleaning hands with soap and water, sterilizing hand gel or antiseptic wet-wipes, particularly before eating and after using toilets, and making sure children don't put anything dirty into their mouths. But think twice before changing their clothes; it's usually not worth it unless the period ahead provides a decent chance of keeping them relatively clean. Good moments to change them include just before they're ready to curl up and sleep, say if you're boarding a plane for an evening flight; or after meals when the worst messes are over.

Another aspect of hygiene relates to **fellow travellers** who want to touch and play with your children; while the gestures are obviously well-intended, babies are vulnerable to infections, so take some extra steps towards keeping them clean. The cordial way to deal with these situations is to discreetly use a wet-wipe to clean your child's hand, face or wherever they've been touched as soon as the person moves off; if someone holds your baby's hand, do so yourself as soon as they let go to prevent your child from sticking dirty fingers straight into their mouth.

It's also worth getting into the habit of placing hand luggage onto seats rather than floors, particularly if these bags tend to find their way onto your lap. And whenever you can, keep bags on trolleys or pile pieces on top of each other rather than spreading them over grime-laden floors. And if your children are at an age when they still want to climb on seats, take off their shoes to keep them and the seats clean; for the same reasons, also change their socks from time to time if they've been padding around in them.

TRAVELLING BY PLANE

Flying with young children can seem a fraught prospect. If you've been on a plane before you had kids, you probably remember being none too thrilled when people with children were seated next to you – it's not surprising that for most families preparing to go away, anxieties tend to centre around keeping the kids occupied and not upsetting other passengers. But plane journeys with your children aren't the huge challenge they might seem at first, and the experience keeps getting easier, largely on account of the enormous improvements to in-flight entertainment. And though there probably will be some stressful moments when you're up in the air, try not to get too concerned about other passengers – you can't please everyone.

SPECIAL NEEDS AND FLYING

If your child has **special needs**, it's worth asking airline staff if there's anything that can be done to make things easier – for example, you might check if it's possible for a touch-sensitive child not to be frisked at security. Getting a wheelchair or someone to help with bags is usually no problem, providing you ask in advance – see p.19 for more details.

PLANE CONTRASTS

"I've had to take many flights with the children, and although each one is different, two stand out. The first was when I was coming back from Tunisia when Cecilia was five and Amaya three. It was ultra-hard from the beginning – a delayed start meant we got on the plane at 4am, and we weren't in the best of shape. The flight was rough and uncomfortable, and when the plane started to lose height for landing, Amaya lost it. She screamed and screamed and screamed. She wrestled and fought her way out of her seat, and sat on the floor refusing to move. I was exhausted and at my wits end – there wasn't anything I could do but watch the tantrum play out. But in the middle of my mustering up the energy to get tough with her, the old lady behind us started up with nasty and judgemental comments. She declared herself a mother of three, a traveller of the world – she'd seen it all and she'd never, ever (ever) seen children behave so badly. If there's anytime I've been close to murder, this was it. But all things pass . . .

The second flight was memorable for different reasons. This time, Eloy was born and the five of us were booked on a really long flight to Chile. I was dreading it. But as it happened, the flight was full of Chilean teachers on their way back from a conference – and they were all in a really good mood. Whenever Eloy or any of the other babies started crying, the teachers started singing, which had a magical effect – the babies just went quiet. Bit by bit, the teachers started getting flutes and guitars out. Before long a real party was in full swing – Mary Poppins couldn't have done better! We were all having a terrific time until one of the first class passengers started complaining. The staff came and asked us to quieten down; we carried on singing of course, but the instruments were put away. That was the best flight ever. You can never tell how things will turn out, but people really make all the difference."

Beatriz Alvarez-Castillo

FLYING AT DIFFERENT AGES

Flying with a **baby** under 6 months is generally pretty easy; unless painful ears or sinuses strike, you can usually expect them to be lulled to sleep by the engine vibrations. **Toddlers** can be a challenge, particularly on long-haul flights, as they generally don't take well to confinement and can find engine noises and the sensations around takeoff and landing disconcerting. However, other **older children** tend to adore everything about flying. Airports provide escalators or trolleys to ride and planes to watch, and following the excitement of takeoff, there's the thrill of being up in the clouds as well as the novelty of watching movies and delving into unusual, daintily packaged meals – the parent's job is usually more about containing excitement than keeping children entertained.

CHILDREN'S FARES

All airlines share a similar pricing framework on tickets for children. As long as you don't want a seat for them, and are happy for them go on your lap or use a bassinet (the airline term for a carrycot – see below for more), the **under-2** – classified by airlines as "infants" – generally fly for free on domestic services, while on budget and international flights, they're charged around ten percent of the adult fare. Bear in mind that **single parents** can only travel with one infant using the discounted rate (even if your babies are twins), the rationale being that one person can only carry and attend to one infant at a time. If you can find another "consenting adult" to share the trip and look after your other child, you can pay the lower rates for both children; the airline will place a remark on your booking so that the presence of the other adult is checked at all stages of your trip. Note that wherever you pay ten percent of the regular fare for infants, you're usually allowed half the standard **baggage allowance**, but do check as things vary between airlines and types of aircraft. If you want to book a seat for an infant, this will generally cost 60–70 percent of the adult fare; luggage allowances vary in this instance, so check with your airline.

Children aged between **2 and 12** are usually charged the full adult fare by budget carriers, or around 67 percent by other airlines, although discounts vary depending on the route and where you buy your tickets. These fares tend to come with the full allowance of luggage.

BUCKLING THEM IN

Airlines can usually provide a **bassinet** for babies travelling on an infant fare, though this is usually for long-haul flights only. Bassinets provide a safe and comfortable place for sleep (though you'll need to bring your own bedding), as well as some relief for parents, allowing you to get your laps to yourselves once in a while. However, airlines

UNACCOMPANIED MINORS

Most airlines allow children to fly without an adult companion – in fact, between ten and twenty-five percent of all children who fly do so as what the industry calls **unaccompanied minors**. The service is usually available for children aged from two (or more usually five), although some airlines take them even younger providing you pay for a full **escort**; in most instances, this means that you'll need to find someone able to travel with your children. The **fee** for unaccompanied minors depends on the length of the flight and periods in transit, but as a general indication, a typical service fee for a single trip within Europe as an unaccompanied minor (above the ticket price for the child) is around £30/US$50; for intercontinental flights, you'll pay around £50/US$100. The cost of having your child travel with an escort boils down to paying for an extra ticket for the adult.

If you're thinking of having your child fly as an unaccompanied minor (with or without an escort), they'll need some extra **paperwork** in addition to passport and tickets. The basic add-ons are parental consent letters (see p.42) signed by both parents and stamped by a notary, and an authenticated copy of their birth certificate; additional requirements vary according to the countries you travel from and to. When booking, you also need to provide ID and contact details for the person that will drop off and pick up and/or travel with your child – the airline will insist on a match of ID before allowing your child to fly and before releasing them at the other end.

If you've organized your own escort, they'll take your child through all the steps from airport to airport, and sit with them throughout the flight. If you're not using an escort, you or whoever you've delegated to take your child to the airport may have to check in, go through security and hand them over to staff at the gate just before boarding the plane. To do this, the adult will need their passport to get a temporary airport pass, which either the airline or immigration staff will provide. Thereafter, a member of the cabin crew keeps an eye on your child during the flight, and makes sure they get safely delivered at the other end. More often that not, unaccompanied children are seated together on flights, the idea being that they might make friends and keep each other company.

differ in the criteria they use to judge the age range which qualifies babies for bassinets. The upper limit is usually between 12 months and 2 years, but some carriers make the cutoff as early as 6 months, others 3 years – always ask before you book, and note that whatever their age, babies over 70cm tall will usually be considered too big for a bassinet. And while some airlines insist on using their own bassinets, others expect you to bring and use yours – another reason for checking in advance.

Things are much simpler when it comes to **seatbelts**, as all airlines will provide smaller ones which fasten around children's waists and connect to your own belt through a loop. Some airlines (and some parents) prefer babies to be strapped into a **child's car seat** if you've booked a separate seat for them, but policies vary a lot. Some airlines (particularly

in the US) specify that car seats are mandatory, while others forbid them, or don't have a policy but allow you to use your seat if you want to. Equally, some insist that you use their car seats, but usually for a fee; check in advance. If you take your own car seat, note that safety specifications vary; some airline staff will look for the certification marks of regulatory bodies recognized within their country, and will not permit anything else – for more on this, see p.59.

CHOOSING BETWEEN AIRLINES

Airlines vary enormously in terms of the aircraft they use and the services they provide. You may not always have a choice in terms of who you fly with, but if more than one carrier serves your destination, it's worth investigating their relative merits in terms of space, entertainment facilities and amenities for children – particularly if you're flying long-haul.

Most airlines offer some of the following **amenities for children**: nappies/diapers and infant food; hot water to make up bottles or warm jars of baby food; changing tables in toilets; bassinets and special seatbelts for babies and toddlers; children's menus (to suit various dietary restrictions); entertainment packs and children's in-flight movies. Although you can ask what's available, and let the airline know what you'll require (24 hours' notice is usually needed), it's always good to come prepared with your own stock of nappies/diapers and food: supplies often run out or turn out to be something you'd prefer to do without. A steady stream of free drinks is always useful and popular with children, and the same applies for handouts of games and toys. But by far the most important of perks to seek out, particularly on long-haul trips, are the in-flight entertainment provisions – individual television screens with channels dedicated to children will keep your kids entertained for hours.

Most large airlines offer some form of **family assistance** that doesn't have to be pre-arranged; this usually amounts to someone on the plane who helps you get seated and fusses a little more than usual over the children, making sure they have things to play with and so on. If you'd like to be met at check-in and helped with the children and the bags all the way to your plane, ask for "meet and assist" services when booking your flight. This is generally provided by the airport and not the airline, and whether or not you get it depends on the availability of staff – but certainly, if you're travelling as a single parent with more than one child, you'll be given priority over others.

Budget airlines

As far as **budget airlines** are concerned, don't expect extra services or personal assistance; and if you don't want to be pestered by your children to buy pricey (and largely poor-quality) snacks, bring your own. However as most budget carriers fly short routes and emphasize getting you on and off the plane as quickly as possible, there are pluses in terms of convenience as well as cost. And because there are usually no reserved seats, and people travelling with children get to board first, there's no pressure to be the first to check in.

Less helpfully, bassinets are rarely offered on the smaller aircraft used by budget operators, and the fact that carry-on allowances are particularly modest can be very inconvenient, particularly if your children can't carry their own hand luggage and need bottles and nappies/diapers. If the flight isn't heavily booked, staff may use their discretion to allow you to carry a bit extra providing the dimensions of the individual pieces do not exceed their specifications – but be prepared to have to check in any extras. Equally, if you're travelling with a collapsible **pram** or **buggy**, you may not be able to take it board. You can generally use it until you get on the plane, when it'll be taken away and placed in the hold – the next time you'll see it will be when you collect your luggage at your destination. The larger the airport, the more likely the lack of a buggy will matter – bear in mind that budget airlines are typically allocated the most distant and inconvenient gates, often with stairs to negotiate. If you want to check what the rules are, look on the airline's website, which will usually have information on flying with kids; some (but not all) budget airlines offer phone numbers for queries.

FACILITIES AT THE AIRPORT

Many trips involve spending more time in the **airport** than actually on the plane, and if you're going to have to wait for hours with your kids, it's worth researching available facilities – particularly if you're making transit stops and have a choice of places to change planes. Things like play areas make a lot of difference, enabling the children to have a ball and exhaust themselves enough to sleep on the flight; public showers or bookable rooms where you can rest (for a fee) are also useful. Almost all airports will have baby-changing facilities of some description, as well as seating areas with a television and shops that sell food, drink and reading materials. Most large airports have a **website** that includes maps of facilities and links to additional services such as car rental, but most sites don't cover things like distances from the departure lounge to the gates and how long it takes to get there, whether or not stairs are involved; ways to get hot water and/or warm up food; and the locations of comfortable seating with or without televisions. If any of these things are important to you, give the airport a ring or send an email.

If you're a member of an airline's frequent-flyer club, you might be entitled to use a **private departure lounge**. While these are primarily geared to business executives (you'll need to make sure your kids behave well), facilities such as a supervised place to leave hand luggage, comfortable chairs, free drinks and snacks, newspapers and magazines, TVs and spacious bathrooms are especially welcome when you're travelling with children. If you're not a frequent-flyer club member, you can often use the lounges if you buy a day pass – if you're going to be in the airport long enough to entail multiple visits to the bathroom, getting a meal or wanting to sleep, it's usually well worth paying the price.

SHORT VERSUS LONG-HAUL FLIGHTS

For **short flights**, planes tend to be smaller, more cramped and without change-tables in the toilets; they're also more subject to turbulence. If these features matter to you, try and get booked onto the largest aircraft you can – just ask. Flying **long-haul** involves very different considerations. As above, ask about the model of the plane: some are a lot more comfortable than others, with larger seats and legroom, individual screens for movies or fewer passengers per toilet. The difference in comfort can be such that economy seats in some planes are equivalent to, or even better than, business class in another. To get the benefits of both classes, some parents book one seat in business class and the rest in economy, and then take turns to stretch out and sleep; others buy business class seats for the adults while booking their children as unaccompanied minors (see p.93) in economy; in other words, you pay extra for the stewards to look after your children while you take it easy.

RESERVATIONS AND SEATING

As a bit of extra space is always useful when flying with children, it's worth asking when flights are busiest when you make **reservations**; if bookings tend to be heaviest on weekends, it makes sense to try and travel during the week – you'll get better service than when attendants are overstretched, and may be able to spread out on empty seats.

When booking your seats, it's worth asking if those around you can be left vacant for as long as possible. Certainly, don't hesitate to ask if you prefer being on your own or seated with another woman, particularly if you're breastfeeding; most reservation staff will try to accommodate you. Generally, though, passengers with infants using bassinets tend to be automatically placed in the **bulkhead seats**, where you have more legroom and a pull-down table designed to take a bassinet. But depending on the type of plane, disadvantages include immovable arm-rests which prevent you being able to stretch out; and detachable tables which are unstable and connect to both arm-rests (and which hem you in throughout mealtimes). Furthermore, you generally can't use the space under the seats to store belongings, which implies a lot of opening and closing the overhead lockers to get at your things.

While children might enjoy and even fight over the **window seat**, make sure one of you has an aisle seat so that you can get in and out without needing to move other passengers – particularly important if you're going to be in the air for hours. Also bear in mind that spreading your party out over a row of **adjacent seats** (rather than seats in front and behind one another) makes it easier to catch each other's attention. Don't expect to be assigned seats near **emergency exits**, though; while these typically have more legroom, children aren't allowed anywhere near handles which open doors. Note also that on some aircraft, more than one infant may not be allowed per group of seats because of a lack of suitable fittings for **oxygen masks**; if you're flying with more than one child under two, ask specifically about this. As for **toilets**, the ideal is to be near without being right on top of them; toilets inevitably get surrounded by queues and having people standing right by you can be a distraction for children. Besides, loos can end up stinking by the end of long flights and contribute to the children feeling queasy.

Finally, if you don't get the seats you want, try again once on the flight – having children works like magic when asking people to swap.

HAND LUGGAGE REGULATIONS

Security-related constraints on what you're allowed to carry in your **hand luggage** keep changing, so it's important to check the rules before you travel; there's usually a list of **prohibited items** on airline or airport websites. The more stringent regulations relate to carrying **liquids**, gels and creams, which of course includes baby foods, drinks and nappy/diaper cream. Where these apply, the standard instructions are not to carry over 100ml of any single item, although exceptions are usually made for essential medicines or supplies for children under 2. You can also get away with more (up to 400ml) in the way of **milk** and drinks so long as these are decanted into bottles and no-spill cups; if you carry the same in the original cartons or bottles, you'll be asked to leave them behind. There are also discretionary set limits for **baby food** – these are generally kept vague, but as long as you don't have more than what security staff deem to be a reasonable amount for the flight, you'll usually be fine.

The best way around the restrictions is to decant creams into small bottles, and bring just powdered milk; you can get hot water to make feeds on most flights, and as soon as you pass security, you can buy bottled water too. Bear in mind that if security machines pick up a

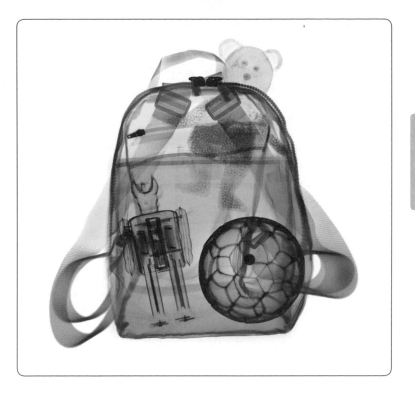

liquid, gel or cream that you forgot, absolutely everything in your hand luggage will be unpacked – this will hold you up and be a real nuisance, so be careful when packing, and avoid the common mistake of hand-carrying the bumper pot of nappy/diaper cream that you'll be using for the whole trip – it's likely that this will be confiscated.

CHECK-IN OPTIONS

Before you travel, it's worth finding out what your airline's **check-in** options are. Some let you do it **online**, which allows you to book preferred seats from home and cuts out both the hassle and the time of waiting in line; when you get to the airport, you usually join a fast-track queue to hand over your checked luggage and get your bag tags. Some airlines have machines at the airport which issue baggage tags as well as boarding cards; in such instances, there's usually someone around to help. Similarly, train stations which feed airports occasionally have check-in facilities, meaning you're then free to board the train with the children but without the bags. There are also instances when you can

check in luggage in advance, sometimes as much as a day before you fly. Though you have to make an advance trip to the airport to do this, the advantages are that you get to turn up a little later than usual on the day, and will have your hands free to tend to your children – this can be particularly useful when travelling as a single adult.

ARRIVING AT THE AIRPORT

Despite what you may feel about **airports**, children tend to find them as much fun as adventure playgrounds. There are spacious areas, slippery floors, moving walkways and escalators, trolleys, shops and, of course, the planes – for many children, the first close-up encounter with mammoth aircraft can be a big deal, making them want to stay put and take it all in. So do allow time for exploring and plane-watching before setting off; your children might just exhaust themselves in good time for the flight.

If your children can read, encourage them to check the display panels to identify your departure gate and when you need to board – they'll usually be pretty impressed by the long list of destinations. Whatever you do, don't leave finding the departure gate until the last minute, and ask how long it takes to get there; check-in staff or an information desk should be able to help, but emphasize that you'll be moving a little slower than most on account of your children. And while there will always be toilets on the plane, you'll probably be strapped in to your seats for some time before you can use them, so get everyone to go just before boarding.

BOARDING THE PLANE

If you have a collapsible buggy, prepare to fold and arrange it ready to hand over to the cabin staff once you get to the departure gate and before boarding the plane. Note that though people with children are usually asked to **board first**, this is optional – if your kids are happy where they are, you might as well wait until the crowds pass. Boarding early adds quite a bit of extra seat time to the trip; and once on the plane, you're likely to be confined to your seats while the other passengers board – if the children are bursting with energy, this could be a bad move. On the other hand, if you're tired or the seats aren't pre-assigned, boarding first has obvious advantages. Either way, ask for help if you need a hand.

Once you're **on board**, cast your eye around to see how full the plane looks; if you didn't get the seats you wanted, or think you might be able to spread out into vacant rows, this is the time to ask. Once you're all seated, remove things from your hand luggage that might spill or that you're likely to need in the next hour: bottles, nappies/diapers, wet-wipes, dummies/pacifiers and infant feeds, as well as some entertainment materials and snacks. Cabin staff may insist on all hand luggage being placed in the **overhead lockers** prior to takeoff and landing, particularly if you're in the bulkhead seats and can't stow it under the seat in front. If there isn't enough room for your bags in the lockers directly above your seats, try to find space between you and the exit of the plane. This way, when it's time to leave, there's no need to go against the flow of disembarking passengers – you can join the exit line and reach for your bags on the way out. If you're in for a long flight, take off the children's shoes, and ask for **blankets** and **extra pillows** before supplies run out; you might want more than the usual ration of pillows to make yourself comfortable if breastfeeding, and to help the kids to get to sleep.

As the children start to explore the space around their seats, either cover up buttons that they shouldn't touch or show them which to avoid (such as the stewardess call one) and why; to avoid annoying those behind you, it's a good idea to stop your children from reclining seats until after the meal has been served. And if there's any chance they might need to go to the toilet, take them quickly before the "fasten seatbelts" sign gets switched on – once they are on, you can expect to have to stay seated for up to forty minutes, sometimes even longer.

Well before takeoff, cabin staff will distribute **safety belts** for babies and toddlers. You'll usually be asked to put these on as soon as you're seated and settled, but once you've worked out how to strap them in, consider leaving seatbelts unfastened until nearer takeoff – if you confine children too early, they might start to protest when they have to wear them. However, keep your children seated, as boarding is usually a very busy time in the aisles. Keep an eye on the cabin crew; when they sit down and strap themselves in, you absolutely must have the children in their seatbelts. If you've requested a bassinet, the cabin crew will help you set it up; however, they usually wait until after the plane takes off to do this, as cots need to be stowed during takeoff and landing.

If your flight is going to or leaving an area where malaria, yellow fever or dengue are present, staff may come through the cabin spraying **insecticide**; while these are quick-acting and harmless pyrethroids, you might want to cover your children's faces – the smell can be strong and it's best to keep it out of their eyes.

THE TAKEOFF AND THE FLIGHT

As the engines rev up in preparation for **takeoff**, double check that everyone is buckled in. If you have a baby, get ready to give them a feed, and hand out drinks or sucking sweets to older children to help avoid painful sinus and middle ear problems (see p.103). Once you've soared above the clouds and the initial novelty of being airborne begins to wear off for the children, start thinking about **entertainment**. If the airline distributes packs of toys for children and you haven't yet been given any, ask one of the cabin crew when they'll be handed out. (Though ask nicely – you don't want to come across as pushy and alienate the crew for the rest of the flight!) You might also check out children's channels for in-flight movies and plug in headphones etc, as well as organizing things you've brought with you to keep the kids entertained. This is also a good time to say hello your neighbouring passengers and the stewards working your bit of the plane. The sooner you break the ice and develop a rapport, the better – and you've more chance of getting a bit of empathy (and possibly some help) if your kids get cranky later on. Sadly, few airlines accommodate children's **cockpit visits** these days, but if you'd like to try your luck, ask early on in the flight, but do so out of earshot of the children to avoid disappointments.

Once the plane is cruising and the **seatbelt signs are switched off**, let the children move around and interact with others if they want to, but make sure they're not disturbing anyone who'd rather be left alone, and always stay with them to make sure they keep out of harm's way – people moving through the aisles often only notice small children once they're right on top of them.

If the flight includes **meals**, ask cabin staff if they can serve the children before you so you can help them eat, then have your meal in relative peace when your turn comes. If you have your own non-spill cups, it's best to transfer drinks into these, and if you need water to prepare a **bottle feed**, it's usually easiest to go to the galley where supplies are kept rather than waiting on busy cabin crew to come to you.

As cabin temperatures tend to fluctuate, you'll need to add or take off layers for babies, and adjust children's clothing as well. And as it nears bedtime, take children to the toilet and check nappies/diapers. Adjust reclining seats, move the arm rests and use pillows and blankets to get the kids comfortable; placing two small children head to toe in adjacent seats allows them both to stretch out. Keep them buckled in even if the seatbelt signs have been switched off; you don't want to have wake them should you hit turbulence and the signs go on. If you

COLDS AND EAR PROBLEMS IN THE AIR

Changes in humidity and air pressure during flights can be quite uncomfortable for children, but there are steps you can take to prevent and alleviate possible problems. Low humidity of cabin air can cause mild dehydration as well as dry and irritated nostrils, so it's important to get kids to drink regularly. If anyone gets a streaming nose (also a factor of low humidity), wet the insides of their nostrils with a finger dipped in water – this often works like magic.

Flying can also prompt air expansion in the middle ear and sinuses, which generally feels like a mild "popping" sensation; it can be painful for babies and infants on account of their smaller ear passages, which are more prone to getting blocked. To prevent discomfort, massage your child's ears from behind and give the earlobes a few gentle tugs from time to time. Toddlers also find it helpful to suck on something or have a drink during takeoff and landing. You could also show them how to clear their ears by yawning, or holding their nose and "blowing" to make their ears pop.

If your child is bunged up with heavy mucous (rather than just a drippy nose), consult a doctor before flying. Depending on how ill they are and the length of your trip, you may be advised to use some medication to help clear the sinuses, or to change your flight dates. Otherwise, there's little you can do other than try to keep their nasal passages clear – get young children to blow noses, and use suction devises for babies' nasal passages. Vapour rubs and mentholated oils can also be comforting, as can regular, short feeds and drinks – each suck will help clear the sinuses. But if your child cries despite your efforts, bear in mind that this can be good news – crying can open the Eustachian tubes and so stabilize the pressure. Certainly, get up and walk up and down the aisle; the movement and distraction might help and will give those nearby some relief as well.

plan to sleep yourself, ask a member of the crew to wake you up a little before descent – you'll need a bit of time to get organized.

DISEMBARKING

As **landing** draws near, get the children to the toilet before the seatbelt signs are switched on, even if it means waking them up; you won't have access to the toilets for a while, and the moment they wake up – which they probably will during the descent – they'll inevitably need to go. Once you land, be prepared for the rush of passengers keen to get off the plane as fast as possible. It's wise to stay seated until the frenzy subsides; if you stand in line with the rest of the passengers, your children might get sandwiched or bashed by other people's luggage. If you wait for the aisles to clear, it's also easier to have a look under the seats and in the seat-pockets to be sure nothing gets left behind.

RECLAIMING YOUR LUGGAGE

Getting off the plane usually feels terrific, what with fresh air and a chance to stretch your legs, so it might be an idea to let the kids run around a little once you're in the terminal building and before you reclaim your **luggage**. Bear in mind that if large items such as buggies don't come through on the belt, this might be because they've been taken to a separate collection point for heavy or fragile items; ask where this is. Before joining the world at large, consider using toilets once again and, if you haven't already got local currency, changing some money.

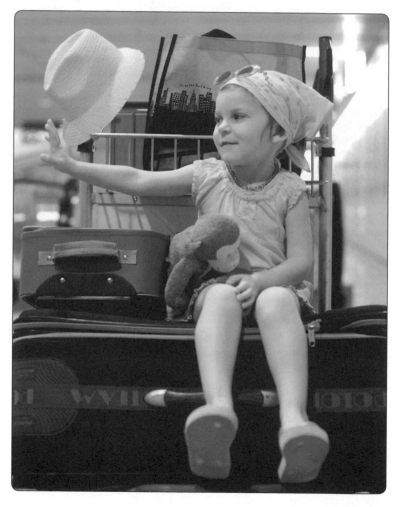

Travel by plane

Check

- ❏ Space, seats, baby-changing facilities, TV screens etc on the aircraft
- ❏ In-flight childcare support, assistance with luggage, availability of nappies/diapers, infant formula, children's meals, children's TV channels, bassinets, car-seats
- ❏ Luggage specifications and allowances, including strollers/prams and hand luggage
- ❏ Transit/connection times and terminals
- ❏ Check-in times and options for early or online check-in
- ❏ Airport facilities baby changing, restaurants, shops, availability of hot water, distance between lounge and gates, play areas, private departure lounges, left-luggage facilities, availability of extra assistance

What to take on the flight

- ❏ Motion sickness pills or bands
- ❏ Decongestant
- ❏ Neck pillow
- ❏ Ear plugs
- ❏ Eye shades
- ❏ Socks
- ❏ Support tights and loose/adjustable shoes
- ❏ Layered clothing
- ❏ Entertainment materials for children

TRAVELLING BY CAR

Travelling by **car** allows you to be master of your own timetable, which can make a big difference when you're with children – as does the fact that the only restriction on the amount of luggage you can take is the size of your car. As a broad rule of thumb, you can expect the odd bad patch on car trips with **babies,** while otherwise enjoying long periods of calm; with **small children,** energies are generally focused on avoiding boredom, fights and car sickness, as well as planning regular stops.

If you're going to be flying before starting a car trip, it's not a good idea to get straight into the driving seat from the plane if there's any chance you might be **jetlagged**. Having jetlag is more destabilizing than a simple matter of a change of hours; you may feel a little dream-like, and reflexes are almost always impaired. Besides, in unfamiliar territory – jetlagged

MOTION SICKNESS

If you've suffered yourself, you won't need reminding that it's worth doing whatever you can to avoid **motion sickness**. Children are particularly prone, and as travel (long journeys in particular) can be the first time it manifests, it's worth taking steps to prevent it even if they haven't suffered before. Motion sickness is triggered by a mismatch of sensory signals reaching the brain. If you're in a car, your body moves up and down, but simultaneously, you'll register objects outside appearing to do the reverse, and might also see other things – say cars in other lanes – moving in completely different directions. This confuses the inner ear, making it hard to know which reference to adjust to: for some, the result is nausea.

Prevention

One obvious step is not to overdo snacks, and avoid greasy, heavy meals and fizzy drinks before you set off. Use over-the-counter **motion sickness tablets** as directed; these generally need to be taken about half an hour before you travel, though they can only be used for kids over 4 years old. Alternatively, **natural therapies** include wristbands, which work on the acupressure principle – these are often referred to as "sea-bands" and are available in most large pharmacies. To make sure you're prepared for the worst, take along several **sick bags**; hair bands and clips are also useful to keep hair out of faces if vomiting strikes.

If you're travelling by **car**, bear in mind that passengers in the back (usually the children) are the most vulnerable; if you know who is likely to feel sick, try placing them up front if you can, and by windows. Do what you can to avoid winding, mountainous roads and driving in traffic that demands lots of starts and stops, both prime conditions for bringing on motion sickness. As far as possible, opt for straight and unclogged roads – highways are ideal, though they have their drawbacks in terms of not being able to stop on demand. If more than one member of the family is prone to motion sickness, swap seats from time to time; otherwise, go slowly and plan several breaks along the way. If your child starts feeling unwell, look for the first opportunity to stop and allow them to recover. Other standard tactics include getting them to focus on the horizon outside the car rather than on moving objects within, and to lie them down horizontally with eyes closed. Certainly, "I-spy" and reading are best avoided; both involve eyes fixing on moving objects, which makes things worse. You can also try getting your child to suck on a bit of lemon or a boiled sweet. But don't lose sight of the fact that they might well **vomit** – apart from not wanting them to suffer to that extent, the mess can also trigger others to be sick as well, so always be prepared to stop when someone starts looking green. If they do start vomiting, comfort them by wiping their face with a wet flannel and giving them sips of water or a sweet drink to take away the taste. After the event, ginger or mint teas help calm the stomach, and ice lollies are usually welcome. Apart from consoling your child, be prepared for him or her to want go to sleep, and be hungry when they awake.

If you're travelling by **plane** or **boat**, the above steps also apply, but as an additional precaution, go for the largest craft as these are the most stable and, therefore, less likely to bring on motion sickness; also opt for centrally placed seats on boats, where you won't pitch and roll as much as those at the extremities.

or not — it takes more than the usual concentration to get used to differences in language, road signs, driving on "the other" side of the road, not to mention simply finding your way about; taking all this in when disoriented and trying to look after your children isn't a fortuitous way to start your travels.

For obvious reasons, the **ideal driving team** consists of two adult drivers, one of whom can manage basic car maintenance.

With two adults, one can do the driving leaving the other free to focus on other things that need attention, from map-reading to general child-care, doling out snacks, changing nappies/diapers, mopping up messes and making phone calls. Furthermore, repairs, stops, and emergencies also become a lot easier to manage with two adults, as one can stay with the children while the other attends to whatever needs to be done.

TAKING YOUR OWN CAR

There are differences in the way you use your car for day-to-day driving compared with **longer trips**, so be sure it's up to the demands of your journey, and that it has enough room for your things; if you're camping, say, you might need to rent or buy a roof-rack or trailer. Once you're confident your car will be fine, get all the usual pre-

"It goes without saying that you should never have more children than you have car windows."
Erma Bombeck (1927–96)

trip servicing and safety checks done, make sure that your tax and insurance are up to date, and that you're fully covered for assistance, breakdowns, and a replacement vehicle. And don't forget to gather (and take) all the relevant certificates and documentation: road worthiness, tax, insurance etc.

RENTING A CAR

Even if you've been used to hopping on and off buses or trains on adults-only holidays, travelling with kids makes **renting a car** a lot more appealing, both in terms of convenience and because it means you won't have to struggle on and off public transport with children and associated paraphernalia in tow.

When you book your vehicle, choosing the right one will make quite a difference in terms of comfort. For instance, upholstery that's reasonably easy to clean means you won't have to worry about every crumb that your children drop; and depending on the weather at your destination, air-conditioning (for air pollution as well as heat), heating and tinted windows might be necessities rather than luxuries, helping your children to be comfortable, stay hydrated and avoid being sick.

When you're driving with children, it's all the more important to get full **backup services**. Always find out what the rental company offers in terms of breakdown cover, and make sure that a replacement vehicle is part of the deal. And if you're going to be travelling in remote areas, opt for a large, nationwide company with many outlets to reduce the chances of being stranded.

If you'd rather not cart your own child's car seat around, ask what the company provides, and get details of the brand and model numbers; it's simple enough to then go online to check that the seat is suitable for your child's weight and height. But bear in mind that banking on seats provided by car rental companies isn't always a good idea – you can't tell how a seat has been used in the past and whether or not it's still structurally sound; and there's always the possibility of the seat not materializing on arrival, leaving you with nothing at all. If you bring your own, though, check that you can use it in the model of car you're renting. It's also a good idea to find out what the car is fitted

CUSTOMIZING A CAR FOR KIDS

▶ Extra rear-view mirrors trained on the back seats allow you to keep an eye on the children without turning around, and are particularly useful if you're driving without another adult. They're easy to get hold of in car accessory shops or online, and attach with suction or sticky pads.

▶ If you're planning on night driving, a useful (if rather hi-tech) accessory is a back seat video monitor (for more on which, see "Equipment", p.62). While more expensive than extra rear-view mirrors, they give you a single-screen view of what's happening in the back in both the night and day.

▶ Sun-screens for the rear windows reduce heat within the car dramatically, and can make a real difference to kids in the back.

▶ Bottle warmers are useful if you're going somewhere cold; they're powered by the cigarette-lighter socket, and are thermostatically controlled. Some versions work with jars of baby food as well as bottles.

▶ Accessories for entertainment such as tape decks or portable CD/DVD players fitted for use in cars (via the cigarette lighter) help to ensure the right mix of entertainment for children. And if you don't want their fun to bother the driver, bring headphones as well.

WE'LL BE THERE BY SIX

If someone is waiting for you at the other end of your drive, be vague about your expected **arrival time**, and discourage immediate or time-bound plans for meals and social events. Hosts who don't have young children can worry when you don't arrive within what they imagine ought to be the normal driving time, and/or expect you to swing into action on arrival. The potential of being a couple of hours late for a planned meal can add unnecessary stress to the trip – besides, your children might not be able to wait, and need feeding before you arrive. Keep things flexible, and use a mobile phone to keep your host informed of your progress.

with in terms of entertainment systems (radio, cassette or CD player), so that you can plan what music and stories to bring. Last but not least, get comprehensive insurance including accident or collision damage waiver; if you don't, the smallest scratch by clumsy children or your buggy could land you with an astronomical bill.

PLANNING A TROUBLE-FREE DRIVE

The most important factor in ensuring a smooth car trip is to study your map carefully and **plan your route** in advance. Preparing small cards to stick on the dashboard with summary directions for each leg of the trip is really useful, particularly if you're the only adult; driving with your kids can be demanding, and the more you do to free up your hands and attention, the better.

If your destination is unfamiliar, find out about informal **driving rules**; most good guide books (including Rough Guides) will have some information, and this kind of insiders' insight can be invaluable. It may be that the horn or dipper lights are used to indicate overtaking, or perhaps next to no rules exist or are respected – whatever the case, it's good to know. Also seek advice on what to do in the event of a **breakdown** or an **accident**, and whether being an outsider makes any difference – for example, in some parts of the world, drivers are advised not to stop after an accident (as everyone would assume it was your fault), but to drive to a police station and seek help there.

Choosing the route

When you're **choosing your route**, think about how long you and your kids will want to be in the car at any one time: take account of how everyone's likely to feel at the end of each leg, and keep each part of the journey well within your individual comfort zones. Give yourselves plenty of time, and plan to stop before you expect the children to get restless. A leisurely pace is best – if you can make impromptu stops to look at things which interest your children along the way, all the better. Feeding animals, having a paddle in a stream or even watching a few minutes of a village football game can prove so popular that they even get children looking forward to the rest of the time on the road.

Highway driving has its pros and cons. The plus points include covering more ground in a shorter space of time, and because the roads are straight and driving speed pretty consistent, motion sickness is less common; children tend to sleep better on long, straight roads, too. However, not being able to stop at will can cause considerable stress if your children need attention. Furthermore, the driver needs to be especially focused on safety at higher speeds, and this isn't always a simple matter with children on board. Motorway driving is best when there's one adult driving and another sitting in the back ready to split up fights, help the children eat, read a story or cuddle them to sleep. If you're the sole adult, pre-empt the need for attention by stopping well before the children start getting restless, and minimize time on highways whilst the children are awake.

Other types of roads have their own specific demands, too: it's easy to underestimate **journey time** through mountainous roads, and forget that queasy children in the back compounds delays. Travel also has a funny way of making you forget rush hour traffic, as well as hold-ups around school drop-off and pick-up times; try to bear such things in mind, and also to research road **conditions** and potential driving hazards, from dirt roads that turn into mudslides when it rains to humungous potholes that you can't see if driving at night. The best way to find out varies depending on where you're driving; most industrialized countries have a national automobile association with facilities for online route planning, and telephone numbers for advice on conditions; alternatively, you could try staff at a car rental agency, or a good, up-to-date guide book.

SMOOTH DRIVING

"We used to drive a lot on short mini-breaks. Rohan would be in the front strapped into his seat. We whiled away the time just talking and singing. He never was a problem. I think I inherited the concept about the journey being a big part of the fun from my parents. I would think of ways to make the trip interesting – we weren't focused on getting there. For example, I never took highways; there's less to see and I don't particularly like driving on them anyway. I was never in a hurry to arrive. We would even take detours, such as following a lane to see where it went – that kind of thing. Rohan still remembers when we stopped to follow a stream to see where it "started" as a grand adventure. Whenever he fell asleep, I would get some serious driving done."

Rebecca Spencer-Smith

Planning stops

Estimating how often you need to stop isn't easy to get right. In theory, children should need to use the toilet every two hours; however, as every parent knows, you might get an emphatic "no" to questions such as "are you hungry/thirsty?", "do you need to go to the toilet?", followed a minute later by "I need to go NOW!". And the more children you have, the less likely it is that they'll all need the toilet at the same time. The safest bet is to plan for a stop every hour and a half, but be prepared to make additional ones as well.

When **planning where to stop**, look for places where you can refuel, rest and go to the toilet; somewhere to buy food or eat your own and space for children to run around and burn up energy are also useful. You might also want to bear the following in mind:

▶ **Fuel** If you're going to be driving for long stretches, particularly in rural areas or in countries with weak infrastructure, be conservative in how much fuel and water the car will need. If there's any chance that fuel stations may be dry or closed, carry reserves, and always stop and fill up when you reach half a tank.

▶ **Toilets** Tactics to avert toilet stops – from allowing otherwise toilet-trained children to wear pull-ups for the trip to using screw-top jars – can backfire, and result in serious distractions for the driver, as well as a mess inside the car; it's always best to stop if you can. If your child won't go to the toilet on the roadside and/or doesn't like using public toilets, a portable potty with disposable liners (see p.68) can be useful.

▶ **Food** Even if you plan to stop and eat, carry snacks to buy time until you're ready to pull over; see p.65 for tips on eating and drinking on the move. Unless you're free to stop at will, limit the amount your children drink to avoid having to stop more than necessary; if it's hot, though, make sure they don't get dehydrated. It's also worth planning for a picnic if you can; it'll add considerably to the charm of travelling by car.

▶ **Exercise** The more exercise your children get, the happier (and possibly sleepier) they're likely to be in the car. Consider taking something along to encourage them to run around during stops, such as a ball, frisbee or whatever the current favourite is.

▶ **Accommodation** As long as you have the time, it can be a lot of fun to find places to stay as you go, and a car gives you the mobility to discover attractive spots and get a first-hand look before making up your mind. Pre-booking accommodation can add to the pressure to make it on time – or frustrate you should you realize you could have gone a lot further. If there aren't many options in terms of places to stay, however, it's obviously best to book in advance.

ENTERTAINMENT

The longer you spend on the road, the more it pays to sort out **entertainment** in advance, from a few audiobooks and music tapes or CDs to a portable DVD player or an MP3 machine that can handle movie files; see p.69 for more ideas. Whatever you take, make sure that it won't distract the driver – **headphones** are a must, because they'll give you some peace and save you having to listen to your children's favourites over and over again. But do bear in mind that reading in cars, and games such as I-spy which mean looking at fixed objects in a moving environment, can bring on motion sickness (see p.106). Lastly, always reserve surprises or the most absorbing entertainment for the final stages of the trip, when diversions are most needed.

LOADING UP THE CAR

Stowing your things within the car so that they're on hand when you need them goes a long way to helping your trip go smoothly. Before you start loading, though, clean out your car or ensure the rental company does – there's nothing like a dirty car to dampen spirits or fast-track car sickness.

THE OVERNIGHT BAG

Even if you're planning to reach your destination long before nightfall, it's wise to be prepared for an overnight stop in case of breakdowns, motion sickness or just getting lost or delayed. Pack an **overnight bag** with a change of clothing, basic toiletries and supplies of nappies/diapers, infant feeds etc. Even if you arrive as planned, it's great to be able to just reach for this bag and leave the rest of the unpacking until the morning.

The front of the car

Ideally, **the front of the car** is the place for your vehicle documents, driver's licence and identity papers, the maps, sunglasses, a cloth to wipe down steamed-up windscreens, and whatever it takes to keep you/the driver refreshed and focused – a flask of tea or coffee, gum etc. If your children can't manage their own supplies, keep snacks and a cache of toys in the front and out of their reach. Wet-wipes or sterilizing hand gel, tissues and a plastic bag for rubbish will also come in useful. Otherwise, get a selection of tapes, CDs or DVDs ready to play when you want them, and get the mobile phone charger, phone, portable bottle/baby food heater and MP3 player ready for use.

The back seat

Before putting anything into the back, tuck a sheet or towel over the seat to protect it from spills (particularly if it's a rental car) and to keep everyone comfortable. If it's really hot you might want to do this in the front, too. Next comes the job of installing the child seat/s (see p.59), and making sure the seat belts strap and fasten as they should. When you're done, it's worth lining these car seats with a protective cloth as well. If you don't have a sunshade to screen the side-windows, you can also use a pillowcase or hand towel: when you need shade, insert one edge of the material at the top of the (opened) window, then wedge the glass shut to hold it in place.

For **babies** that can't support the weight of their heads, stringing up something colourful within eye range gives them a more interesting view than just the back of the front seat, as well as something to play with; strings of beads or coloured cloth are good. To keep these from falling, fasten them to the baby's seat or the back of the front seats, and check from time to time that your child doesn't get tangled up in them.

Children love the novelty of snuggling up with blankets and pillows in a moving car, so organize some bedding and keep it in a plastic bag under everyone's feet, or in the boot/trunk, until you need it. And if your children are old enough to manage their own supplies of toys and snacks, arrange these within their reach as best you can.

Finally, some parents swear by a bit of chalk or adhesive tape to mark a line on the back seat between children that tend to fight, and make it a rule that each child sticks to their side, and we've detailed some more subtle tactics for keeping the peace on p.88.

GAMES FORBIDDEN IN THE CAR

"Our children love hearing stories of the antics we used to get up to when we were small. My siblings and I were a particularly rowdy pack, but when it came to car trips, it was mostly my brother and myself who acted up – my sister was usually too ill. We used to throw things around and scream, and our definition of a successful trip was based on how many times we made the parents stop. I'm not sure how they coped, but I remember once when even we felt we had gone a bit too far. This was on a trip around Ireland, during which my sister had been throwing up as usual. This time, my brother Anthony started trying to hit other cars (while we were driving of course) with full sick bags – and he succeeded. The parents went ballistic. From then on we had to quieten down, and made do with pulling faces at other drivers from the back of the car. My own children are under no illusions of what I'd do if they tried pulling anything similar: stop the car until they simmered down and, if necessary, leave them tired and hungry until they behaved."

Ben Stringer

Packing the boot/trunk

You're going to be travelling with lots of paraphernalia, and it makes a real difference if you organize the storage space so you can easily put your hands on the things likely to be needed most. Start by organizing tyre-changing equipment and anything you might need in the event of a breakdown, and stow it all as deep into the boot/trunk as possible. If you're taking things like a baby bath or a sterilizer, stuff the dead space within them with bedding or towels. It's also helpful to pack things you'll use a lot into open boxes rather than suitcases; this way, you can see where everything is at a glance, and don't need to dismantle your packing – or worse, try and open suitcases each time you need something. Any supermarket cardboard box will do, although collapsible plastic boxes are perfect; and waterproof roll-top sailing bags are great for things that need to stay clean such as food and bottles; you can buy both online or in hardware/sailing shops. For obvious reasons, the last things you pack should be toys for the kids to play with at exercise stops as well as the overnight bag, medical kit and picnic items.

HIRING A DRIVER

In many countries, renting a **car with a hired driver** is a standard (and inexpensive) option with many advantages, particularly if you're travelling without other adults. Apart from freeing up your hands, a local driver will be familiar with driving conditions in your destination, and their understanding of local customs can help avert many misunderstandings or problems. And if you don't speak the language, a driver usually ends up being your translator and informal guide as well. If you're lucky, you also get another adult to help with everything from hauling luggage to finding socks under seats or forgotten toys – not to mention impromptu childminding or providing diversions for the children. In countries where driving licences are bought rather than earned, consider a **test run**; and while this may sound a little extreme, some advocate getting an independent person who knows the local system to check the driver's papers – it obviously depends on where you are.

SETTING OFF

No two car trips are the same, except that **setting off** always takes longer than you expect, and once on the road, everyone seems to get remarkably hungry. Before you leave, make sure that everyone's been to the toilet, and those prone to motion sickness have taken medication or are wearing an acupressure band (see p.106). Once everyone's in, set the child locks on the doors, but if your children have a tendency to undo seatbelts, don't be tempted to modify the arrangements to prevent them from doing so – the risks associated with having to keep refastening seatbelts are said to be far lower than not being able to work the quick-release system in emergencies. Make a mental note of the time as you drive off, and according to your circumstances (number of children, fast/slow roads), figure out when you next need to stop.

ALONE IN THE CAR

Leaving your **children alone in the car** is never recommended, but there might be times when it's difficult not to such as an emergency tyre-change. If you do have to, make sure you have the keys with you rather than in the ignition, and that the handbrake and door locks are on; it's also sensible to park on level ground so that the car won't roll if the handbrake is released. You should also leave the windows rolled down a fraction, as cars can quickly heat up and children dehydrate fast, leaving them highly susceptible to heatstroke – if you're not inside yourself, it's easy to misjudge the temperature.

SETTLING IN FOR THE NIGHT

If you're still driving at bedtime, it's worth getting prepared before the children fall asleep: put their pyjamas on, organize bedding, play some calming music or start a bed-time story. But if your children tend to drop off only after a last burst of energy, it's best to stop or drive slowly until they do.

Car trips

Car checks

- ❑ Tyres
- ❑ Spare wheel
- ❑ Lights
- ❑ Brake fluid and pads
- ❑ Water
- ❑ Oil
- ❑ Antifreeze
- ❑ Heating and/or air conditioning
- ❑ Repair kit including jack
- ❑ Fuel specifications/capacity (for rental cars)
- ❑ Child seat(s) and seatbelts
- ❑ Airbags
- ❑ Child locks

Essentials

- ❑ Driver's licence
- ❑ Car registration papers
- ❑ Owner's manual
- ❑ Insurance policy
- ❑ Rental policy
- ❑ Anti-pollution/motor-test certification
- ❑ Road-tax stickers
- ❑ Phone numbers for emergency breakdown service
- ❑ Detailed maps of route, and abbreviated sets of directions
- ❑ Sunglasses
- ❑ First-aid kit

Things to bring

- ❑ Mobile phone and in-car charger
- ❑ Extra set of car keys
- ❑ Coins for tolls
- ❑ Extra rear-view mirror to watch the children
- ❑ Flashlight and spare batteries
- ❑ Blankets and pillows
- ❑ Detachable sunscreens for rear windows
- ❑ Large umbrella, weatherproof coat and walking shoes for breakdowns
- ❑ Motion sickness pills
- ❑ Flask of coffee or tea
- ❑ Plastic bags
- ❑ Tissues and wet-wipes
- ❑ Spare toilet roll
- ❑ Blankets and pillows
- ❑ Baby bath
- ❑ Overnight bag
- ❑ Guide books
- ❑ Portable potty
- ❑ "Baby on board" stickers
- ❑ No-mess snacks and drinks
- ❑ Waterproof tarpaulin or plastic sheet to sit on and protect luggage from dust
- ❑ Picnic gear
- ❑ Bottle/food warmers

Entertainment

- ❑ Toys suitable for inside the car
- ❑ Toys for exercise stops
- ❑ Tapes, CDs, DVDs, audiobooks
- ❑ Walkman/MP3 player and headset, plus spare batteries
- ❑ Portable DVD

TRAVELLING BY TRAIN AND BUS

Regardless of how you get to your destination, you may well want to use public transport at some point while you're there. **Train travel** has several advantages when you're with kids, as you have more room to spread out your things and can get up and walk around, and although bus journeys can bring on motion sickness, they do at least free you

> *"If God had intended us to fly, he would have made it easier to get to the airport."*
>
> **George Winters**

up to eat, doze, play with your kids or just enjoy the changing scenery through the window.

Whether you're going on a bus or a train, it's worth arriving early if starting your journey from a major station to give the children a chance to absorb the scene, from streams of people weaving in different directions to the trains themselves. Getting there with plenty of time to spare also means that you're more likely to find seats together.

TRAVELLERS' TALES

THE CAUCASUS BY TRAIN

"In the summer of 1986, I took a trip to Adler, a small resort town on the Black Sea in the Caucasus, on the border of Russia and Georgia. I was working as an engineer in a big electronic factory and my employer sponsored the trip and paid for my daughter (aged 8), but not my husband, to come along.

In those days, when Estonia was part of the USSR, some places in the country weren't well provided with food, but in Tallinn, where we lived, you could buy almost anything. After visiting various shops around the city, we got a good selection of things to eat, and began our journey south by train in high spirits.

As the train started, the conductor walked through our sleeper-car, checking tickets, distributing bedclothes and offering tea in tall glasses set in iron holders. The smells of food started spreading from one cabin to another as passengers took out their grilled chicken, boiled eggs, tomatoes and, sometimes, bottles of spirits. It didn't take long before we were acquainted with the two other passengers in our cabin of four; this was our 'hotel on wheels' for the next three days.

The journey broke in Riga, where our car was re-attached to a different train. During the long wait, Kristina enjoyed the chance to go into the city, visiting the zoo and the market followed by a meal in the train station restaurant. After the busy day out, we were glad to be back to our simple routine on the train: reading, talking to other passengers and having frequent meals. Kids were never a burden as they would always find something to do together and, if there were no children of the same age around, there was always the changing scenery out of the window, which Kristina could follow for hours – she loved everything about the train.

But Kristina was always accident-prone. This time, she managed to cut herself trying to catch a falling knife. Fortunately, on trains you're surrounded by people whose luggage miraculously contains unthinkable supplies ready at hand. Everyone rallied round and in no time, Kristina's wrist was bandaged, and she was given hot tea with sugar – after which she promptly fell asleep, forgot about it all and woke up her usual cheerful self. After that trip, I knew that I could travel with my daughter any time, anywhere."

Ljubov Mänd

FAMILY TICKETS AND DISCOUNTS

As a general rule, the more children you have under 5, the cheaper train or bus travel is likely to be. Children of preschool age usually go for free, as will older kids on occasion, though this depends on whether you want a reserved seat for them and/or are allowed to have them on your lap. Children over 5 will usually be charged half the adult fare, whereas those over 11 or 15 (depending on the country) might qualify for "young persons" discounts or student rates. In some countries, limitations are placed on the number of children entitled to discounted tickets, usually a maximum of two per adult; so if you're the sole adult with three children, two would travel half-price, but the third would have to pay the full fare.

When booking tickets, make a point of asking for **deals for families** and young people. In many instances, a family travelcard reduces the cost of regular tickets so much that it's worth buying one even for a single trip. Such deals are usually restricted to travel outside rush hours, but this is likely coincide with your preferences in any case. To buy a card, you usually need to show identification for one or both parents, and have photographs with you.

BUYING TICKETS AND MAKING RESERVATIONS

While there's plenty of online information on fares, routes and journey times, many Internet booking sites aren't geared up for families, and getting quotations that include deals for children and families often has to be done by phone. Get a basic idea of prices and routes from the websites, and then ring or visit stations in person to ask about special deals. Make sure you outline all your travel plans, as there are often **special deals** which apply across countries or that extend over periods of time. However, think twice about all-you-can-travel deals such as monthly rail passes; with children, you always want a leisurely pace, and are unlikely to get the full value of these tickets. But combination packages which cover more than one country or form of transport (buses, trams, metro etc) can be very useful in terms of simplifying logistics. Also ask what the options for flexibility are; in addition to the obvious virtues of being able to change travel dates and times, you might want to be able to break your journey if you spot somewhere interesting, or chose a different route for the return trip. Finally, find out the length of the journey; some trains stop everywhere – which might be exactly what you want; alternatively, you might prefer faster options. Also ask how long you have to board and disembark; some stops are so short that if you aren't quick with the bags and the

TRAIN TRAVEL IN SOUTH ASIA

"I frequently travel by train with my grandchildren and my children. Here, the trains are very dirty but we're used to it – it's not a problem. We go first class to keep the crowds and beggars out, and we always clean the carriage before sitting down as the children touch everything. If we have really small children with us, we're particularly careful. I take along everything we need for this: a bucket, a large container with soapy water, some towels, sheets to cover the seats and a large piece of plastic, big enough to cover the floor. The floors have to be covered as these are the dirtiest of all surfaces and impossible to clean, and the plastic sheet gives toddlers more room to play. When we're finished cleaning, we hand over the dirty cloths to beggars who are happy to have them. The other passengers don't mind at all, as they like having a clean carriage too. We all take off our shoes and place them under the floor mat. But no matter how hard you clean, there are always things that the children touch that you'd rather they didn't. I take along a bottle of drinking water, soap and a clean cloth to keep washing their hands. And when we finally get to our destination, we fold the plastic sheet around the dirty surface to keep it from touching other things. Later on, we wash it down with soap and a hosepipe ready for the trip back."

Jahanara R. Choudhury

children, you stand a real risk of leaving something or, worse still, someone behind.

If you're thinking of buying tickets over the phone using a credit card, note that quoted prices can change, and delays in processing payments can mean that the amount you're eventually charged can be a lot more than the quote – quite a shock if you're buying for the whole family. To avoid surprises, it's best to pay in person if possible.

Choosing your seat

When it comes to **selecting seats**, go for the non-smoking section even if you smoke – smokers' carriages can get very stuffy – and if the weather's likely to be hot, aim for air-conditioning, which will be particularly welcome when the bus or train is stationary. Ask how the seats are arranged; on trains and some long-distance buses, you might be able to get groups of four facing each other around a table (particularly useful for carrycots and games); and if you prefer to face the direction you're travelling, mention this too. If you're going on a train with a buffet or restaurant carriage, don't book seats close by, as these are likely to be noisy and possibly smoky, and you'll be pestered for treats by the kids. Some trains (and newer long-distance buses) have toilets for the disabled, baby-changing facilities and special places for leaving your pram – ask. Finally, if you think you might need **assistance** – either on board or at stations – mention this when buying tickets and find out what the options are.

TRAINS AND BUSES IN DEVELOPING COUNTRIES

Assumptions about public transport being a pleasant way to travel can be completely off the mark in countries with weak infrastructure, and it's worth spending a bit of time researching track/road conditions and train stock/bus fleets. Standards can vary tremendously: you might get the best of old-world comfort, or a decrepit contraption on its last legs; equally, you may get there on time or suffer a series of infuriating delays.

The difference in comfort between **seat classes** can also be dramatic. It's usually assumed that international travellers want the most expensive tickets, and going first class will certainly mean more room and comfort, and may be the only means to guarantee a seat. If you're travelling with more than one child and you want space for them to play, or prefer to avoid being squashed by other passengers, it's a good idea to buy more tickets than you need, or book out an entire compartment. This might sound elitist, but sharing a packed carriage can be overwhelming when you're with small children. If you don't travel first class, it's all the more important to arrive early to claim seats; and if you think the train itself might be filthy, go prepared with ample supplies of wet wipes to clean your space (and everyone's fingers); a roll of insulating tape can come in handy to seal off broken fixtures or wires on old trains, too. As the refreshments sold on the train or at stations may be unhygienic or just too strange to appeal to the children, take your own supplies of **food and water**. And lastly, anticipate delays: apart from maintenance problems with the roads, train or track, holdups might come as a result of anything from animals on the track to a local dignitary running late – it's important to be able to be flexible.

INDIA BY TRAIN

"We went rock-bottom class on the trains when travelling around South India. The kids (three and all under 10) loved it. I remember one time we had the usual crowds and animals but also a troupe of travelling circus performers. That took care of Krishna, Arjuna and Shanthi. They were riveted watching the artists perform their tricks – we had non stop entertainment all the way. The toilets were definitely on the rough side and the train wasn't exactly clean. But we always drank bottled water and carried a picnic with us on the train; we also took along some soap and a cloth and I kept watch over the need to clean hands. We had a terrific adventure, traversed vast distances, and didn't have a single bout of diarrhoea between us!"

Elizabeth Mason

TRAIN TRIALS OF A SINGLE PARENT

"I was dreading travelling with the two kids. We were on our way back to Marseilles from Paris, only this time I was on my own with them. Apart from the children, I had heaps of luggage, which meant I could carry one or the other, but never both, and this caused a lot of stress. But once on the train, all went much better than I imagined. The kids stayed put and were happy just looking out of the window, playing with their toys and the colouring materials that the train company provided. (That was a happy surprise.) The toughest part was going to the toilet. I couldn't leave either of the two children behind, so each time any of us wanted to go, we all went together. Getting all three of us into the tiny toilet was a squeeze. All in all, we spent quite a bit of time jammed in there together."

Charles Dunant

ON THE BUS OR TRAIN

When you're boarding a bus or train, decide who'll get on first, who'll go last and who's stowing the luggage so as to be sure nothing and no one gets left behind. Once **on board**, organize yourselves so that your children and the luggage remain in view – particularly when nearing and during stops – see p.132 for tips on keeping your things secure on public transport. If you're the only adult travelling, and the ride is going to be a long one, think about starting up conversations with those immediately around you; sooner or later, you'll need a trip to the toilet, and it's likely you won't be able to take everything with you – make a broad announcement to those nearby, asking them to collectively keep an eye on your (less than vital) things.

If you're on a train, establish limits in terms of how far older children can stray and how long they can be away for, emphasizing that they always need to come back to you when the train slows down to stop; to start with, wander around and explore the length of the train with them. Children tend to enjoy tracking progress of the journey, so do get them to help you watch out for the station that comes before your stop.

 Bus and train travel

Check
- ❏ Family or child discount deals
- ❏ Flexibility of tickets and routes
- ❏ Length of the journey and of stops
- ❏ Seating: non-smoking, air-conditioning, class, groupings, direction of travel, proximity to restaurant car on trains
- ❏ Toilets for the disabled/changing tables
- ❏ Conditions on board and of the road or track
- ❏ Availability of assistance

Consider
- ❏ ID and photos for buying tickets
- ❏ Food and drink ▶▶ p.65
- ❏ Entertainment ▶▶ p.69
- ❏ Cleaning materials and tape for securing loose fixtures on trains

BEING THERE 3

BEING THERE

Once you arrive, you don't want to waste holiday time grappling with the very chores you meant to leave behind, or find yourselves bogged down with logistics of travel. This section provides some practical tips that should help free you up to enjoy your break, from checking in to your accommodation and keeping everyone fed and clean to handling some of the challenges that can crop up. We've also given some suggestions to help you get the best out of time at the beach or on the slopes, as well as walks, bike rides and camping trips.

ARRIVAL

If you've travelled by plane, train or bus, your arrival will coincide with that of hundreds of others. Your first few minutes in a new place can be disorienting, so try to be on the alert for opportunist pickpockets, and keep a close rein on the children. As it can be difficult to manoeuvre both your children and your bags, you might want to make use of a porter – even if it's not something you've done before; just check that they're bona fide (official porters will be uniformed). Before heading out into the open, it's a good idea to use the toilets so that you don't have to circle back the moment you set off.

CHECKING IN TO YOUR ROOM

It's impossible to fully visualize what your hotel or guesthouse will be like in advance of pitching up, and when you arrive at the place you're going to stay, you're almost always in for a few surprises. If they're not of the pleasant kind, there are things you can do to rectify things. Before completing the registration steps, ask to see the room/s you've been assigned, mentioning that you'd like to check the quality of the room and bathroom. If standards between rooms vary – and they almost always do – this may well result in your being offered something better. But if you still don't like the room, there's always the option of asking to change, and perhaps limiting your booking to one night so that you can find somewhere else the next day.

CHILD-PROOFING YOUR ROOM

Most tourist accommodation isn't particularly child-friendly, so you'll probably need to make some adaptations yourself. Start off by checking

locks on doors and windows – you don't want your children to be able to let themselves out, and obviously you'll want the room to be secure. Check the sturdiness of the **fittings** – while wobbly balconies and railings are unsafe and mean you should change your accommodation straight away, loose towel-rails or curtains that are easy to pull down are manageable; just point such things out to the staff and either agree that you can't be responsible should they break or fall down, or ask for them to be fixed or removed. Have a look at the electric outlets, checking for exposed wires or sockets; use insulating tape to make them safe, or block them off with furniture that's too heavy for your children to move.

Next, have a look at the **furnishings**, checking for sharp edges and fragile objects; you could tape a rolled-up towel over corners of tables, or ask for them to be taken out of the room. Similarly, move fragile things such as glass ashtrays and porcelain lamps out of harm's way, or get them removed. As to the **bathroom**, if the floor is slippery, cover with towels or ask for rubber non-slip mats. It's also a good idea to check the temperature of the hot water; it's often scalding, so you might need to warn your children. If your accommodation comes with a **stove**, you might want to tape the knobs down so that they aren't easy to meddle with; matches and candles are best put away, too. And if there's a **minibar**, either make sure it stays locked or get it emptied – particularly if it's packed with (expensive) alcohol and chocolates.

Beyond your rooms, think through wider **access issues**: if you've a balcony and it's not safe for the children to stray out there alone, make sure they can't access it without your help by locking connecting doors and the like. Similarly, if the grounds are unfenced and border a busy road, or if there's no lifeguard in the pool, it's best to be forewarned.

SETTLING IN

As you get settled in, do what you can to keep things clean and organized. Start by putting dirty cases in places where they're least likely to be touched by the children, and get the kids to leave their shoes by the door. Within seconds of entering rooms, children usually find their way onto the beds, perhaps for a bit of a jump. But before they get inside the sheets, give them a wash and get them out of their dirty travel clothes. It's also a good idea to take off and put away the bedspreads straight away; bedspreads are the least frequently washed of bedlinen items.

If you have a baby, you'll need to organize an area to set out your changing mat and creams; if the tables look unsteady, try a corner on the floor instead. And if you haven't already run out of energy, unlock your cases and take out some start-up supplies (including your toiletries); otherwise, keep your bags closed if there's any chance that your children might disrupt the rest of the packing.

GETTING THE BEST OUT OF THE STAFF

It's easy to overlook the fact that staff are often able to help with services beyond those officially on offer (as long as requests are within reason, of course). For instance, if you return to your hotel at the end of the day and realize that you forgot to buy something, you could ask if there's anyone who could get it for you (and how much it'll cost), rather than getting all the kids dressed and trooping outside again.

If everyone's boots are muddy or your clothes are sodden, staff might prefer to clean or dry these for you rather than having you muck up the rooms doing it yourselves; asking where you might clean dirty gear is usually enough to prompt an offer of help. It's also worth asking if you've a lot of ironing to do or need to post something. You'll probably need to clear these sorts of things with the management first, but either way, a tip will be expected.

FOOD, WATER AND HYGIENE

Your children's ages and your destination will determine how difficult or easy it is to maintain your usual standards in terms of **food**, **water** and **hygiene**, so choosing somewhere that's appropriate for you and your family makes it a lot easier to stay clean and avoid upset tummies. If your kids are at an age when they love playing on the ground, heading off to a developing country or spending lots of time in grimy places means you'll have your work cut out for you.

Food

Even if your children aren't picky with what they eat, finding **food** when they need it requires more than the usual advance planning when you're travelling. If you don't think ahead, you can end up either stuffing them with ridiculous amounts of junk food or stopping at restaurants and spending small fortunes when you'd much rather be doing other things.

Eating in

When you're holed up in your accommodation after a long day out, you won't want to leave in search of food each time someone wants a nibble, and there will also be times when you just feel like staying in.

So, keep some **fruit** and **snacks** in your room; if you have a kettle, you can also whip up instant noodles or soup, and if there's a fridge, you can store bread, sandwich fillings and the like. For more substantial **hot meals**, don't forget there's always the option of getting a takeaway delivered, or ordering in room service if it's available.

If the drinking water in your destination isn't safe to drink, or if it's a place where traveller's tummy and other stomach bugs are common, don't forget to follow stringent **hygiene measures** if you buy food to eat in your room. Wash raw vegetables and fruit thoroughly or soak it in a bowl of water with sterilizing tablets; rinse with pre-boiled water before you eat to get rid of the chlorine taste, and throw away any fruit with a broken skin. If you have a kitchen and are going to be cooking meals for the family, prepare dishes that require high temperatures and prolonged cooking rather than, for example, quick stir-fries – and always avoid raw or underdone meat, fish or eggs. If the tap water isn't fit to drink, you can use it for boiling rice, stews and pastas, as the cooking process will render it safe. But be careful to only add in pre-boiled water thereafter; it's easy to forget that water added in at the end of a cooking session might not get hot enough to kill bugs. And before eating, check that plates and cutlery are both clean and dry; to be really safe, give them a rinse in pre-boiled water.

Eating out

Eating out when travelling is usually as much of a pleasure for the children as it is for adults, but to start out on the right foot, make up your mind about where to go before everyone is hungry. Apart from deciding on the kind of food you want, think about how your children will be received. Places filled with families or advertising children's menus are clearly a safe bet, but the reverse is true for places with elbow-to-elbow seating, linen tablecloths and crystal glasses – unless, of course, your children happen to be exceptionally well-behaved. If the layout of a restaurant has a lawn or open space where children can go to give them a break from sitting at the table, or has things that might interest them such as a colourful fish tank, then all the better. It's also a good idea to bring things with you to keep children amused at the table – books to read or paper and coloured pencils make excellent distractions when you're waiting for the meal to arrive.

"When you go abroad with your kids, one of your main worries is probably a food-based one. This guide makes the whole holiday thing easier – fantastic!"
Jamie Oliver

Though it can be notoriously difficult to gauge, the length of time

between placing your order and having food served makes a lot of difference. Even if your children aren't hungry when you arrive at a restaurant, they can quickly become ravenous when they smell food and watch others eat, and a long wait is a sure route to crankiness. It helps to arrive before the bulk of the crowds descend, but unless you opt for fast food, the surest bet for quick service is to find a **buffet** (though only if you're in a place with high standards of hygiene). As well as enabling you to eat as soon as you're ready, buffets allow everyone to be experimental – particularly valuable in places where local dishes aren't familiar. Pizzerias are also a good standby for families; food tends to arrive quickly, and there will usually be something besides pizza or pasta to keep the adults happy. Another way to make sure your meal gets to the table quickly is to **order in advance**, either over the phone or by turning up before you plan to eat, placing orders and taking a stroll together until the food is ready. But if your meal takes an eternity to arrive despite your efforts, ask for bread but defer ordering drinks until the food is served – otherwise, children tend to fill themselves up to the point of not eating. Besides, bread is usually free, whereas drinks – in terms of value – are often the most expensive thing on the menu.

Assuming that a children's menu isn't on offer, ask about **portion sizes**; you might want to order starters instead of main courses, or

DINNER AT *THE CARNIVORE*

"We were in Nairobi on holiday. Our daughter was just four months old, and having had to miss out on safaris (which every traveller we met kept raving about), we were feeling a bit sorry for ourselves. One day we decided to make up for this by splurging on a night out. When we got to the restaurant, people had just started to arrive. We chose a corner table and placed Ellie on the end in her carrycot. The decor was rustic – heavy wooden tables, set in a garden with pretty light bulbs threaded through the tree canopies. Huge joints of meat were roasting on open fires tended by chefs wearing starched aprons and hats. The babble of people and the music made us feel we were in for a good night – something that we hadn't managed since Ellie was born. The place started to fill up fast with an interesting-looking international crowd.

We were feeling pretty good halfway through our first glass of wine. Before, that is, the waiter brought two people to our table and then dashed off. The four of us looked at each other awkwardly. We didn't want company and it was pretty obvious that sharing wasn't on the other couple's minds either. The fact that they were the picture of elegance also didn't help – it made me feel tatty and underdressed. But we had no option, so we just made room. In the shuffling of our things, they noticed we had a baby (she was sleeping), and the ice broke. From that moment on it was all "oohs" and "aahs". And when she woke, they took over. This turned out to be one of the best evenings we had. They had just got married and were expecting a baby. Not only were they desperate to practise, but this made us suddenly feel like experts – which frankly we didn't up until that point."

Sarah Cohen

something that you can share with the children. And if there's nothing suitable for the kids, most restaurants can accommodate an off-menu pasta, salad or omelette. But whatever you order, ask for your children to be served first so that you can help them get stuck in before you eat. And as children often don't finish their food, take along an air-tight box for leftovers – doggy bags tend to become a greasy mess when you lump them together with everything else you need to carry.

Keeping tummy bugs at bay

When eating out in countries with **poor standards of sanitation** and hygiene, always eat at busy places where the turnover of food will be fast and, unlike in more conventional destinations, avoid buffets. They're notorious for harbouring the bugs that cause diarrhoea: the food might have been contaminated by hands or dodgy water, and once bugs are introduced, a buffet provides the perfect conditions to help them multiply. Obviously, steer clear of anything exposed to dust and flies such as sliced fruit or ice-cream sold at street stalls; children are often sucked in by such tempting offerings or by the persistent sales patter of vendors, but if you're unsure of hygiene standards, stand firm and be ready with substitute snacks of your own.

When eating in **restaurants**, have a look at the crockery and cutlery; if anything is wet, giving it a dry wipe with a clean tissue will lower any potential dose of bugs dramatically. Otherwise, check that bottles and cans are unopened before handing these to the children (and use straws or clean the can or bottle before they drink), and get them to avoid ice and leave salad untouched, even if it's just a garnish. If the **tap water** isn't safe to drink, you'll need to boil, filter or sterilize your own, or buy bottled water. If you plan to use bottled water to make up formula feeds, aim to get the lowest mineral content you can. As well as getting into the habit of either buying or treating enough water for everyone's use, make sure the children don't drink from taps; this can be a hard habit to break, particularly when brushing teeth. Keeping a bottle of drinking water by the sink is a helpful reminder.

DOING THE LAUNDRY

You don't want to spend your entire holiday washing clothes, but as kids tend to go through outfits like the clappers or cover things in sticky messes that need cleaning immediately, you'll probably have to do some **laundry** while you're away. Most hotels will wash clothes for you, but it's usually expensive and you'll probably have to count out each item as you hand it over (one sock, one bib, another sock etc). It can be a bit embarrassing as well as time-consuming to hand over bed-wetted nightclothes or food-encrusted tops, though the satisfaction of collecting clean, neatly folded clothes takes some beating. It's also worth bringing some travel soap from home to sort out the odd milky bib or stained outfit; soak things overnight to make the job easier.

KEEPING CLEAN

When **washing in public places**, bear in mind that taps will have been touched by many others, and using them might mean walking away with more germs than you had in the first place; best plan is to rinse off the handles with soapy water before you begin. Obviously, don't use shared towels in public bathrooms; leave your hands to dry naturally, or use your own.

At some point, you'll probably need to deal with spills, dirty bottoms and the like while out and about. If you plan to put your child into a **sink** to wash them, be sure to check that it can stand their weight, clean the sink and tap handles with soapy water before you start, and get a plastic mug or something similar to collect and pour water.

TOILETS

Wherever you go, it's inevitable that you'll develop a sixth sense for spotting the nearest **toilets** (note that we've given a very generalized idea of the availability of public loos in the "Around the world" section; see p.174). Apart from being prepared with your own supply of paper, and coins in case you need to pay, try to accompany the children each time they go – the facilities might be different to the ones they're used to, from holes in the ground to flushes in odd places or different systems for disposing of toilet paper and washing hands. If you're concerned about security, don't think twice about taking children of the opposite sex into your own toilets – people will understand. Alternatively, stay just outside and talk to them from wherever you are.

see p.174

TOILETS IN UGANDA

For a child who used to be reluctant to poo away from home, Ruby (aged 4) developed a fascination with the weird and wonderful toilets we encountered in Uganda. The loos were often the first thing she wanted to check out when we arrived somewhere new. She remarked on the doors (or lack of), the various flush mechanisms, garish air fresheners, decorated seats, the number of geckos on the wall – and of course their smell.

The eco-flush loo in a tented camp was a source of wonder to her – it looked almost throne-like and had a complicated flush mechanism that required strength and skill (probably a good thing, otherwise Ruby would have flushed it repeatedly just for fun). Many of the toilets in Uganda were traditional pit latrines under a basic shelter. The smell and the flies came as a shock to a child brought up in London, but she was always very keen to assess the (in)accuracy of previous visitors' aims, and to get a good look at the pit below.

Perhaps Ruby got off lightly with only one brief bout of traveller's tummy. While clearly unpleasant, this did bring the excitement of pooing in a bush – for her, this was the highlight of a long drive up-country.

Lorna Fray

USING PUBLIC TRANSPORT

When leaping on and off **public transport**, there are a couple of things to bear in mind. In new places, it's easy to forget the importance of thinking through who goes first and who carries what, particularly if you're carrying a lot of luggage as well as the children. If there are two adults in your group, one should get on with the children while the other deals with the luggage, handing pieces to those installed inside. When you get to your stop, one adult should get out and receive the luggage and the children, and when everything is out, the other adult should follow; this type of "drill" will help everyone (and the bags) stay together. See p.161 for tips on what to do should you and your children get separated.

INTERACTING WITH PEOPLE

When travelling with children, you'll find that you meet many more people than you would at home, or if you were travelling on your own. The fact is that kids interest others – you can't stop anywhere for long before people recognize you as the parents of your children, and kids tend to make friends long before you do. You won't need any tips on breaking the ice, but it is a good idea to start interactions on the right foot. It goes without saying that **good manners** are appreciated everywhere, and getting your children to follow simple courtesies (and perhaps say the odd word in the local language) will stand the whole family in good stead – misbehaviour and mishaps will be excused, and antagonistic reactions to foreigners are likely to be targeted elsewhere if it's clear that your family shows respect. Also caution your children against voicing negative opinions, such as "Yuck! That's so stupid/ filthy/disgusting!" – explain why these won't go down well, using the "imagine if someone came to our home and said/did . . ." trick. It's also worth reinforcing that there are people who'll speak your language everywhere, so you can't assume those around you don't understand what you're saying. And for times when children want to convey something potentially indiscreet, get them to whisper or use a code (even a dig in the ribs) so that you know when they want to tell you something in private.

BREASTFEEDING AND TRAVEL

Breastfeeding in a new, unfamiliar destination can be a worry, and as it's hard to predict whether you'll feel at ease, it is worth doing some research into local attitudes towards feeding in public before you go. But whatever you think reactions might be; the best approach is to prepare yourself for all eventualities. Wearing the right bras, loose, front-opening clothing and having a shawl to cover up with are obvious starting points, but you could also try finding some female company, such as you might expect in a women's clothing shop, where you're more likely to feel at ease than out in the street. Another idea is to head for the ladies' toilets of a posh hotel; these are usually spacious, with seats and pleasant surroundings allowing for a quiet and peaceful break for you and your child to feed in comfort. You could also try asking women working in shops or restaurants where you might feed. With or without the right language, it's likely you'll be understood, and you may well be ushered into a comfortable back room.

When you go out on **day-trips**, take a flannel and drinking water to give yourself a sponge-down whenever you feel sticky. As long as your breasts remain covered and clean, there's no need to use soap when on the move; soapy residues, while unlikely to do much harm, are not intended to be ingested by babies, and can end up irritating them. However, if you've been swimming and may have contaminated water or sand on your breasts, use a wet-wipe, and then rinse off with drinking water before the next feed.

ACTIVITIES

If you've spent some time reading your guide book before arriving, you've probably got an idea of what you'd like to do and see, but it's worthwhile going a step further and pre-preparing **lists of activities** which take various lengths of time and suit different weather conditions. You can then start each day by focusing on getting everyone up and out, and when you're ready to go, just check the time and the weather, and finalize what to do. This helps deflect the feeling of constantly running against the clock, being too late for "x" or getting rained out for "y". If your children sleep in the afternoons, another way of freeing up your options is to find makeshift places for them to nap while you're out rather than working day-trips around the usual routine.

But do prioritize what you really must fit in – for instance, if you're passionate about seeing Michelangelo's *David* in Florence, say, make a beeline for it; once you have, you can relax and take in other things as time permits – the policy of leaving the best till the last doesn't tend to work with children. Similarly, if you're going somewhere with plenty for the kids to do, such as a museum or theme park, start with the prize treats; once these are out of the way, you can just explore at will until the children run out of steam.

To **get your children involved** in deciding what to do, let them choose from a selection of possibilities on your activities list. If you've more than one child, give each a turn to make choices. This way, everyone gets a sense for what it means to be responsible, and the fact that expectations sometimes don't match the reality. If you can all joke your way through the odd disaster, your children will quickly pick up the art of making the most of whatever's on offer, and avoid blaming whoever's "fault" it all was.

Lastly if you're travelling with more than one adult, try **splitting up** from time to time, either having one-on-one time with the children, or heading off without them to do something you can only enjoy on your own – having a break from the children will recharge your energies and enthusiasm, which is good both for you yourself and the rest of the group.

SHOPPING AND BARGAINING

When in new places, children's enthusiasm for shopping can be boundless. They tend to want everything in sight, but everyone finds it grating to keep up the "please!" followed by "no!" routine. One way of pre-empting this is to warn your children in advance that there will be lots of things that will interest them, and that it's best to buy

TRAVELLERS' TALES

STANDING YOUR GROUND

"Rome has horses and carriages dotted around the city. Our children spotted them immediately and begged for a ride. It was relatively easy to put them off the first time as our youngest was asleep – I argued with the others that it wouldn't be fair to him. Later on, when leaving the Colosseum, there were seven horses and carriages lined up waiting. The children started begging again. We told them we would check the prices, but that we weren't making any promises. It was our last day, so we thought we would give it a go, but the first driver had the cheek to ask for 150 euros. He obviously thought we were an easy catch with the kids, and hadn't taken into account that we have no problem saying 'no'; we feel our children are privileged enough to begin with. So we thanked him but kept walking. Sure enough, we were approached again. This time the offer was 100 euros; again, we declined. The kids, meanwhile, were looking sadly at the line of horses as we kept walking on. A third driver came forward and offered 75 – there was clearly some communication going on between the drivers. This time – and as part of the overall bargaining game – we explained that this was our last day in Rome and we needed the cash for a taxi ride to the airport. He then asked how much we were willing to pay. We told him 50 euros; he offered 60. Again we declined and started walking. We were approached once more, this time with the offer of 50. But before we had a chance to respond, the children had leapt into the carriage. So in we got too. The children were ecstatic and it was a wonderful ride for everyone with the exception of my husband. He kept mulling over the thought that he could have got an even lower price; on reflection, there were many carriages and we seemed to be the only prospective customers. I told him to sit back and enjoy the ride! A few days later, in another town – surprise, surprise, more horses and carriages. The children started up again. This time we said nothing doing – we had done that in Rome."

Melissa Reardon

towards the end of the stay – by then, they'll have had the chance to see what's on offer and learn how much things cost. If this sounds far too rational an approach, decide on an amount of **spending money** that they can use to buy whatever they want (but perhaps with the exception of live animals). Reserve a small budget for the first day to get them get started, although be prepared for this to disappear pretty quickly. They'll soon get the hang of it and give you some peace, but be firm about the fact that this amount is all they can have.

Vendors can be ruthless when they spot children; some not only target you, but jack up the price too, and have a tendency to count on the adults being pressured to give in. Don't let yourself fall for this: either bargain till you're happy, or walk away. Bear in mind that as you turn your back, this is probably when the meaningful bargaining starts. At this point, however, the children might have lost interest – which means you can keep on walking.

Picking up souvenirs

Apart from taking **photographs**, there are lots of ways to help your children preserve memories of your trip. You could buy a **postcard** for each destination and help them to note a single memory on the back, alongside the date or their age. This could lead to a **collection**; postcards fit perfectly into shoe boxes, and children can spend hours sorting through their selection – and usually end up putting other things into their "travel box" besides. You could also get them started on collections of things that can be found in most places, such as badges, snowball paperweights, model cars and boats or toy animals. An unusual idea is to collect a piece of material in each place you visit, and eventually stitch them into a quilt or keepsake; this kind of collection can keep going for years.

If your children are keeping a **journal** of some kind, encourage them to draw and list things they see and eat (writing about food has a way of getting kids engaged); they could also collect autographs and doodles from people they meet – particularly interesting if the entries are written in a different language – as well as ticket stubs and colourful bottle labels to stick in. If free mini-maps (the kind usually handed out to tourists) of places you visit are available, get extras for the children to stick into their books, and help them circle the places you've seen. You might also try recording special events yourself ("x drew this while y happened"), and save space to stick in photographs later on. Certainly, if you're encountering different languages, put in lists of new words and add more as they learn one set. And if you've planned a "traveller's bingo" (see p.76) for the children, help them get started with this, too.

ENTERTAINMENT

There are plenty of ways to keep children **entertained** whilst travelling beyond the usual holiday activities. Local papers should have details of any festivals, exhibitions, plays or films that might interest them, but watching people at work can also be fascinating, from cottage industries such as chocolate-making in Switzerland or cigar workshops in Cuba. Don't overlook what's happening on the street, either; watching cooking at a stall is an all-time favourite, particularly if some sampling of the food is on offer, but anything will do, from shoe mending and tailoring to carpentry – and people generally warm to requests to show off their skills when children are in the audience, possibly even allowing the kids to have a go themselves.

Local toys are also often worth seeking out, and make great gifts to take home, too. Apart from the novelty value, kids tend to like playing with the same things that local children have, and it can help with making friends, too. Wherever you go, you're bound to find some surprises if you look, be it exotic kites in China or ingenious beach toys in Brazil. Similarly, local **bookshops** often stock things that are very different to the storybooks back home, which can provoke some interesting discussions and give your children some insight into what life is like in your destination.

BEACH HOLIDAYS AND SWIMMING

There's nothing that comes close to the beach for keeping both children and parents absorbed. Kids are inevitably bewitched from the moment you arrive (and usually need a considerable amount of coaxing to leave), and you might find that the seaside allows you to rekindle your own ability to just play, too. From digging in the sand, walks around the coast, watching creatures in pools or collecting shells and bits of polished glass – not to mention the sea itself – the beach really has it all.

When **choosing your beach**, bear in mind the differences between sandy and pebbly seasides. Sand is a lot more fun for the children to work with, and is less likely to hurt delicate feet than pebbles; obviously, it's also more comfortable to lie down on. But a pebble beach has its advantages, too: there'll be no sand in eyes or picnics, and it's easier to clean up at the end of the day – sand-soaked towels can be a nightmare. There's also the question of **shelter** from the sun and the wind; if there aren't natural or man-made shelters, you might need to take along umbrellas and wind breaks, or spend less time outdoors. **Showers** or a tap on the beach are a real bonus when you consider just how mucky everyone can get; and as salt water can be uncomfortable

for children's delicate skin, it's great to be able to rinse them off if they start feeling itchy or complain of "burning" skin (usually from salt in a scratch). Finally, there's the **sea** itself to consider, from the tides and currents to how calm or rough the water will be, what might be in it and immediately underfoot. If there are no lifeguards or designated swimming areas, always seek local advice before getting in, and think twice about swimming if no one else is – there's likely to be good reason. Conversely, bear in mind that the more people there are, the harder it is to keep an eye on your children.

What to bring to the beach

Essentials include the full range of sunblock, towels, clothing and hats to protect sensitive skins, as well as swimsuits, and swim-nappies/diapers for little ones who aren't yet toilet-trained. T-shirts and pyjamas also provide protection from the sun. Pebble beaches call for waterproof sandals with good tread and ankle straps to keep them in place, while scuba divers' foot-socks will protect little feet from sea urchins and sharp coral or stones underfoot. You'll also want something to lie on as well as snacks, drinks and water; even if there's plenty on offer from vendors and restaurants, it's annoying and expensive to keep getting up to buy things. When deciding what **toys** to take with you, a mask and snorkel will help young swimmers explore even if there's not much to see, while a bucket and spade will keep them busy for hours on end. But don't forget age-old **games** like throwing stones and shells into the sea, making moats for sandcastles, collecting shells or getting your children to lie down while you cover them with sand, maybe even crafting shapes to turn them into mermaids – with fish tails and all. But save the lilos and inflatables for swimming pools, as they can buoy children quickly out to sea. Finally, bear in mind that it's almost impossible to get rid of sand if it's wet, so try to time your last dip so that swimsuits and towels will have dried off by the time you're ready to go; and if you're driving, keep a bottle of water in the car so that you can rinse off sandy feet before getting in.

PLAYING IN THE SNOW

If you're planning to spend your holiday in the snow or happen just to chance upon it, your children won't need much encouragement to go out and play. As well as **dressing to stay warm**, use sunblock and sun goggles if the sun is strong. If your children are ready to ski, it's best to rent equipment while they're still growing; and as for renting snow shoes to go trekking across the countryside, bear in mind that kids generally prefer to stay put and just muck about in the snow. Otherwise, make sure they wear brightly coloured clothing that's easy to pick out from afar, both to help everyone stay together as well as to make sure they're visible should they accidentally stray. Extra sets of gloves are definitely worth having – once they're wet, little hands will quickly be smarting with cold, and you'll have no option but to call an early end to the fun.

In terms of **things to play with**, rubbish bags make an inexpensive alternative to a toboggan, and last a fair while before they get torn up. But don't forget trying your hand at a snowman – if you have a secret stash of stones and a carrot to make the face once the work is done, you'll make their day. But no romp in the snow is complete without a snowball fight – you might want to try setting up bases with something hard (a wall or a toboggan, perhaps) to act as a defence; while the real hilarity comes with hitting a person, smashing snowballs against something hard results in spray which is fun in itself. And do caution your children against eating yellow snow – although once you explain what it is, be prepared for them to want to produce their own!

It's important to keep track of how cold children get, as they lose heat faster than adults; if they get wet, either from too much rolling around or from wetting themselves, it's time to head indoors. Just before you head home, get them to make a **snow angel**. Lie them on their backs in reasonably soft snow, and get them to wave their hands up and down and push the snow apart with their legs. When they stand up to look back at their impression, the angel shape can come as a wonderful surprise.

CAMPING

Going **camping** is one of the most popular options for a family holiday – children love sleeping and waking up outdoors, and the fact that their parents are less likely to fuss over how they look, whether or not they eat with their hands or, for that matter, play with fire; and given that children tend to be happy left to their own devices (particularly if you go with friends or can bank on other children being around), parents also get time to relax. And as everything to do with camping has got a lot easier, from tents that practically erect themselves to a huge amount of choice in terms of where you pitch, a camping holiday doesn't have to be about roughing it.

Choosing the right campsite

Campsites vary hugely, so when you're choosing where to pitch your tent, it's important to consider the needs of the whole family, asking yourself if you want peace and quiet and plenty of nature, or lots of company and activities for the children. Generally, **large sites** with extensive facilities (from swimming pools to movie halls) are less private, and can be lacking in aesthetics or even downright noisy. That said, you and your children might welcome the company and enjoy laid-on recreation. In contrast, **smaller sites** tend to be more private and peaceful, which usually means more time together as a family, but the fact that there will be fewer facilities means a bit more work to manage cooking, washing and keeping everyone entertained.

If your children are very young, you might feel that things like hot-water showers, a laundry or electricity outlets for sterilizing bottles are essential; but if you associate camping with making fires, find out if these are permitted – they aren't at many sites. Also bear in mind that an indoor cooking area or a large covered space where children can run around and play will be very welcome if you get rained out. Finally, do try to check up on whether your destination is home to ticks, mosquitoes, ants, poison ivy and the like – when you're camping, these kinds of things can ruin your trip, so do what you can to avoid them.

Getting the right tent

While camping does require equipment, it's easy to get carried away. In terms of your **tent**, the first thing to think about is whether the children will sleep with you or on their own – and if they'll be with you, whether you want a separate tent for them to play in during the day; having the option of space to yourselves, even if just for afternoon naps, can make a real difference. If they're having their own tent, look for ones with zips, locks or tie-tags that will stop them from straying out on their own should they wake up.

Always opt for tents that are simple to erect, with short ropes and neat pegging systems that reduce the risk of children tripping over and bringing everything down. Many tents come with a porch, essentially a few flaps of extra material which provide cover around the entrance, and serve as a useful dumping ground for toys or dirty shoes that can otherwise muck everything up within the tent or get forgotten outside in the rain. If the campsite's likely to be muddy, spreading a large tarpaulin from the porch provides a clean place to play.

Sleeping under canvas

Children can find it hard to sleep in tents, particularly on the first few nights when the sounds of nature or the absolute dark can seem pretty scary; if you're sleeping in separate tents, make sure there's enough room for them in yours, as they might well want to migrate in the night. When choosing **sleeping bags**, don't buy cotton or down-filled versions if your children wet their beds; instead, go for synthetic fabrics which are easy to wash and dry, and put a plastic undersheet beneath their sleeping bags. As children get colder than adults, you'll need to be sure that their sleeping bag is warm enough; novelty ones made for sleepovers and napping in nursery aren't a good idea. You can buy bags specifically designed for children, or adapt adult ones by just folding them in half, which reduces the internal volume and makes it easier to heat up the bag from within; you might also stuff some spare clothing inside for extra warmth. Having a zip up the side is always useful in case the evenings turn out to be warmer than you'd expected, and lining bags with cotton cocoon-sheets adds comfort. **Pillows** or **cushions** are also useful for sleeping or propping yourselves up when reading; a less bulky alternative is to take pillowcases and stuff them with clothes. When you're done with your basic packing, fill any extra space with additional blankets and duvets – you're bound to use them, although bear in mind that whatever you take is likely to get pretty dirty.

For babies and toddlers, take a portable cot; if you choose one that sits off the ground in a frame, you can use it as a (clean) outside playpen as well as a bed. Other **accessories** which go down well with children are head-torches, which have a good novelty value and make night-time exploration more fun. Torches with handles that glow in the dark are also useful, as kids invariably forget to put them back in their designated place. Hot-water bottles are great for warming up damp sleeping bags and taking the edge off cold evenings.

Eating alfresco

Plenty of fresh air and running around means that kids are usually famished on camping trips. **Hot meals** are always welcome and often end up being the highlight of the children's day, particularly if they get to help with the cooking. For ideas on camping food, get hold of one the books listed on p.70, which detail meals that kids can cook on the end of a stick or in foil, as well as more sophisticated things for you to attempt.

Even if you cook some meals on open fires, it's best to bring a **portable stove**, too; you can't guarantee that you'll always get your fire burning merrily, and a stove is really useful when you want to get food ready quickly or just boil a kettle. (On that note, if your children are bottle-fed, bring a thermos flask and fill it each time you boil water; you can

CAMPING REFLECTIONS

"Camping has always been a feature of holidays with my three children – they've camped as little babies, toddlers and now teenagers. As a single parent on a limited budget, I tend to go camping with other friends and their children as our main holiday, but also for the odd weekend when we just want to get away from the city. We have several favourite sites which offer relative freedom – in a forest, by rivers or the sea – and the capacity to make fires at night. Camping is a great way to holiday with friends and meet new people without having to live with them.

We keep things simple. We have a couple of small tents which the children can put up quickly on their own. Good sleeping bags for the cold are important; we sleep on 5mm mats; and if it is really cold, we put a blanket or duvet underneath the sleeping bags as well. Clothes are also best kept simple. We find that we quickly degenerate into wearing the same things day after day (kids will also sleep in the same clothes). Nobody minds, it's very liberating!

All our trips have been enjoyable and memorable in their own way, even last summer in Wales when it poured with rain most of the time. These occasions can feel challenging – a good sense of humour and relaxed attitude are important, but you learn to appreciate the beauty of lying in your tent listening to the rain falling, the wind in the trees, or cuddling up with your youngest because she's a little afraid of the new sounds of nature, and enjoys the cosiness of being in that tent with you. Then there's days spent doing the crazy things you would only consider on a rainy holiday in Wales, like bowling, swimming, watching a movie at the local cinema, and playing running games to keep warm on a freezing beach.

There's always a unique sense of closeness with my children and friends as we all open up, relax and enjoy a different way of living for a few days. The kids grow up in front of you and enjoy a new independence and freedom. It's a vital way for us all to holiday together while still finding a lot of personal space – I sneak off and read or sunbathe when everyone is happy.

Group camping helps me share the work. We all chip in with preparing meals, keeping camp and entertaining the group. We set up activities; usually the children will organize their own games or just hang out chatting or making things. The evenings (which can otherwise be tough if you're on your own with young children) are wonderful spent with friends around a camp fire. We've had many magical times lying in sleeping bags in large plastic (bivvy) bags while someone plays the guitar and we sing our hearts out to old Beatles and Led Zeppelin numbers, fuelled by wine and cocoa; or just lying back watching the stars and shadows, the odd animal passing, children and adults falling asleep. The next morning, the first light of day warms the sleeping bags and reveals a series of sleeping bundles around the fire. With luck, the embers are still warm and someone gets the fire going again. It's chilly and the beauty of the morning is so uplifting, everyone smiles. The smell of campfire in your children's hair is so good, so is the smell of some food cooking on the fire and a pot of coffee. Little by little, the bundles start to stir and another day kicks into action.

Generally, everything takes longer when you camp, but I have more time to notice and enjoy simple things like the sky, the changes of the day, the long shadows of the evening, eating outdoors, basking in the sun, games with my children, preparing a meal with friends. Go with the flow, don't organize or expect too much and enjoy all those beautiful moments we usually don't notice."

Katherine Lowe

also use a pressure cooker for sterilization.) A two-ring stove is ample for feeding four, though there are plenty of meals you can cook on a single ring.

Things to do in camp

As camping often means the odd day stuck in the tent when it rains, you'll want to bring some toys (see p.69 for ideas); playing cards, board games and equipment for listening to taped stories or music are especially good. If it's not pouring down, you might want to think about ways to help your children engage with the Great Outdoors. The camping books listed on p.70 have lots of ideas, but it's easy to improvise: you could take simple things like a jam-jar to catch (and release) insects, small fish and tadpoles (and a magnifying glass to look at them with), a bit of toilet paper and a book to press leaves and flowers, and ropes for climbing trees or making swings. And at the more sophisticated end of the scale, telescopes and binoculars are great for exploring things big and small.

Arriving and setting up camp

If you've driven to your campsite, try and park fairly close to where you'll be pitching your tents, as your car will serve as storage space for luggage and food. Give your **pitch** a good once-over to check for insect nests or anything that could puncture the floor of the tent. Also consider proximity to toilets; if you'll have to tramp through dew-soaked long grass to get to them in the wee hours, you might want to camp elsewhere on the site.

If you and your children have separate tents, pitch them with the openings facing each other; if they sleep with their heads at the entrance end, they'll be able to see and talk to you.

Keeping a tight camp

Establishing a few **rules** at the beginning of your holiday makes camping a lot easier. Start off with banning shoes and eating in tents – even the smallest biscuit crumb will mean ants at bedtime, and shoes not only dirty the interior but can damage the floor. Do what you can to keep belongings organized inside the tent, designating areas for toys, shoes and clothes, and make it a rule not to leave things lying around outside other than in the porch area. Besides losing things, a sudden downpour could mean wet sleeping bags, jackets and shoes, which could ruin the trip. You'll also need to establish boundaries in terms of how far your children can roam on their own, and reinforce all the usual "do's and don'ts" about playing with fire. It's also sensible to tell the children what to do with rubbish and leftover food: set up a rubbish bin/bag somewhere, preferably off the ground but within the reach of the children.

Don't forget to share out the **chores**. Camping tends to make children more willing than usual to help out, so get them involved in collecting firewood, helping with cooking, cleaning up or making fires. And well before nightfall, be sure to set up lights and establish a place where the torches are kept.

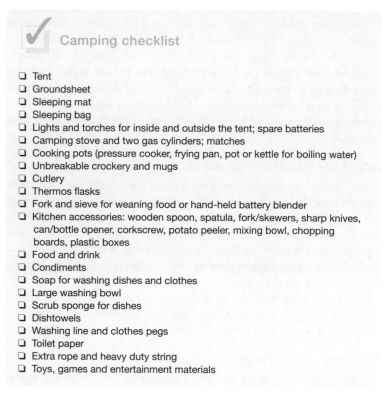
✓ Camping checklist

- ❑ Tent
- ❑ Groundsheet
- ❑ Sleeping mat
- ❑ Sleeping bag
- ❑ Lights and torches for inside and outside the tent; spare batteries
- ❑ Camping stove and two gas cylinders; matches
- ❑ Cooking pots (pressure cooker, frying pan, pot or kettle for boiling water)
- ❑ Unbreakable crockery and mugs
- ❑ Cutlery
- ❑ Thermos flasks
- ❑ Fork and sieve for weaning food or hand-held battery blender
- ❑ Kitchen accessories: wooden spoon, spatula, fork/skewers, sharp knives, can/bottle opener, corkscrew, potato peeler, mixing bowl, chopping boards, plastic boxes
- ❑ Food and drink
- ❑ Condiments
- ❑ Soap for washing dishes and clothes
- ❑ Large washing bowl
- ❑ Scrub sponge for dishes
- ❑ Dishtowels
- ❑ Washing line and clothes pegs
- ❑ Toilet paper
- ❑ Extra rope and heavy duty string
- ❑ Toys, games and entertainment materials

WALKING AND CYCLING

If you're keen on **walking** or **cycling**, you won't want to stop when you have children – and the sooner you start them off, the more likely they are to want to do more as they get older. Though there are the obvious drawbacks in that babies have to be carried and young children can only walk or cycle for short distances, a bike ride or a gentle hike allows you to enjoy the scenery at close quarters and at a pace which perfectly suits children; it's also easier to interact with people you meet

WALKING IN THE HIMALAYAS

"Ben Heason had something to prove to the world. Anything his brother could do so could he. Better, in fact. It was ten days into the trek, and we had stopped for lunch between boulders on the bank of the swollen river, eating fingers full of rice and chillies cooked on a small smudge fire, washed down with tin mugs of black, sweet tea. Progress that day had been slow, as there was always something to startle or amaze, from Annapurna II leaning over us far above to ice-falls grumbling. Frequent avalanches were causing icy blasts of wind to shriek up the valley. Winter was fast approaching and we would be some of the last people to cross the Thorung-La pass (at 17,700, some 3000 feet higher than Mont Blanc) that year. There were perhaps two and a half hours of daylight left as we buried the fire, shouldered our rucksacks and trudged slowly uphill towards the col. Ben started off first, impatient and eager to keep ahead. It was his first Himalayan season, and he was mildly resentful that we had not taken him with us until he was a venerable four and a half years of age; whereas his brother, Mathew, had celebrated his fourth birthday at the Mustang border some years earlier.

The clear skies of morning had gone. Cold grey clouds rolled in from the southern plains and sank ever lower towards us. We chatted easily together, remarking on how well the lads were coping and, in particular, how well Ben was moving. He had already reached the col and disappeared from view. Perhaps ten minutes later, we breasted the col ourselves, and saw our well-defined track descending steeply to a flat-bottomed valley, another river, and far away beneath the awesome flanks of Annapurna III, our intended campsite for that night. But there was no sign of Ben. We looked at each other, both assuming that there was a simple explanation. There was the mule-path, clearly visible. There were no folds in the ground where he could be concealed, just stark, grey, ice-rimed scree.

We raced back to the top of our ascent path, sure that we must have passed him earlier. No sign. It doesn't take long for a feeling of helpless panic to set in. It was too early for recrimination, too soon to hypothesize, but we had absolutely no contingency plan, and just stared wildly about, eyes straining to

along the way. You'll need to be prepared for the times when your children can't or won't walk any longer; if walking, this means using a sling or backpack (see p.58 for more on these), while for cycling you'll need a child seat that fixes to your bike – most rental companies won't have these, so you'll need to bring one from home.

Planning a walk or ride

Young children won't want to focus on getting from A to B, but on following their interests, so if you want to build their enthusiasm for cycling or walking, don't hurry them on when they're happily exploring. Expect plenty of stops and detours (the more children you have, the more there will be), and don't try to cover huge distances – in fact, it's a good idea *pick out the slightest sign of our child.*

And then, the wind must have dropped briefly, for we heard the faintest of sounds – a dislodged stone. We saw him, but only just. He was far above, a minuscule figure climbing steadily upwards. Scudding sheets of cloud tore against the brutal flanks around him. Never have I moved faster, at altitude, than then. I had to move at least three hundred feet before he heard me shouting his name.

It was difficult to refrain from berating him, to blame him; but I managed, I think calmly, to explain that he had gone a little off track, and we descended together to the col. It was easy to see the mistake he had made. The track he took twisted suddenly. Retrospectively, we saw how Ben, eyes on the ground immediately ahead, had missed the left turn and continued to climb onwards and upwards.

And so, a small episode in life, but one that lives on in our memories. Of course, we learned from it. It had seemed so admirable that he was eager to lead the way. And it was a simple matter to introduce a new rule that he never went further ahead than within speaking distance."

Alan Heason

"I celebrated my fourth birthday trekking in Nepal, and remember bits of that trip to this day. I was there again three years later with my younger brother who managed to get himself "lost" in the foothills of Annapurna. It didn't seem that serious to us at the time, but I guess my folks were pretty worried. From what I recall, inspired by plenty of chapattis, dhal bhat, boiled new potatoes, salt and butter, most of the three-week trek was spent discussing catering plans for an impending birthday party. Tape recorded diaries (which our parents kept) are similarly biased towards the food we ate: 'On the airplane we ate sausages and mash with a can of tomato juice', and also the animals we saw and monkeys we quarrelled with! My recommendation for anybody travelling with youngsters would be to make sure there is a ready supply of interesting food and plenty of wildlife. We'd always return home with notebooks full of sketches and heads full of ideas for the next trip."

Matt Heason

to plan your route around the capacity of your youngest child and your ability to carry them. Try to choose a route where the scenery will change frequently – children get bored of vast landscapes where distant landmarks never seem to get much closer. And if you're going to be carrying your kids, avoid trails that could hamper balance, and bear in mind that slopes which you find steep will be twice as hard for small children to manage – though they'll probably need restraining as they race you down the other side. Good choices for walks or rides include following a river or canal tow-path; there are no hills to negotiate, and there's the possible bonus of water to play in and birds to feed. It's also a good idea to combine walks or rides with a side activity such as swimming, taking a short train ride or crossing fields with animals to feed.

On the road

Your kids are likely to **overheat** and feel **cold** in quick succession, so you'll need to add or remove clothing as appropriate – if you don't want to be lumbered with a heap of small jackets, make sure there's room in a backpack to carry discarded items. If you're cycling and have more than one adult in the group, one should lead while the other brings up the rear, making sure the children stay safe. But whether you're walking or on bikes,

Walking and cycling checklist

Check
- ❑ Your capacity
- ❑ The route: scenery, inclines, traffic, distances
- ❑ Availability of places to eat and rest

Take
- ❑ Child carriers and bike seats
- ❑ Water and snacks
- ❑ Layered and all-weather clothing
- ❑ Extra socks
- ❑ Walking shoes
- ❑ Sunglasses, sunhats, sunblock
- ❑ Mobile phone

make a rule that everyone has to stay within earshot.

Children might get more exposure to sunshine than adults if carried in backpacks or on a child seat at the front of a bike; and if they're not walking or cycling themselves, they'll get colder than everyone else as they won't be warmed up with exercise – protect them accordingly and have layers to pull on and take off. Finally, if the children start flagging, do make a stop; you could try rekindling interest by getting them to lead for a change or getting out the maps to let them see how much progress you've made.

CHALLENGES

It's inevitable that things will **go wrong** while you're away: kids get sick, your partner and you argue or the interactions with new people become draining. But there are always ways of coping with challenges, and much of the advice in this section centres around preventing problems before they arise. Bear in mind, though, that while we touch on some health issues, we by no means cover them all or aim to replace specialized medical advice. If you're concerned, it's well worth visiting a travel clinic or investing in a book on travel health; we've suggested some further resources on p.40.

As the challenges of travel with children are so varied, we've included a summary list of subjects below to help you navigate the information.

ALLERGIES

You're probably already aware of your family's predispositions to **allergies**, but previously undiscovered ones can manifest for the first time when travelling in response to things like higher levels of pollution, more contact with animals, chlorine in pools and the like. It's worth travelling with a non-prescription **antihistamine** such as Piriton, which you can quickly administer should symptoms such as sneezing, streaming noses or itchy eyes or throat start up. For skin allergics, try applying over-the-counter hydrocortisone cream on the spot itself; natural alternatives include drinking honey and apple cider mixed to taste with warm water, a spoonful of honey or, particularly for hayfever, nettle tea. If your child is wheezing, finds breathing difficult, or has widespread or painful rashes, see a doctor.

ALTITUDE

Bad reactions to high altitudes can start at 2400m, and if you're pregnant you'll be advised not to stray higher. Oddly enough, children and adults are at equal risk; and if you've had altitude sickness before, you are likely to get it again. If you're considering going higher than 2400m, get medical advice.

BITES

Being **bitten** by insects and animals is part of growing up, and insect bites in particular can be a real nuisance when travelling – they make children itchy and uncomfortable, scratching can lead to infection and allergies, and whining mozzies or a slew of bites can lead to sleepless nights and grumpy kids. It's always best to do what you can to avoid getting bitten, and it's even more crucial if there's malaria and rabies in your destination.

Insect bites

Start off by finding out what biting insects you'll come across in your destination, and do what you can to avoid the worst seasons. If there will be a lot of bugs, always go for accommodation that has insect screens on windows; air-conditioning also works wonders to discourage mosquitoes. But bear in mind that it's impossible to avoid getting bitten altogether – don't get anxious every time you discover a bite, but do follow the preventative steps below.

Prevention

Standard bite avoidance measures include covering limbs with long-sleeved shirts and trousers in the evenings and keeping ankles covered. Apply 0.5 percent permethrin cloth sprays directly on to clothing (socks in particular), and **insect repellent** on all exposed areas of skin. DEET is the most effective and safe repellent to use. For the spray to work best, it needs to have 30–35 percent DEET in it; skin reactions are uncommon but even if they occur, having malaria is always a lot worse. Natural oils such as citronella don't work nearly as well, if at all; if malaria is a concern, don't gamble, use DEET. Note that while DEET-impregnated wristbands are widely marketed, they don't seem to work (possibly because the chemicals aren't freshly applied) and are a waste of your money. Rub the repellent between your own hands before applying it to your children, as this results in a more even spread, and follow the application instructions on the bottle in terms of avoiding delicate and broken skin. If you find that DEET badly irritates your children's skin, apply it to clothing and/or bedclothes instead.

In the evenings, spray your rooms with a **knock-down insecticide** and use **insecticide–impregnated bed nets** (see p.63); always check that nets don't have holes in them or mosquitoes inside the net before tucking your children in. Wherever possible, encourage your children

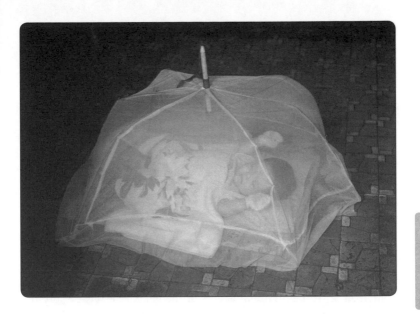

to read and play under nets; they usually won't take much persuading as there's something particularly cosy about the space within. And once your children fall asleep, check from time to time that their limbs don't end up right against the netting where the mosquitoes will still be able to get a good bite.

If **ticks** are a problem, dress your children in tops with long sleeves, sturdy shoes, and tuck trousers into socks if moving through undergrowth. Brushing past bushes, sitting on bare ground, and outdoor toilet stops are prime times to pick up ticks. Rather than constantly worrying about ticks, get into the habit of looking over the children each time you bathe them; ticks and mites retreat to armpits, genitals and folds of skin, so examine them really well.

The most common and ubiquitous of insect nuisances are **ants**; if you can't avoid them, you can try decoys of sticky sweet drinks spilt onto a patch of floor or ground, which will temporarily draw them away. If ants get onto the furniture, give the legs (especially on beds) a good spray with insecticide, then stand them in a beaker of water; the "moat" will keep new invasions out. Also be scrupulous about not leaving food and drink around – you might even forbid eating inside your rooms or on beds. And to avoid other creepy crawlies, get in the habit of checking shoes and beds before you put them on or get between the sheets.

Treatment

Most insect bites eventually disappear without needing any attention, but an antihistamine cream provides some relief for swelling, itching and pain; calamine and calendula lotions and creams are also helpful. The homeopathic alternative is ledum for mosquito bites, and apis for bee stings. No matter what you tell them, most children will **scratch bites**, which of course makes them itch even more and can lead to broken skin and infections. Cut their nails very short, and try using cotton mitts for babies. If bites get **infected**, keep them clean and use antiseptic sprays or powders, but leave them open rather than covering them up with plasters, as they'll heal faster. If the infection persists (and certainly if you notice pus and red tracks radiating from the bite), see a doctor.

Should you discover **ticks**, don't try to pull or flick them off; the head or mouth-parts often get left behind, which can lead to nasty infections. The least invasive removal method is to smother them with a blob of teething gel, which seems to act through suffocation combined with the numbing agents in the gel. Otherwise, apply the lit end of an incense stick to the tick's abdomen, but only if it's large enough and you can keep your child very still. The tick will release its jaws from the skin, although you might also need tweezers to prize it off completely.

Mites or **lice**, on the other hand, require treatment. You can find effective products at any pharmacy – but do treat for the whole family. Infestations spread rapidly, and if you've spotted mites or lice on one of you, it's highly likely that others have them as well, even if you can't spot them straight away.

Animal bites

If **rabies** is endemic in your destination, don't stray far from health services, even if you've all been vaccinated. Watch your children when animals are around, regardless of whether the animals look healthy or not, and make sure they don't provoke them in any way. Toddlers need more supervision than older children, as they're prone to misjudge animals' reactions or put themselves in harm's way by reaching into holes in the ground and the like. Bear in mind also that children might not tell you if they get scratched or licked, so press home the fact that they need to speak up if this happens.

If you visit tourist attractions that have resident animals such as monkeys or squirrels, do be careful, as they often survive by taking food from tourists and can be aggressive – just carrying food or drink can prompt them to attack. That said, some tourists will always **feed** animals and it can be fun; if you want to join in, start by watching others for a while to judge safety as best you can, but never allow your children to feed animals from their hands – instead, they should throw it from a safe distance. If an animal comes too close, throw the food further away to get them to go after it. Bear in mind that animals can turn on people who get too close to their young – and of course, baby animals inevitably hold the strongest attraction for children, so be especially careful.

Wherever **leeches** and **snakes** abound, wear sturdy boots and thick trousers tucked into socks, and stick to well-trodden paths rather than tramping through the undergrowth.

Treatment

If your child gets bitten, scratched or licked by an animal that could carry **rabies**, wash the area thoroughly with soap and water, apply ethanol or iodine, and get post-exposure rabies vaccinations without delay. Think twice about telling your child that you're going to get injections, as they're likely to be upset enough as it is.

Leech bites are simple to deal with. Once a leech has taken hold, don't flick or pull it off, as this will usually result in its head getting left behind under the skin. Instead, cover the leeches with salt (this sucks them dry) or burn them off with a cigarette; alternatively, if the children aren't overly bothered by the leech, let it drink its fill – it will drop off eventually. It's quite a sight watching leeches ooze and shrivel up in front of your eyes – if your children are fascinated rather than frightened, let them watch. Once the leeches are off, clean the bite with plenty of running water, and use antiseptics until the skin break heals.

Snakes are a different matter; if someone is unlucky enough to get bitten by one, make them lie still and keep the bitten limb below the level of their heart until you get medical help. Even though very few snakes carry serious venom, it's always worth being on the safe side. If you can, kill and hang onto the specimen, or try to remember its markings to help with identification.

CONSTIPATION

Constipation is a real inconvenience when travelling, and often takes hold simply because toilets aren't available when your child needs to go; it can also be caused by dehydration or changes in diet. To prevent constipation and recognize the onset of it, pay particular attention to how often your children move their bowels while you're away, all the more so if you're changing feeding regimens or starting new medications. Otherwise, be sure to give children all the time they need to use the toilet; watch that they drink enough when it's hot; and do what you can to maintain a balanced diet, which isn't always easy when travelling. While children vary in their habits, there's cause for concern if your child has less than three bowel movements per week. If your baby hasn't passed a stool in three days and/or has hard stools, shows signs of colic, eats less than usual, and perhaps retches when they do, suspect constipation. In older children, symptoms can include hard stools or difficulty passing them, as well as abdominal pain and cramps, nausea and vomiting. Bleeding from the rectum (caused by straining to open bowels) is another clear sign.

Treatment

There are other methods to treat constipation besides laxatives. Give **babies** water to drink, use a light oil to massage their tummies, and bring their knees up to their chests a few times. You can also gently rub a button of Vaseline over their anus; this often brings on instant results, so get ready with a nappy/diaper. Give **older children** water and a few teaspoons of a light vegetable oil to drink, as well as trying the Vaseline and abdominal massage. Whichever method you use, be patient, and provide for plenty of time on the toilet.

CUTS AND SCRAPES

Children are no strangers to **cuts and scrapes**, but if you're travelling in hot or humid conditions, you need to treat them particularly carefully, as even minor grazes can become **infected** fast. Clean wounds scrupulously, and apply antiseptic spray or powder rather than cream, as these stay put for longer and will help to dry cuts out. It's best not to swim until cuts are properly dry and scabbed over, but if you do, make sure the water is well chlorinated and reapply antiseptics whenever your children get out. It's also important to be fastidious about regular bathing, and to change clothing around the affected area more frequently than usual.

DEHYDRATION

Children are particularly prone to dehydration, mostly because they don't drink unless they feel thirsty, which isn't the best gauge of how much fluid they need. If your **baby** is exclusively breastfed, you should drink more whenever it's hot so that you produce slightly diluted milk; but if temperatures are particularly high and you don't have enough milk or sense that your baby isn't sucking enough, give them some

TUMBLES IN ITALY

"After having just seen Michelangelo's David (whom the girls kept referring to as "the big naked guy"), we gave the children a ride on a carousel in a piazza. Before we knew it, my son Mitchell (aged three) fell on a jagged barrier gate and cut his chin. We found the first pharmacist we could, and asked him if the cut needed stitches. He said that he thought it did, and wrote down the name of a hospital for us to go to.

We had a few moments when we weren't sure what to do next – we were a big group, four kids, ourselves and the grandparents – the detour could ruin the day for everyone. But I took the decision that it was best to go, rather than worrying about it all day. After a mini conference, we agreed that my husband would stay with everyone else, and I would take Mitchell to the hospital. We fixed on a place to meet afterwards – fortunately, we had two mobile phones between us.

I found a taxi without any problems and once Mitchell and myself were in, the driver commented that the hospital suggested by the pharmacist was rather far away and suggested a closer one. I went with his suggestion. Sure enough, it didn't take us long to get there.

When we arrived, we were met by a kind elderly volunteer. He spoke English which was such a relief! After giving us detailed instructions of where we should go and what we should do, he obviously decided it was going to be easier to take us himself – my face must have registered a blank. I was really thankful – I would never have found the little clinic myself. He then went to the front of the line in the crowded waiting room and spoke in Italian to the person at the desk. All I understood was "Americano" and "insurance". To the latter cue, I dug through my wallet, pulled out, and handed over my son's insurance card. To my surprise and somewhat embarrassment, we were ushered to the front of the line and, of course, I didn't object. The staff were incredibly kind, they washed the cut and decided it didn't need stitches after all. They put a little purple "glue" in it and taped it together. The doctor then even gave my son a small candy bar – they were all really lovely to us and it wasn't long before we were walking outside once again. I looked for the taxi driver and asked him to take us to meet the rest of the family. Again, this man was unbelievably kind. After having waited for us he told us that we were only 200 meters from the place, and showed us how to get there ourselves. Once we were all reunited, we realised that the whole episode – from being split up to getting back together again – took just an hour! Looking back, that was incredible. In the States, my son would not have been seen within an hour of waiting. And here we were, walking out of the hospital without paying a dime. They marked our address as "touristo"; they didn't even take down our personal information. It's been a year since then, and we haven't been sent a bill yet – I presume it's not going to come."

Missy Reardon

water to drink, too. Keep **older children** out of strong sun and give them drinks at frequent intervals. Also check all your children's urine from time to time; if it's darker than usual, cloudy or strong-smelling, insist that they drink more, giving in to their favourite sugary drink if necessary.

The main **sign of dehydration** is dark or strong-smelling urine or no urine at all; for babies, look for a depressed fontanel (the soft spot on the top of their head). Other things to watch out for are dizziness and headaches, dry mouths and sticky saliva, and possibly cramps in the arms and legs. Symptoms of moderate to serious dehydration include fainting, severe muscle contractions in the arms or stomach, convulsions, sunken eyes, rapid and deep breathing, and listlessness – and at the very worst, unconsciousness.

Treatment

For **mild dehydration**, simply increase the amount of water your baby or child drinks. You can also try giving oral rehydration salts, which are available in most pharmacies; you can also make your own by mixing six level teaspoons of sugar and one level teaspoon of salt into one litre of drinking water. If your children won't drink this solution, try adding extra sugar and lemon juice; you could also give them water, and/or any other drink they prefer, but make a point of getting sugar and salt into them in other ways, as their supplies are likely to be depleted. Rest assured that as long as your children are drinking, all should right itself soon enough. For **serious dehydration**, you must seek medical help immediately; children can deteriorate fast, so treat it as an emergency and go to a hospital rather than a clinic.

ORAL REHYDRATION

The table below details the approximate amount of oral rehydration solution to give your children in the first four hours of dehydration. In the initial stages of rehydration, children of all ages can drink as much as 20ml per kilogram of body weight per hour, so don't worry if anyone wants to drink more than the volumes below.

Age	Under 4 months	4–11 months	12–23 months	2–4 years	5–14 years
Ml	200–400	400–600	600–800	800–1200	1200–2200

DIARRHOEA

Diarrhoea can be an unfortunate side-effect of travel, and while rarely serious, it's no fun being chained to the toilet for hours on end. The runs can be triggered by a range of bugs and toxins, as well as a change in diet or water, jetlag, tiredness or just plain excitement, and can indicate an infection as well as the system purging toxins in bad food or water. Children are at greater risk of getting diarrhoea, as they're not very careful about what they put into their mouths and their immune systems aren't yet fully formed. Unfortunately, they also tend to feel pretty poorly if diarrhoea strikes, as they dehydrate more quickly than adults.

The first precaution is to watch what's going in or near your children's mouths, and do your best to keep food and fingers clean. It's worth bearing in mind that medicines designed to temporarily stop diarrhoea actually inhibit nature's way of getting rid of toxins; and depending on the bug that's responsible, they can do more harm than good. Either way, you can't give them to children under two, or take them yourself if pregnant.

Treatment

Full-scale diarrhoea is defined as three or more loose, watery, stools a day – some count five or more, but it's best to be conservative with children. The biggest danger is **loss of fluid**; going without food for a few days isn't a problem, but you must get your child to drink – the table on p.158 gives an indication of the volumes to aim for. To avoid spreading the bug around the entire family, be extra scrupulous with **hygiene**; make sure the bathroom stays clean, and that everyone washes their hands with soap after using the toilet. If the diarrhoea continues, start with oral rehydration solution on the second day, and help your child eat as normally as possible; if you're breastfeeding, keep at it and drink more than usual yourself. If your child has difficulty with drinking and is nauseous, see a **doctor** as soon as you can – apart from providing a definitive diagnosis, they may prescribe anti-emetics to help keep fluids down. In theory, so long as you can keep replacing lost fluids and other minerals with rehydration solution and your child doesn't feel too ill, you can wait for the diarrhoea to resolve itself – most bouts settle on their own within five days without treatment. The general rule of thumb is to see a doctor if the diarrhoea lasts for more than three days and/or there are very frequent watery bowel movements, blood in the stools, repeated vomiting or fever. However, it's best to see a doctor as quickly as possible if your children get diarrhoea while travelling. If it's been caused by an **infection**, then the longer it's around, the more likely it is that other members of the family will catch it – besides, you'll want to help your child get back into shape as quickly as possible. As soon as you suspect your child has full-blown diarrhoea, make a tentative appointment to see a doctor the following day; if symptoms persist the next day, see the doctor, taking along a fresh stool sample

The recommended volumes of oral rehydration solution for children with diarrhoea are as follows:

Under twos: quarter or half a cup (50–100ml) after each loose stool
Two to ten: half a cup to cup (100–200ml) after each loose stool
Older children and adults: according to thirst

in something clean such as a jam jar. Usually, your child will be seen and sent home without treatment while their stools are tested; full tests can take three to five days, another reason why it's important to see a doctor early – the sooner the cause is known, the sooner treatment can start. If you need to move on before test results come back (assuming your child is well enough to do so), you can always call the doctor from your next location to find out what the problem is and what the medication should be.

EAR AND EYE INFECTIONS

Eye and ear infections are common in children whether you're at home or on the road, and though they're simple to treat they can make kids miserable, so it's sensible to take steps to avoid them. **Eye infections** are contracted via dirty fingers or unclean water, so keeping hands clean and away from eyes, as well as washing and swimming in clean water, are the basic steps to avoiding them. If one member of the family gets an eye infection, it's very likely that others will too, as they tend to be highly infectious – so keep everyone's hands scrubbed and away from eyes as best you can. **Ear infections** are frequently brought on by swimming in public pools that haven't been properly chlorinated. Make sure you can smell the chlorine before letting the children swim, and always dry their ears when they get out.

Treatment

Because ear and eye problems are so common, it's sensible to travel with combined **ear and eye antibiotic drops** (the same ones work on both ears and eyes). **Eye infections** are easy to spot. If the eyes are just itchy, the cause may be an allergy, but if they're red and gummed up, it's likely to be an infection. Either way, children will want to rub their eyes, so show them how to do this without fingers touching the eye using a sterile cotton ball or a folded tissue. And when applying drops, always treat both eyes, not just the one that appears infected, and always finish by washing your own hands.

As far as ears are concerned, the first sign of an **outer ear infection** is usually a fever. Small children rarely verbalise that they have problems with their ears, so as soon as you suspect an ear problem, tug gently at their ear lobes. If the ear is infected, this should result in some yelps. Don't prod anything into their ears, but look inside as best you can – if it's oozing, it's infected. (You can also look on your child's pillow for signs of pus.) Keep applying the drops until the course is finished; if you don't the infection might return with a vengeance. It can be hard while you're on holiday, but try not to let your child go swimming until the symptoms have subsided and the treatment over. If the infection is in the **middle ear** (usually following a chest cold), there's little you can do other than offer something for the pain. It isn't always easy to tell which kind of ear infection a child has, so see a doctor if unsure.

GETTING SEPARATED

If one of your children goes astray, it's obviously very worrying, and all the more so in new places, but the chances are that you will be reunited soon enough, and find your child happy, if a little disoriented, in the midst of a host of people spoiling him or her. We've given some tips to make sure you stay together on p.33, but if you do get **separated** from your child, stay calm and cast your mind back to where you last saw them. If you haven't already agreed on what to do in such an event, stay where you are. Look for a chair or something to stand on to make yourself easier to spot as well as to get a better view. If you have more than one adult in your group (or a responsible elder child), split up, with

THE LIME GREEN TOWEL

"We were on Polzeath beach in Cornwall. We regularly went there, but this time it was in the height of summer and heaving with people. We had spent all day playing in the pools at one end of the beach and were on our way back. While walking, I looked back and there were the three children, ambling along. But the next moment, our 6-year-old daughter was gone. She had been wearing a bright lime green poncho-type towel. It was the kind of colour you couldn't miss but I couldn't spot it anywhere. After moments of looking, we started calling and then shouting for her. People became aware something was wrong and started coming forward to ask questions. One woman alerted the coast guard. When I heard the announcement over the loud speaker describing a lost 4-year-old girl with black hair, I crumbled – my description of a 6-year-old girl with light brown hair had been distorted like Chinese whispers. I tried to keep it together whispering over and over again to myself 'It will be fine, it will be fine' – but somewhere I was imagining the worst – that I would never see her again. I stayed with the other two while Ben went off. After a while he came back with the little one in tow. She had found her own way to the car and was wondering what had kept the rest of us – and of course why Leila and I were in tears."

Lilly Stringer

TRAVELLERS' TALES

one part of the group staying put to keep watch and remain visible while the other retraces the steps to where you last saw your child, surveying the route for things that might have attracted/distracted them.

If you're close to the place you're staying, bear in mind they might have strolled back, so check there too, but if you're somewhere crowded such as a train or bus station, an airport or a shopping mall, find an official and give them a good but brief description of your child's features and clothing so that they can spread the word quickly via a tannoy announcement. And in the very unlikely event you don't get reunited quickly, leave your contact details with people close to where you got separated (such as shopkeepers), and then contact the police and your embassy and provide them with a photograph of your child. In the very, very rare cases of children being abducted, the person responsible is almost always the other parent – so be sure to let authorities know if this is a possibility.

JETLAG

Although **jetlag** (see p.82) usually subsides in a couple of days, it can be really disruptive at the time, but unfortunately there's not much you can do to prevent it. While there are sedatives on the market designed to help you sleep when your body clock is out of synch, it's difficult to recommend anything that makes sense for the family as a whole – the possibility of being knocked out yourselves when the children are wide awake is something you want to avoid. The best way of dealing with jetlag is just to let your body clocks readjust naturally. Spend time outdoors, especially if it's sunny, and aim to sleep and get up at the normal local times. However, anticipate everyone waking and sleeping at odd hours for the first few days; if you don't have 24-hour room service, make sure you have food in your rooms for an impromptu midnight feast.

MALARIA

If your child runs a fever within six days of entering a malarial region, rest assured – it's not due to **malaria**. However, see a doctor immediately if the fever is higher than 40°C, it probably isn't malaria, but it's best to be safe – and with malaria, it's crucial to seek help fast. Also remember that malaria can kick in anything up to ten weeks after leaving infected regions, although it's far more common to appear within sixteen days of being bitten.

For more on malaria, see p.37.

MASTITIS

If you're **breastfeeding** while away, it can be hard to find places to feed, and holding back can be a factor in getting **mastitis**, or engorged and infected breasts. The warning signs are discomfort in one or both breasts, as well as warm patches, lumps or taut areas. With any luck, you'll be carrying some just-in-case antibiotics to treat it (see p.35), but starting feeding the moment you feel some discomfort can help to stamp mastitis out before it takes hold.

A headache and light fever indicate **infection** and the need to begin antibiotics. If you get either symptom, it's really important to continue to express milk and massage the area until the fever, local heat and pain subside; your child needs the milk, and antibiotics prescribed for mastitis are completely safe for babies.

PRICKLY HEAT AND NAPPY/DIAPER RASH

When travelling in hot climates, children – particularly those in nappies/diapers – are prone to uncomfortable bouts of prickly heat and/or nappy/diaper rash, both of which can make them quite uncomfortable. Brought on by excessive sweating, **prickly heat** occurs when sweat gets trapped under the skin. It appears as a rash of tiny reddish pimples or blisters which itch or burn, usually in sweaty areas such as around the neck, shoulders, armpits, groin and waist. **Nappy rash** is caused by insufficient cleaning, keeping children in dirty nappies/diapers for too long, and humid conditions; it typically presents as flat, red, irritated patches of skin around the groin and buttocks.

Keeping cool and having frequent baths or showers or a quick sponge down whenever sweaty help prevent both forms of rashes. When you're in a hot climate, it's also important to be particularly careful to clean skin thoroughly after each nappy/diaper change, and use a generous layer of barrier cream. If possible, leave your children naked from time to time, particularly after showers and baths, and make sure that their bodies are completely dry before dressing them. Avoid using plastic pants over cloth nappies/diapers as these trap humidity, and dress your children in clothes made from natural fibres.

Treatment

As with any skin irritation, start by cutting your child's nails short to avoid skin breaks caused by scratching, as this can make matters worse. To get rid of **prickly heat**, increase the number of times you wash your child, use an antiseptic soap and apply medicated talcum powder on the affected skin after each wash. Calamine lotion also calms itching to some extent, but antihistamine creams are more effective. For **nappy/diaper rash**, step up the washing (so long as the skin is unbroken) using soap and plenty of water, pat the area dry (rubbing will make it worse), and apply calendula or regular barrier cream. If the skin starts to flake or break, use a dry antiseptic spray before putting on barrier cream; alternatively, use gentian violet – it's messy and stains, but it works for longer than most antiseptics. Whenever you can, take nappies/diapers off to allow your children's skin to breathe, and change them the moment they get wet or soiled. If the rash starts looking raw or inflamed (more like a burn), you'll need to see a doctor.

REJECTING OFFERS OF FOOD

Most parents find themselves having to turn down offers of **food** whilst travelling, whether from a kind stallholder on the street, a guesthouse owner or a well-meaning person who invites you into their home. You might want to say no for a variety of reasons: eating what's offered could interfere with mealtimes, there might be concerns about hygiene, or you might be worried that the children won't like the food. If hygiene or mucking up appetites is the issue, you might try claiming that you've all had bad stomachs, or that you can only eat food you prepare yourselves due to allergies or religious reasons; provide profuse apologies and compliments that the food looks lovely, and consider offering something you have to share with them instead. If you're worried that your children won't like the food, accept some yourself, try a bit and then judge whether or not to signal to them to ask for or accept some. While this can feel a bit awkward, it avoids the children making faces – or, worse still, spitting it all out.

SUNBURN AND HEATSTROKE

The depressingly familiar sight of an uncomfortable, tomato-red child on a beach is an obvious reminder of why it's important to limit your children's exposure to the sun, particularly if they're fair-skinned. Ultraviolet light is strongest near the equator, either side of noon, at high altitudes, and when reflected off water or snow. Keep children away from the sun when it's at its height and be particularly vigilant with babies; those under 6 months should be kept out of direct sunshine altogether. Older children should start off with small doses of sun, but even if they're dark-skinned and take the sun well, encourage them to play in the shade. Always use a combination of protective clothing and apply sunscreen of at least SPF 25, taking care not to forget necks,

ears and shoulders, which often get the brunt of the sun; feet are easily forgotten, too. You might also consider body suits or T-shirts for swimming, as well as hats with visors and flaps to cover the back of the neck. Children's **eyes** are especially vulnerable to sunshine, so if the glare is strong enough for you to put on some shades, your children will need goggles or sunglasses too.

Symptoms and treatment

If your children do get **sunburn**, apply the usual soothing aftersun creams or aloe vera gel, and keep them out of the sun until their skin is no longer painful, and stops looking tender and feeling warm.

Heatstroke is a lot more serious, however. It can accompany sunburn, but can also occur without, and is characterized by nausea, throbbing headaches and a high temperature, as well as disorientation and dehydration following prolonged exposure to heat. Delirium and collapse happens in extreme cases. Should you suspect heatstroke, treat it as an emergency and head straight to a hospital – this is a serious condition in children. On the way there, keep your child as cool as you can, and get them to drink if at all possible.

TOO MUCH COMPANY

Interacting with other people when you're away can be a strain, and all the more so when you're with children, as people may well be especially curious and want to spend time with you when you'd rather be on your own. In some cultures, the locals can come across as intrusive, putting questions to your children that they're not accustomed to, or that you'd rather they didn't answer, such as matters that relate to your religion, finances or marital status. Help your children out by telling them that whenever in doubt, they should be polite but say nothing at all, or that they don't know the answer. In particular, tip them off not to share your address, either back home or wherever you're staying – and to tell you should anyone ask. If the problem is too much **touching**, the simplest tactic is to take over yourself – people won't disturb a parent's caress to pick up or pet a child.

Classically, though, the phenomenon of too much attention has a way of creeping up on you in stages. It's typical to start off by finding someone's company refreshing, and then rather wishing they would go away. There are also moments when you clearly want to be alone, but others don't read the signs – you might spend hours finding a deserted beach only to be joined by a family that homes in on you, placing their mats right up against yours and looking forward to spending the afternoon together. Another common scenario is trying to have a quiet dinner when people at the next table pull up their chairs to play with your children and talk to you. It pays to keep in mind that in many parts of the world, privacy carries little meaning and in some cultures, only social outcasts are left on their own, particularly at mealtimes. Don't take offence, but do be prepared to be a little devious; try the following ploys: "Could you please excuse us, we

need to pray/breastfeed/have to help our children prepare for a test";
"This is the day that x (family ancestor) died. We have a tradition to
talk about him/her on this day – could you please excuse us?".

If you're dealing with **beggars** or people poor enough to be hungry
(for more on which, see p.77), bear in mind that handing over money or
treats may result in being surrounded by many others, and increasing
rather than diminishing the attention. Your children might also want
to know why you give money in some instances or choose not to at
all – so be prepared to offer some guidance and try to be consistent
if you don't want to face a barrage of questions later on. But if you

(for more on which, see p.77)

ORCHESTRAS AND BABIES

*"When travelling with an orchestra, taking your baby with you makes you
an instant social outcast. It's not just that musicians are obsessive about
quiet, but everyone looks forward to these trips to have some footloose
time away from home – the last thing they want is a colleague with a baby
to cramp their style.*

*One of the conventions for travelling orchestras is that seats are
always booked in alphabetical order – so the same poor young chap
got me and us every time, whether it was on planes or worse still, on
buses. Fortunately, he was and is really mild-mannered. He never overtly
complained and my babies were actually pretty well behaved – mostly at
least. He quickly got the hang of being our assistant.*

*The first time I travelled as a mother, my baby was 4 weeks old. I borrowed
my sister's au pair and off we went to Naarden in The Netherlands. That
worked as well as I might have hoped; I managed to rehearse and play
reasonably without incident, but I was absolutely exhausted. Apart from the
breastfeeding, the three of us slept in the same room; and for some reason
the au pair and I had to share a bed, and she talked in her sleep. So, between
the night feeds and the au pair's cryptic dreams, I didn't get much rest. The
days also had problems, the auditorium had to be kept below four degrees
to protect the artwork. It was freezing and being tired, I really felt the cold. By
the end of that trip, I was a wreck. The next few years were very stressful. In
the first place, the conductor did not approve of the arrangement at all and
made that perfectly clear to everybody. I felt more than usually under pressure
to pull it all together for rehearsals – not to mention performances. And of
course, I couldn't join in with the fun after concerts – I'd try sometimes, but the
inevitable interruptions made it rough going. I resigned myself to spending all
free time with my babies. In other words, I was working around the clock – all
hours.*

*It was probably three years later (after my second baby) when I had my first
trip alone. We were going to New York and I felt ecstatic at the prospect of
a bit of freedom. But after checking in at the hotel on arrival, a baby-laden
colleague approached me. She said that she had just booked herself into the
room next to mine: "I knew you wouldn't mind", she said. She couldn't have
been more wrong; needless to say, I immediately changed rooms. It didn't
take long to get back to my old and very enjoyable habits."*

L.C.

find yourselves being hassled by beggars and the children beginning to worry, remain polite but keep moving, and if necessary, dive into a shop and ask the shopkeeper for assistance – being rude, especially if you're an outsider, can result in ugly scenes which could frighten the children. Similarly, if sights of poverty disturb your kids, it goes without saying that you should go elsewhere as soon as possible. When it's all over, allow some time to reflect together over what happened, but rather than focusing on the upsetting circumstances of people they've seen, you might try emphasizing just how lucky your children are; certainly, comparisons can have a very positive effect on children, making them appreciate their good fortune.

TRAVELLING FOR WORK

Parents often find themselves having to take their children along on **work** trips for a variety of reasons, and although you might not have much choice in the matter, there are ways to make it smoother for everyone. In the first place, aim for accommodation and childcare that's as near to your work location as possible, so that you can breastfeed and/or check up on things during the day. Conversely, it's best to be out of earshot while you work; hearing your child will distract you, and they'll want to come and find you just because they know you're there.

When your working day is over, avoid rushing back to resume duties on the home front straight away – this is a recipe for exhaustion. Instead, try to **extend childcare**, even if it's just for half an hour, to allow you to rest. And if you could do with some sleep, either during or at the end of the day, consider arranging for the children to be taken for a walk, so that you can have some rest on your own.

VISITING PLACES OF WORSHIP

Perhaps because places of worship are frequently dark or have strange acoustics, children often want to make more noise than usual. Even if you aren't devout, you don't want to annoy others who are, so talk to your children about the need for quiet; it's unrealistic to expect them not to speak at all, so suggest whispering only. As well as adhering to local dress codes and taking shoes off wherever required, be prepared to keep the children away from some of the things inside. If candles are on display, young children can be sorely tempted to blow them out, so keep watch. Similarly, touching offerings of food, flowers or even interfering with the rise of incense smoke in temples can be considered

CHILDREN AND CHURCHES

"Living and travelling in Europe has taken us into countless cathedrals. We have prepped our two year old son to be respectful whenever entering "God's house", and he is usually very good. Once in Lyons, France, he shushed a woman who was continuing a conversation with someone while walking into the cathedral. I'll never forget her expression – it was priceless. Later on, in Lisbon, every time he saw pictures of their patron saint – the one with arrows all through him – Mitch would look up and say, "That man is dead!", and people nearby would always swing around to see what he was talking about. However, later on, and after a great deal more cathedrals that week, he had had enough. We knew he had reached this point when he started yelling at the top of his voice, "I don't want to go to God's house!" *whenever we approached a church. I imagine some thought he was possessed by the devil. And of course, that was it. For quite a while later, we had to split up to take turns to hang about outside with him".*

M. Reardon

as an interference to worship. If the challenge of containing themselves proves too much for your children, be ready to make a quick exit, and remember that places of worship are frequently surrounded with excellent places to play, such as grand stairs, squares or courtyards.

WATER HAZARDS

Safety is obviously paramount when you're near water with children, but bear in mind that the most common problem isn't drowning, but slips and trips that lead to injuries. The first precaution is to explore your surroundings whenever you're around water. Check access to the water, familiarize yourself with the depth of swimming pools and how steeply beaches shelve off from the shore, make sure you're aware of what's available in terms of life-saving devices or lifeguards, and think through what you might do in an emergency. If you're by a beach or river, ask after the currents and be wary of swimming in built-up areas, where there's a higher risk of pollution and sharp bits of garbage that you might tread on.

It goes without saying that you've always got to **keep watch** on what your children are up to around water. Make a rule that they can't swim without you, or that they have to tell you before they do – this is all the more important for smaller and less able swimmers, but is also advisable for older children. Furthermore, remember that young children often have no fear at all; first-time snorkellers might try to chase rays or catch conger eels just because they know no better, or jump into water when they've no idea of the depth or what lies below. Always talk your children through the risks, tell them not to touch or disturb anything – for their own sakes, as well as out of respect for preserving wildlife.

If you're swimming in a **public pool**, you'll probably have to temper your children's excitement, particularly if it's likely to interfere with safety or annoy others; get them to respect the usual rules of not running if there's a chance they might slip, and not jumping into the deep end (or on top of people). If you'll be spending a lot of time in and around pools, it's a good idea to buy swimwear with inbuilt floats (see p.50); apart from helping with staying afloat, these give you more time to jump in and fish your child out should they jump into water that's outside their depth. For more on swimming, see p.137.

Rescuing someone from water

People having difficulties in water classically get in a panic and are desperate to grab and climb on top of anything they can; having someone – even a child – trying to get on top of you when you're trying to rescue them is a real danger when you're out of your depth. So, even if your own child is in trouble, look for floats and tow ropes,

TRAVEL AS A COUPLE

"Our first trip as parents was when our son was just 4 weeks old, when we went to introduce him to my husband's parents. My husband and I hadn't been together long as a couple. Visiting the in-laws came with more than the usual stresses including the fact that I was seriously tired. I had met them before, but this time, I was mother, and mother of the only boy who would carry the family's name – they made a huge deal out of it. I got no practical help but was inundated with 'advice' – all of which resulted in my feeling either irate or incompetent. After two weeks, I was desperate for breathing space, and so was my husband. Fortunately, we had enough sense to head off to the coast. Once we arrived, I felt an immediate sense of relief. No more forced smiles, trying to be the perfect mum, holding back my tongue and tears.

The sea air and warmth was lovely. But while walking along the beach, I kept feeling pangs of longing for the old days. The very places I was drawn to felt inappropriate – wrong for babies and/or out of synch with my new status as a married woman – a mother no less. It felt hard passing by beach bars with loud music and cocktails. I even had to stay away from strong sunshine which I yearned for – all for the sake of our newborn baby. I kept my thoughts to myself but felt pretty low.

On the second or third day, a splitting headache and fever began to creep up on me. My husband went off to get some aspirin while I drifted off to sleep in the hotel room – baby by my side. He left at around 4 in the afternoon, but when I woke hours later, he hadn't returned. By 9 o'clock I was really worried; and not long after, I was seriously frantic. I imagined all sorts of things that might have happened to him. I still had the fever and the headache was worse than ever. But I pulled myself together, got dressed and went down to the or grab a piece of clothing such as a cotton blouse (not a towel, as it'll be too heavy when wet), and call for help while swimming out. Get your child to grab onto the other end of the material and tow them to safety; so long as they are conscious, they will hold on and keep their heads out of the water. Once you have them out, lie them down on their side with their chin tilted upwards and neck extended – they're likely to have swallowed a lot of water and may well vomit, and this position helps prevent choking. But if your child is unconscious, pull them out in the quickest way you can, and start mouth-to-mouth resuscitation and heart massage while calling for help.

YOU AND YOUR PARTNER

Relationship issues between couples classically surface in the first three to seven years, and it's no coincidence that this corresponds with the time when most start families together. Even if you're deliriously happy with being a parent, the new realities always come with compromise and curtailed freedoms, and there are bound to be patches when someone

reception with our baby. I conveyed that my husband was missing, and that I was worried. I remember the glances exchanged between them; the kind that say 'well we all know what he's up to'. I felt furious and helpless. Hours later and after a few more visits to the reception, I gave up.

But at around 4am, there was a knock on the door. There he was, totally drunk, just like in the movies, swinging a bottle of spirits. From worrying about his life, I switched to wishing he didn't exist. And of course, there I was with a baby – feeling just about as trapped as you can get. The next few days were rough. Some nights later, however, I found myself insisting on having 'my turn', even though I knew I couldn't go far or for long as I was breastfeeding. I dressed up and left the hotel, leaving husband 'carrying the baby'. I was finally on my own, alone, on the streets as my own person – neither wife nor mother, and I felt transported with joy. I ended up in a little bamboo bar on the beach to watch the sun set. There, I enjoyed a bit of harmless flirting. Somehow, even though I couldn't have been out for more than a couple of hours, this time to myself was hugely important for me.

It probably sounds silly, but while I had wanted a baby more than anything else, there were many things I hadn't bargained for. Both of us had been – and still are – fiercely independent people; the transitions that we had to go through individually as well as together were enormous. That trip made us face these issues head on and share what each of us was going through. If we had been at home, working, with the usual distractions, who knows if we'd ever have worked things out. But just a few days later, we were out together on the town accompanied by our baby in his carrycot; and while it wasn't exactly smooth sailing, things started getting steadily better. Whenever we travel, if there is something we need to work out (isn't there always?), it comes up. These days (twenty years later) we reserve making complex decisions for trips. In no small way, I reckon our travels have been a very important ingredient in our relationship."

Anonymous

feels stuck, overly dependent or responsible. The odd meltdown is inevitable, particularly when you're on holiday and the responsibilities of being a parent are brought into sharp focus. So don't be surprised if the odd niggle surfaces in the midst of otherwise serene moments of watching horizons and sipping cocktails, prompting profound discussions and arguments. But rather than see this negatively, take it as a good thing: sorting out the kinks while having fun and accomplishing new things together is a brilliant way to strengthen your relationship.

To help things go as smoothly as possible, take turns having some **time without the children** – even if this means some late-night partying and being out of synch the next day when one of you has a hangover. You might also avoid spending too much time visiting each other's friends, family and old haunts, as it tends to be more mutually refreshing to explore places and people that are new to both. Make a point, too, of **sharing childcare and decision-making** for the trip – try swapping roles from time to time. Not doing this can lead to unexpected problems: the person left to "chill out" with the kids can feel left out, while the one "released" to figure out the next adventure can feel lumbered with a sense of ever increasing responsibility, or maybe even guilt for having chosen a horrible hotel or disastrous day-trip. So if (or when) you have a spat, tell yourselves this is all fabulous therapeutic stuff: one down and out of the way.

AROUND THE WORLD

WORLD

4

AROUND THE WORLD

The more you know about your destination before you go, the better time you can expect to have, and it's crucial to do some research before leaving to find out what's in store, from the availability of nappies/diapers to cultural do's and don'ts. Though it's necessarily random given that space prevents us giving a detailed country-by-country coverage, the information in this section serves as a taster for the kind of things you need to find out about the practicalities of travel with kids wherever you're going.

For ideas on how to research your destination before you go, see pp.10, 30 and 41.

AFRICA

Angola, Benin, Botswana, Burkina Faso, Burundi, Cameroon, Cape Verde Islands, Central African Republic, Chad, The Comoros, Congo, Côte d'Ivoire, Democratic Republic of the Congo (Zaire), Djibouti, Equatorial Guinea, Eritrea, Ethiopia, Gabon, Gambia, Ghana, Guinea Republic, Guinea-Bissau, Kenya, Lesotho, Liberia, Madagascar, Mali, Malawi, Mauritania, Mauritius, Mayotte, Mozambique, Namibia, Niger, Nigeria, Republic of Guinea, Réunion, Rwanda, São Tome and Principe, Senegal, Seychelles, Sierra Leone, St Helena, Somalia, South Africa, Sudan, Swaziland, Togo, Uganda, United Republic of Tanzania, Zambia
Note that North Africa is covered on pp.197–201.

Infectious diseases, a relatively weak (and sometimes non-existent) infrastructure and occasionally harsh conditions and climate make **Africa** a fairly adventurous destination. But if you prepare well and plan your trip wisely, it can be fabulous for a family trip. Apart from the vast landscapes, Africa is home to some incredible animals, some of which your children will probably be seeing for the first time, perhaps bringing kids' staples such as Tarzan and The Lion King to life. And if you don't want to rough it in Jeeps on hot, dusty roads, there's plenty in the way of poolside, air-conditioned luxury experiences on offer, too.

BACKPACKING AROUND THE WORLD

"Our first family odyssey was a round-the-world backpacking trip that began in 1999. We had to persuade our children (then Lucy, 14; Katie, 12; Georgia, 10; and Arthur, 7) that this would be a great thing to do. Once all were in agreement and we had beaten the mindset that says 'the world is a dangerous place and why are we doing this?', there was no stopping us. As for schooling, we took along a teacher who followed the curriculum as best she could. Any sensible school would agree that to travel the way we did is the best education a child could get; in fact, it should be compulsory!

We bought a small library of travel books and maps and eventually honed down our schedule to cover six main countries. Our equipment for the various climates and locations had to fit in our backpacks, and each member of the family had to carry their own stuff. Apart from the twenty train and plane tickets per person, accommodation and the itinerary were usually organized on arrival. The sight of four backpacking children diminishing in size and programmed to look frazzled in times of need often helped our situation.

The dangers are the same the world over; you can be run over anywhere, but it's more likely in Cairo, which seems to operate as a permanent racetrack. You could fall off a mountain in Nepal, or a tree in your own back garden, as Georgia did when we got home. If you're worried about being mugged, even the world's meanest people think twice before taking on a whole family.

I complicated the travelling process by making a documentary. This necessitated taking fewer clothes to make space in my backpack for the cameras. The discipline of charging batteries, logging shots, begging your children to wear radio mics, cajoling people to respond to the camera and covering twice as much ground as everyone else was exhausting.

The highlight of our expedition was the trek in the Langtang Valley, Nepal, to nearly 5000 metres – even though tears were shed for Katie, who got altitude sickness and mild hypothermia at a high pass. Next on the 'great moments' list was a walking safari in Zimbabwe, where sightings of a pride of lionesses, bird-chomping crocodiles, laughing hippos and perhaps the oldest elephant alive, whose single tusk skimmed the dusty savannah, were thrilling. Our penultimate destination, the Manu rainforest in Peru, was the most challenging. Our night-walk encounters with marauding army ants, giant slugs and spiders as big as a dinner plate had us all checking for the slightest hole in our tents.

Canoeing on the river by day, we trailed a family of giant otters squabbling over a breakfast of catfish. Add to this a stunning eclipse of the sun in Hungary, a sail to an island paradise in the South Pacific, weekends in Paris, Rome and Venice and, finally, Christmas in the Caribbean, and you have the whole story.

The documentary series we made was broadcast on the BBC as Travel Bug, and followed up by a further series to China (Chinese Breakaway) and more recently to India (Arthur's trip to India) which was shown on Channel Five.

One of the end results in taking your kids on big adventures is that it carries on for them as they get older. Lucy is in Beijing studying Mandarin, Katie went back to South America, Georgia is planning a gap year to remote places and Arthur wants to travel the world as a sports journalist."

Peter Duncan

Visit ®www.heresoneimadeearlier.com for more on the family's travels

Before you go, it's worth talking to your children about the issues surrounding **poverty** and, if they're old enough, HIV/AIDS in particular, as they'll probably want to ask about the things that they see, from child workers to impoverished homes. Cultural research is also crucial here given the extraordinary diversity of African tribes and peoples, each with their own language and ways.

LOGISTICS

Child's car seats

▶▶ These won't be widely available, so you'll need to bring one from home, but rear seatbelts aren't standard in rental cars, so check in advance.

Food

▶▶ Don't expect Western-type fare outside urban areas. Local cuisine doesn't tend to be especially spicy throughout the continent, but the main difficulty when it comes to feeding your children will be lack of variety, as there are few ingredients available in many places. If anyone has dietary restrictions or food allergies, take particular care: in West Africa, for example, peanuts and peanut oil are used extensively in cooking, and you'll find it hard to avoid them.

TRAVELLERS' TALES

FIRST-TIME UGANDA

"We wanted to have a term-time long-haul trip before our 4 year-old daughter started school. A good friend had been based in Uganda for a couple of years and regaled us with tales of beautiful lakes, friendly people and gorgeous butterflies, so we decided to plan our travels around seeing her.

This was our first trip to Africa, and our daughter's first time in a developing country. Friends, family members and even some guide books suggested we were mad to take a blonde child to sub-Saharan Africa, citing the dangers of sunstroke as well as malaria, bilharzia and all sorts of other diseases. The naysayers were even more concerned while we were away, as our trip happened to coincide with a period of political unrest caused by two separate events: the arrest of the main opposition leader before the national election, and the International Criminal Court issuing a warrant for the arrest of the leader of the Lord's Resistance Army, the rebel group operating in northern Uganda. There were riots in the capital and an unprecedented level of attacks on muzungus (whites) in the north. These events did have an impact on our trip, in that we met some very distressed people and amended our itinerary to avoid riskier areas of the country, but our daughter was oblivious to these political events, and we all had an amazing time.

Starting out in the capital, Kampala, we travelled to the small town in southern Uganda where our friend lives, then passed through a succession of towns and villages on our way to Kibale, a forested region renowned for its primates, crater lakes and tea plantations. From there, we moved on to the Mweya game reserve before travelling to Ishasha, by the border of the Democratic Republic of Congo, to see the tree-climbing lions. Somehow we managed to fit in a trip to Jinja, then believed to be the source of the Nile, before returning to Kampala and then chilling out in Entebbe for our final couple of days.

Prams and strollers

▶▶ Think twice before bringing these; many cities won't have pavements, making backpacks and slings a better bet.

Public transport

▶▶ As buses and trains tend to be privately run, there are no hard and fast rules concerning discounts for children. Visitors will often be charged more than locals in any case, making it worthwhile to get a rough idea of the going rates to be sure you aren't (too) badly ripped off – consult a good guide book.

Safaris

▶▶ If you're planning a safari or a stay in a game park lodge, check if there are restrictions for children, as lower age limits are often set to prevent kids from disturbing the animals.

Supplies

▶▶ With the exception of capital cities on the tourist trail in eastern and southern Africa, baby food, infant formula and nappies/diapers are hard to find, so if possible, bring all you'll need from home. Once you leave big cities, you'll also need to take adequate supplies of things like wet-wipes, extra bottles and teats – and a good medical kit is essential wherever you go.

We saw an amazing array of wildlife, from outsized grasshoppers to enormous hippos and herds of elephant. We saw butterflies the size of birds and birds (marabou storks) the size of dogs. Our shy child, who normally hates car journeys, happily went on long-distance cross-country trips, meeting and waving to people along the way. Some people claimed she was the first white child they had ever seen. She played with Ugandan children, ate nsenene (grasshoppers), used hole-in-the-ground toilets, went rafting, swam in a hotel pool while listening to warthogs grunting and a hippo grazing, and had her first drink of Coke. Gecko counting became a mealtime game; and she rated each place we stayed on the basis of their desserts (fresh pineapple or ice cream being the winners).

Our daughter's recollections of Uganda are quite different to ours. She was completely unfazed when our car got stuck in lion and elephant country, meaning that some of us had to go to seek help on foot, but freaked out when she was bitten by an insect while swimming. Our photos are of landscapes, bustling markets and grazing game, whereas she favoured dogs, cats, lizards and flowers.

One year on, I asked her what she remembered about Uganda. 'We went on two boats and there was a big splash on one of them and I got my knickers wet'. 'We saw lots of animals and we had a Halloween party and we ate grasshoppers . . . There are bicycles with bananas on them, green and yellow . . . The people had black faces and were smiley and friendly. I played with Lucia and Isaac and other children. The beds had nets, didn't they, so the flies didn't get in . . . I remember that massive elephant!'

Travelling with a child did slow our pace and ruled out mountain gorilla trekking, which some would say is the highlight of any trip to Uganda. But being with our daughter was a great way to meet local people and get some sense of what it's like to live in Uganda – what we feel travelling is all about. We don't regret a thing."

Lorna Fray

Toilets

▶▶ In cities, Western toilets are the norm, but outside of touristy areas, they're few and far between. In rural areas, things can be very basic: little more than a fenced-in patch of ground with a couple of bricks to squat over. In the heat, the smell can be overbearing; and in the rains, children will need help to tip-toe through the fenced-in area to get to the hole-and-bricks business end of things without getting covered in crap.

▶▶ If you need to make toilet stops during journeys, it's usually far better to stop in the middle of nowhere than look for places to go in villages. Take your own wet-wipes or toilet paper, and a plastic bag to stash them in once used – in many instances, there won't be anywhere to dispose of rubbish.

CUSTOMS, ETIQUETTE AND CULTURAL INSIGHTS

General etiquette

▶▶ Children are expected to show particular deference to those older than themselves in terms of things like never being seated themselves if it means leaving adults standing.

▶▶ In many African countries, children usually use both hands or even kneel when offering things to adults or accepting something from someone older.

▶▶ Avoid touching heads of children, as this isn't welcomed in many countries.

Clothing

▶▶ You won't have to think too much about dress codes for kids, although in some areas, nudity and skimpy clothing will be frowned upon even for very young children.

Eating

▶▶ In many parts of East Africa, eating while walking will offend local sensibilities, so even if your child is just having a chocolate bar, get them to sit down somewhere. It's a good idea to prime your kids on general mealtime etiquette; if you're invited to share a meal where everyone eats from one platter, they'll need to first wash their hands, and should take food only from the area directly in front of them. Bits of food elsewhere on the dish will be intended for someone else, but you can assure your children that as guests, they'll probably be offered more of whatever they like.

▶▶ In Zambia, children are expected to wait for adults both to wash their hands and eat before they themselves wash and tuck in.

Greetings

▶▶ Actual greetings vary hugely, but in general, it's important for children to acknowledge the presence of those around them. While a hello will be understood in most places, tell the children that whenever greeted (in Swahili) by a "*jambo*" or "*habare*", "fine" should always be their first reply; cheerfulness in all people, but especially in children, is highly prized and considered a virtue. In West Africa particularly, greetings can be much more elaborate, involving a series of questions as to how things are; once again, the expected response from children is that everything is OK.

▶▶ Amongst many tribes, handshakes may not be expected or welcomed between children and adults, as such physical contact can be considered forward or disrespectful. In some places – Uganda, for example – youngsters aren't supposed to look elders directly in the face; while in Zambia, children are expected to bow without an exchange of words, and should only speak if first addressed by an adult. But pretty much everywhere, children should address adults using formal terms such as Mr, Mrs or "*tata*" – which means "my elder" – rather than first names.

ASIA – THE FAR EAST

Brunei Darussalam, Cambodia, China, Hong Kong, Indonesia, Japan, Laos, Macau, Malaysia, Mongolia, Myanmar (Burma), North Korea, the Philippines, Singapore, South Korea, Taiwan, Thailand, Vietnam

Though you might have a few difficulties with indecipherable scripts on packaging and street signs, the **Far East** is a great destination for children, what with dragons that don't breathe fire to fireworks which do, as well as martial arts in all their incarnations, and circus gymnastics where the artists and their ribbons of silk take on seemingly impossible contortions. Infrastructure and healthcare are pretty good, but you might want to prepare your kids for getting lots of attention from local people; the relatively large eyes of non-Chinese children are considered particularly beautiful.

LOGISTICS

Child's car seats
• Most rental companies won't have seats for children, so bring your own, but cars are generally fitted with seatbelts in the back.

Food
▶▶ Eating can be tricky, as food tends to be highly seasoned; ask for no chilli when you order, and research the names of local dishes that are likely to go down well with your children before you go. If all else fails, bland rice and noodle dishes are always available.

Public transport
▶▶ Pre-school children either travel for free or get discounted prices on public transport; in China, all children under a metre in height travel for free.

Supplies
▶▶ Nappies/diapers and baby or infant food are widely available in the large

TRAVELLERS' TALES

THAI MASSAGES

"We are already planning our second trip to Thailand as my son Arthur and I had such a wonderful time last summer. If we had to choose one highlight, it would be the massages. All the hotels seem to offer them, and after the long flight there, I couldn't resist booking one to try it out. Arthur watched while I had mine, and then wanted one himself. From then on, we were both addicted, and managed to fit one in most days. In Bangkok, we visited a temple which seemed to double up as a massage school, and both of us had a massage in their shady courtyard. I fell asleep (this is a wonderful remedy for being on your feet all day); this particular massage ended up being so good that we went the next day for another. When we turned up, an old man recognized us and couldn't seem to stop laughing at the sight of Arthur enjoying himself; the young aren't supposed to need massages, and adults who do generally only get one every two weeks – so we were clearly overdoing it.

That didn't stop us, though. When on the beach, south of Bangkok in Hua Hin, there were people offering massages once again. After dinner each night, we had sublime massages on platforms built above the sand with awnings flapping in the sea breeze, facing the sunset while we were pampered for an hour – sometimes even two.

Eating did present some problems as the food was invariably spicy – but we found that menus often indicate the strength of chillies with little pictures of one to three chillies by the side of the listings. And yet mealtimes were also unusually relaxing; people came forward to play with Arthur, and I got to take my time, even have a second drink. Once, while eating at a market 'restaurant' (a few tables and chairs by the roadside), a young lad offered Arthur a ride on his motorbike. I agreed – and of course, five minutes later I was worrying about whether this had been a good idea. But sure enough, he was returned safe and sound, completely exhilarated and ready for bed (without a massage that night). It's not always easy for single mothers to manage alone, but Thailand really was different – everything seemed so easy."

Lydia Piguet

cities of Brunei, Hong Kong, Japan, Malaysia, the Philippines, Singapore and Thailand, although look for larger shops in affluent neighbourhoods. As babies tend to be toilet trained early here, expect to find only smaller nappy/diaper sizes. Away from large cities and in rural areas, you'll need to travel with stocks of whatever you need.

▶▶ Brands will be unfamiliar and labelling on packaging won't be in English, so you'll probably need help with translation wherever you shop – you can always ask someone at your hotel to write down what you need in the local language.

Toilets

▶▶ Toilets vary from the squatting to the Western variety, but there are few public facilities. You may have to pay a small fee to use toilets in shopping malls and the like, so have some change at the ready; and as most only have water to wash with, you'll need your own toilet paper or wet-wipes.

CUSTOMS, ETIQUETTE AND CULTURAL INSIGHTS

General etiquette

▶▶ Strangers might want to touch or photograph your children, or even place their hands on their faces for good luck; if this starts to worry your kids, just pick them up yourself.

▶▶ Bad-tempered children are frowned upon throughout the region, and displays of frustration or anger won't go down well. Kids here are taught not to show anger, and especially not to cry, from an early age; for instance, in Thailand, kids who make light of inconveniences are thought to be especially well brought up and show *jai yen* ("cool heart").

▶▶ In cultures influenced by Buddhism, try and get your children to understand the concept of not harming any living thing – including insects and trees – and bear in mind that raised voices and hitting can be construed as violent on your part as well as theirs.

▶▶ If your children's pranks are met with giggles, don't assume their antics haven't offended anyone – in China, the Philippines or Japan, laughter could indicate embarrassment rather than amusement. Similarly, if people don't correct your children for bad manners or point out that your child's nose is running, it's likely to be because they don't want to embarrass you – sparing one another from losing face is seen as very important.

▶▶ In Chinese-based cultures, your children might be offered gifts of money in red or green paper envelopes, particularly around the Chinese or Lunar new years; if this happens, always allow your children to accept graciously after a preliminary show of "Oh! But you shouldn't have!" resistance. When giving or receiving gifts, use both hands; using just the left hand can be considered a subtle insult.

▶▶ Visiting children often find shaved heads fascinating, particularly in other children; restrain your kids from pointing (which is offensive), or laughing – in many instances, the person will have shaved due to religious reasons or following the death of someone close in the family.

▶▶ Patting children on the head is considered disrespectful in many countries (Cambodia, Laos, Thailand and Indonesia, for example); likewise, feet are considered impure and shoes dirty, so get your kids to take off their shoes before entering homes, and avoid touching objects and people with their feet.

▶▶ If you or your children want to point at something, use your whole hand rather than just a finger; the latter is considered rude.

Clothing

▶▶ Visiting children won't usually be expected to observe dress codes other than in places of worship. You might pay particular attention to the state of your children's socks, though, as shoes will inevitably be taken off when entering homes – in countries such as Japan, local children tend to be immaculately turned out, which includes spotless socks.

Eating

▶▶ The range of customs that relate to food is vast, so don't expect to get it right all the time, but it's worth learning the basics. The first thing to find out (and pass on to the kids) is who gets to eat first. In Vietnam, for instance, youngsters are traditionally expected to wait for the others to be seated before eating, and to ask their parents or the eldest person at the table to eat first; children are supposed to start only once the adults begin. Don't let your children use chopsticks as drumsticks or as makeshift weapons in swordfights, as this will be seriously frowned upon; crossing chopsticks is said to bring bad luck. For tips on using hands to eat, see p.188.

Greetings

▶▶ Spend some time researching local greetings and teaching your children the significance of them, as well as the postures that they should adopt. Kids generally adapt fast – if anything, you're likely to find that yours end up a bit like performing monkeys, using bows and the like to get attention wherever they go, and learning new words much faster than you.

▶▶ Greetings can be very different (not just between but within countries), but there will always be slight adaptations expected of children – bowing lower than adults is common in Thailand and Japan, while in Malaysia and the Philippines, children will kiss adults' hands or cheeks. Throughout the region, get the kids to refer to adults by titles rather than first names.

ASIA – THE INDIAN SUBCONTINENT

Afghanistan, Bangladesh, Bhutan, India, the Maldives, Nepal, Pakistan, Sri Lanka

Many children's preconceptions of the **Indian subcontinent** come from stories such as the *Jungle Book*, and in most places, they'll get to see some of the characters for real, from snake charmers to performing street monkeys and elephants. The ornate local clothing can quickly turn children into shopaholics – girls may want to emulate bejewelled young ladies with hennaed hands, and if your boys are game for dressing up, you can transform them into little princes wearing flowing robes, sashes and filigree curly-toed sandals.

Aside from India, the Maldives and Sri Lanka, where you can travel from one end of the country to the other in an air-conditioned five-star bubble if you choose, you'll need to do more than the usual research to make sure you get a child-friendly place to stay and access to healthcare, as well as the most comfortable seats on public transport. This is also one region where you absolutely have to discuss poverty with the children before you leave, and prepare them for street filth as well as crowds, who can be inquisitive and invasive (see p.77).

SRI LANKA WITH FOUR CHILDREN

"Sri Lanka is incredibly child-friendly: it's not over the top, but children are just fully accepted as part of life here. As we were there with our four kids (aged 4 to 11) this accepting attitude made our lives much, much easier – elsewhere, we've been glared at for seemingly having dared to reproduce. At a hotel on the coast, the waiter was quite happy for the older kids to help him set the tables and serve breakfast. One day, the gentleman who did the sweeping shinned up a palm and got a coconut for the children. He later appeared with a plastic horse for our youngest, which she was still playing with a month on. Our van driver was also incredibly sweet with the children, finding sandals stuck under seats and helping put them back on, picking up things the children dropped in cafés, or catching the small one as she almost toppled off her chair. The kids consequently had a holiday that I don't think even the youngest will ever forget.

We went all over the island, and the children particularly enjoyed the Kosogoda turtle hatchery (which they referred to as a turtle factory); our second-eldest was allowed to put a newly hatched turtle she'd spotted struggling on the sand into the water. Our eldest is still delighted with the memory of the elephant sanctuary.

On our last journey back to the airport, the driver stopped as he always did when he passed the Buddhist shrine coming out of Kandy, and prayed for us to have a safe journey home. He then hopped back into the car with his usual handful of flowers to scatter round the little Buddha on his dashboard, and some extra lotus and frangipani flowers for the girls. Once in the airport, I looked back to see him in the doorway. He was still watching. I waved, he waved – it had been a real pleasure knowing him."

Becca Stanford

LOGISTICS

Child's car seats

▸▸ You'll need to bring your own seats from home. Hiring a driver rather than a car is the norm here, but check in advance if their vehicle has rear seatbelts.

Child discounts

▸▸ As everything from transport to tourist attractions tends to be privately run, there are few standardized rates for children – expect to do some haggling.

Food

▸▸ Food is invariably spicy and it can be hard to find things that children will enjoy; however, fresh *chapatti* and *parata* breads, dhal or bland lentil dishes will usually be available everywhere.

Prams and buggies

▸▸ As there won't be much in the way of pavements or pedestrian zones, standard buggies or prams are probably best left at home.

Supplies

▶▶ Other than in Bhutan and Nepal, you can buy basic baby food, nappies/ diapers and infant supplies in capitals and other major cities, but it won't be a simple matter to get brands that are common in the West.

▶▶ Be particularly careful about checking sell-by dates for food, as finding items long past the expiry date is pretty common.

Toilets

▶▶ Toilets can be a major problem away from hotels. Apart from being few and far between, public facilities will generally be of the squat variety (with or without water to wash), and can be a stinking, unhygienic mess; and because of the region's high population density, it's not always easy to find somewhere private to go in the open. Plan day-trips carefully, factoring in the availability of toilets, and always carry your own toilet paper and wet-wipes.

▶▶ In Bhutan and Nepal, toilets in mountainous areas may not be able to take paper even if they seemingly flush with water due to water shortages or low pressure; use the baskets provided for dirty paper, or be ready with a plastic bag to take yours away with you.

CUSTOMS, ETIQUETTE AND CULTURAL INSIGHTS

General etiquette

▶▶ Prepare your children for inquisitive people and some rather direct questioning, starting with "what is your name?" and going quickly on to other topics such as "what is your religion?" or "why don't you have more sisters/brothers?"; talk through possible answers with your children in advance.

▶▶ If you visit someone's home, everyone should take off shoes before entering. Remind the kids to ask adults before using anything, particularly electric appliances like TVs – these are usually the domain of grown-ups. It's also a bad idea for them to explore alone; in some households, places such as the kitchen, family prayer areas or altars are out of bounds to visitors. If your children do wander, ask your hosts to find them rather than going after them yourself.

▶▶ Wherever you are, get your children to apologize profusely if they inadvertently touch someone with their shoes, as this is considered especially offensive.

Clothing

▶▶ Small children won't be expected to follow any special conventions, although in Afghanistan and Pakistan, the customs can be more akin to those in the Arab states (see p.197). But wherever you are, children will be expected to be freshly bathed and dressed in crisp, clean clothing when invited to people's homes.

▶▶ On special occasions, children tend to be ornately dressed, with girls in frilly things and ribbons, and boys wearing adult-like garb such as long-sleeved, button-up shirts, trousers and slicked-back hair,

Eating

▶▶ Conventions around food can be intricate here, governing how you eat as well as the combinations and order of dishes, but visitors won't be expected to know it all. When eating with hands, get the children to use only their right hand, and not to share sips of drinks or bites of food with anyone else – this is considered unhygienic and rather gross. It's also important to teach children not to get "dirty" above the first joint of their fingers while eating; holding a ball of food and letting it ooze out between fingers won't be considered particularly elegant. Equally, it's bad manners to suck fingers clean, or use your eating hand to pick up a glass or serve yourself. As young children are likely to forget all of this, keep an eye on them.

▶▶ The old Asian tradition of treating guests as revered and offering generous hospitality still stands. Even the poorest of families may want to serve you the very best meal they can prepare, so if asked what you like beforehand, try and go for something simple and relatively inexpensive which everyone (including your children) will enjoy and not waste.

Greetings

▶▶ Given the diversity of languages spoken here, there are a great many specialized words or phrases used by children when greeting adults, but when speaking English, get them to use either Mr or Mrs or the more endearing uncle or auntie, which reflect intimacy as well as respect. Should your children be addressed as "sister" or "brother" by local kids, explain to them that this is a compliment, and maybe get them to try the same with other children, particularly those older than themselves.

▶▶ Children are sometimes expected to touch the feet of the elderly or revered as a greeting which shows great respect; watch what others are doing, and encourage your children to do the same. If your boys hate being kissed, they will usually be spared this in countries such as Afghanistan, Nepal and Pakistan, but they might get the odd hug, particularly from men.

AUSTRALIA, NEW ZEALAND AND THE SOUTH PACIFIC

American Samoa, Australia, Christmas Island, Cook Islands, Federated States of Micronesia, Fiji, French Polynesia, Guam, Kiribati, Marshall Islands, Nauru, New Caledonia, New Zealand, Niue, Northern Mariana Islands, Palau, Papua New Guinea, Pitcairn Island, Samoa, Solomon Islands, Tokelau, Tonga, Tuvalu, Vanuatu, Wake Island, Wallis and Futuna

A relaxed attitude, wide open spaces and plenty of sea, sun and sand (not to mention koalas and kangaroos) make **Australia, New Zealand and the South Pacific** a relatively easy region in which to travel with children – providing, of course, you don't underestimate the vast distances. In the larger islands, you'll find lots of great supervised activities to suit kids, from walking trails and camps to beaches with every recreation facility imaginable, as well as ways to look at sea creatures and coral, either at aquariums, via glass-bottomed boats or just by taking a dip.

LOGISTICS

Bugs
▶▶ In some areas, flies can drive children to distraction; wherever they're a problem, fly-nets and hats with dangling deterrents are widely available.

Child's car seats
▶▶ Child's seats are available from larger car rental firms in Australia and New Zealand, but not in the smaller islands. Most cars come with seatbelts in the back.

▶▶ If you're planning on island-hopping by boat, enquire about life-jackets suitable for children or bring your own.

Child discounts
▶▶ Expect reduced fees or free entry for pre-school children on pretty much everything.

▶▶ As infants' fares are very affordable, domestic flights are a viable alternative to long road trips.

Food
▶▶ You'll be able to find something that suits children in most places, so take only basic start-up snacks from home.

Mobile phones
▶▶ If you're planning cross-country trips or visits to islands, bear in mind that many areas aren't served by networks that support the use of mobile phones, meaning that you can't call for help if you get stranded. Before making long journeys, check coverage with network providers, and avoid being out of range with small children.

Sun
▶▶ Skin cancer is taken seriously here, and you'll often see adults painting children's faces with coloured sunscreen products, which makes it easier for you to follow suit.

Supplies
▶▶ In Australia and New Zealand, the full range of supplies for babies and children will be available wherever you go, but stock up before heading for the islands – things like nappies/diapers and baby food are imported, so they're expensive and availability is patchy.

Toilets

▶▶ These will invariably be of the Western type, but take your own toilet paper and wet-wipes when travelling in the more remote islands.

CUSTOMS, ETIQUETTE AND CULTURAL INSIGHTS

Clothing

▶▶ In Australia and New Zealand, children can wear pretty much what they want, and even stay in their swimwear and flip-flops all day. On the Pacific islands, it's best to get them dressed before visiting villages – bare chests, shorts and swimsuits can be considered disrespectful.

Eating

▶▶ On the smaller islands, extensive exchanges of compliments are common while eating and can take children by surprise; for instance, if the children say "thank you" for the meal, they're likely to be thanked in return for eating the host's food – rather than bursting into giggles, get them to reply with "thank you for inviting me" and so on.

Greetings

▶▶ Australia and New Zealand are refreshingly casual "no problem" destinations; there's no special etiquette for children to follow, and everyone quickly gets on first-name terms. If you visit Maori areas, it's fun to get your children to do the "*hongi*", the traditional Maori greeting of nose-rubbing.

▶▶ In Samoa, youngsters are expected to respect not only their elders, but their "betters" too, which can include visitors and people in professions such as medicine; to avoid offending anyone, get your children to greet every adult they meet.

▶▶ There are lots of different customs to bear in mind when entering people's homes, from taking off shoes to bowing down when crossing the threshold as a sign of respect – consult guidebooks for each destination to get an idea of the specifics. In Fiji, for instance, you should wait to be welcomed into village compounds before walking around – this means restraining the children until village leaders formally invite you in. The welcome can then involve an exchange of greetings, gifts and sharing of a drink, which can seem to take an eternity to children – take something along that they can play with on their own.

THE CARIBBEAN

Anguilla, Antigua and Barbuda, Aruba, the Bahamas, Barbados, Bermuda, Bonaire, the Cayman Islands, Cuba, Curacao, Dominica, the Dominican Republic, Grenada, Guadeloupe, Haiti, Jamaica, Martinique, Montserrat, Puerto Rico, Saba, St Kitts and Nevis, St Eustatius, St Lucia, St Maarten, St Vincent and the Grenadines, the Turks and Caicos Islands, Trinidad and Tobago, the Virgin Islands

With its mirror-calm warm seas, sandy beaches, lack of serious disease (which means no jabs or antimalarials) and great tourist infrastructure, the **Caribbean** is a popular destination for families. Given the history of colonial settlement here, visitors from English, French, Dutch and Spanish-speaking countries will find plenty of common ground, from language and food to what's on the TV. Equally, most children are thrilled by the Caribbean's history of piracy, much of which is easy to bring to life – you might take a walk on the very stretch of sand where Henry Morgan once beached a ship, or sail between the same peaks as the silver screen's Captain Jack Sparrow and Elizabeth Swann. Children are usually fascinated by the bright colours and elaborate costumes of the Caribbean's many festivals and carnivals; kids as young as 4 regularly take part in the parades, and adults are welcome to join in too. Carnival in Trinidad also features stilt-walkers known as *moko jumbies*; children as young as 5 or 6 walk and dance on stilts that are double their natural height – an impressive spectacle for kids.

The fact that the Caribbean has a hedonistic reputation means that locals can be a bit jaded by visitors who assume that everyone smokes marijuana and spends most of their time at reggae parties; it's likely that people will assume that as a family, you'll be a lot more sober, thereby affording you and your children a special welcome.

LOGISTICS

Child's car seats

▶▶ Rental cars will have rear seatbelts, and larger firms can almost always provide children's car seats.

Child discounts

▶▶ Tourist attractions aimed at children will usually have some kind of discount for kids, but as much of the public transport is privately run, don't expect reductions for children.

Food

▶▶ It's usually simple to find things that children will like and be familiar with in the resorts, from pasta and pizza to burgers. Local food isn't usually that spicy, as chilli is added at the table via a dollop of pepper sauce, and there will always be bland rice dishes available.

Supplies

▶▶ You can count on getting basic supplies for babies and infants in the larger cities and towns, but as most islands rely on imported goods, prices tend to be high.

Toilets

▶▶ Public facilities are few and far between, but toilets will invariably be of the Western kind, although not always very nice outside of tourist restaurants or hotels.

CUSTOMS, ETIQUETTE AND CULTURAL INSIGHTS

General etiquette

▶▶ In terms of breastfeeding, local women tend to be fairly discreet, so either feed indoors or find somewhere quiet and away from the action.

▶▶ It's customary for children to give up seats and places in queues for the elderly throughout the Caribbean, so get your kids to follow suit.

Clothing

▶▶ Displays of skin – even under-5s naked on the beach – are generally frowned upon.

▶▶ If you plan on attending church or formal occasions, take smart clothing for all the family.

Greetings

▶▶ Get your kids to refer to elders as Miss/Mrs or Mr across the various islands – using first names might be seen as disrespectful. Note that it's "Don" and "Doña" in Spanish-speaking islands rather than "Señor" and "Señora".

EASTERN EUROPE AND THE FORMER SOVIET UNION

Albania, Armenia, Azerbaijan, Belarus, Bosnia/Herzegovina, Bulgaria, Croatia, Czech Republic, Estonia, Georgia, Hungary, Kazakhstan, Kyrgyzstan, Latvia, Lithuania, Moldova, Montenegro, Poland, Romania, Russia, Serbia, Slovak Republic, Slovenia, Tajikistan, Ukraine, Uzbekistan

From folk singing and finger puppets to Russian *matryoshka* dolls, children and adults will find plenty to entertain here, and wherever you go, expect a high degree of cultural and ethnic diversity. Logistics tend to be easier in countries within the EU as opposed to those closer to Asia, and English and German will get you further within the region than you might initially think. Travelling as a family pretty much guarantees a hearty welcome – apart from other children and parents, expect to make friends with many a *babushka* (grandmother) as well.

LOGISTICS

Child's car seats

▶▶ As the international rental companies don't operate throughout the region, the availability of child seats is patchy – check before you go or take your own.

Child discounts

▶▶ Expect generous discounts or free travel for pre-school children on public transport, and free or discounted tickets for national parks, museums and the like – this is particularly the case in countries of the former USSR.

Food

▶▶ Russian food is quite common throughout the region, and though the names of dishes are different, many are pretty similar to Western standards. Traditional local food can be hard to find, but potential favourites with kids include *pelmeni,* little dumplings with meat inside, or *pirozhki*, little pies with various fillings – and don't forget to try *kievskaya kotleta*, or chicken Kiev.

Supplies

▶▶ Nappies/diapers and baby/infant food will be widely available within the EU countries and in major cities elsewhere; labels will often be translated into as many as six languages so you should be able to understand what you're buying.

Toilets

▶▶ Facilities vary from Western to squat versions, and the farther east you travel, the more you'll see the latter variety. In remote rural areas, you might find another version of the Western standard: toilets capped with a board to sit on that has a hole set in the middle – these are easier for children to manage than squat loos. But in general, public toilets aren't as readily available as elsewhere in Europe, so the only option is to ask at shops and restaurants.

CUSTOMS, ETIQUETTE AND CULTURAL INSIGHTS

General etiquette

▶▶ Get your children to take off their shoes when entering private homes, even if they're not asked to – adults will usually be given a pair of slippers to wear

inside, but children will be left in their socks, so make sure they're presentable.

▶▶ It's common to see children walking hand in hand with their parents in the street here, even as adolescents, which is a great help in persuading your own kids to hold hands when you need them to.

▶▶ While the usual standards apply for children's behaviour, explain to your children that those who are moody or argumentative (particularly with parents) are frowned upon and strictly dealt with here.

▶▶ Strangers may tell you if they think you should be caring for your child better or in another way, that they should be fed more or less or dressed differently for the cold or heat; these are common social interchanges, so don't take offence.

▶▶ The tradition of taking children to cultural venues is strong, so it's no problem going to theatres, museums, concerts and the ballet with kids – not to mention the circus.

Clothing

▶▶ While women will be expected to cover heads in some Muslim areas, young children won't be subject to dress codes. Nonetheless, there's quite a lot of emphasis on dressing up, so take smart clothing for social events.

Eating

▶▶ The tradition of eating together as a family or with friends is strong, and as a rule people tend to prefer to eat at home rather than at a restaurant. If you get invited to eat at someone's house, prepare the children for quite a lot of bustle, and for the fact that while people may be pressed up together around the table, manners are quite formal and polished – remind them not to eat with mouths full, make a noise with utensils and so on.

Greetings

▶▶ Initial interactions with people can seem overly direct at first – Russians, for example, tend to dispense with opening remarks like "how are you" and go straight to the point, perhaps asking the children what they want in a shop without greeting them.

▶▶ Get your children to learn appropriate ways to address their elders: in Russian-speaking areas they could try *"Gospozha"* for Mrs and *"Gospodin"* for Mr, the more intimate *"tyotya"* or *"dyadya"* for auntie and uncle, or *"babushka"* and *"dedushka"* for grandma and grandpa in Russian.

THE MIDDLE EAST AND NORTH AFRICA

Algeria, Bahrain, Cyprus, Egypt, Iran, Iraq, Israel, Jordan, Kuwait, Lebanon, Libya, Morocco, Oman, Qatar, Saudi Arabia, Syria, Tunisia, Turkey, United Arab Emirates (including Dubai and Abu Dhabi), Yemen

From tales of the prophets to spooky, bandage-swathed mummies, your children may well be familiar with the history and culture of the **Middle East**, so make the most of it with plenty of storytelling, and invest in some books to read together. However, given the political volatility of some parts of the region, where situations can change from one day to the next, be sure to get a security update before you go; see p.30 for resources. With urban developments centred around rare (and often long-gone) watering holes, infrastructure is sporadic – it can be fantastic in some areas and nonexistent elsewhere, which means planning carefully if you want to travel overland between cities or go off the beaten track.

Israel is quite different from the rest of the region, so much of the advice below doesn't apply here. There's no segregation of the sexes (apart from in places of worship), you can expect to breastfeed as you would elsewhere in the Western world, and you won't need to worry too much about clothing or customs. Bear in mind, though, that on the Shabbat (sundown on Friday till sundown on Saturday) and other religious holidays, orthodox Jews will neither work nor travel, or operate technical appliances. This can extend to not touching a light switch, so stop your children from touching appliances and get them to leave all switches the way they find them – even if lights are switched on during the day.

LOGISTICS

Child's car seats

▶▶ While cars will almost always be fitted with rear seatbelts, most rental firms won't have child seats available.

Food

▶▶ Western-style food, including fast food, is readily available in the large cities that get a fair amount of tourist traffic. While Middle Eastern food can be highly seasoned, it's not necessarily chilli-hot, and there are plenty of staples such as bread, stews and roasted meats to keep children happy.

▶▶ Be mindful of religious restrictions applied to food here, and be careful not to take or offer pork-based, non-halal or non-kosher food to other children – even artificially flavoured "smoky bacon" products are taboo.

Supplies

▶▶ In well-travelled areas with large expatriate populations – in effect, most of the region's capital cities – you'll have no difficulty finding baby food, infant formula and nappies/diapers; when travelling elsewhere, bring what you need with you.

▶▶ Buy baby and infant food from air-conditioned shops and examine the packaging carefully; even if the products are within their sell-by dates, the heat can spoil contents.

Toilets

▶▶ Public facilities are fairly widespread in Israel, Turkey and Cyprus, but the Arabian Gulf states are a different matter. Here, public toilets tend to be scarce, and while men and children will usually have somewhere to go, women won't, making spontaneous travel hard. Accommodation designed for international guests will have Western toilet fittings, although others may be of the squat variety, and some local toilets (in Yemen, for example) are designed to use as little water as possible, with a hole for faeces to drop elsewhere and slabs which channel the urine to dry immediately outside the building; children will get used to it, but they may need help to begin with.

CUSTOMS, ETIQUETTE AND CULTURAL INSIGHTS IN ARAB COUNTRIES

General etiquette

▶▶ The importance placed on religion here means that many people you meet may ask about your faith, so it's worth priming your children with diplomatic answers.

▶▶ Political sensitivities govern more than the obvious topics, and your "allegiances" can be defined by the smallest detail, such as whether the children order Western or local brands of soft drinks, bottled water and so forth; to play it safe, stay away from specifying altogether.

LEILA AND ISTANBUL

"On my 40th birthday, my husband booked us on a surprise trip Istanbul. I grew up in the Middle East and was prepared to be watchful of local customs, but fitting in was easier than I expected. People were relaxed, warm and welcoming, and obviously appreciated our interest in Turkish culture and ways. The bigger surprise was learning soon afterwards that I was carrying the child we so wanted. For her second name, we chose Leila, which means "headiness of wine" in Arabic. Nine years later, the three of us returned to Istanbul. Each time our daughter heard "Allahu Akbar" – the call to prayer – she'd stop and cross herself (she's deep into catechism). It didn't seem to make any difference to her that this was the Muslim version; church bells, muezzin – it was all the same to her.

We stayed in a "boutique" hotel, and although the minibar was out of order and the swipe key had to be replaced every day, the service was wonderful. Late one night, our daughter felt like having some loukoum (Turkish delight). She mentioned it to the concierge, and he promptly asked the waiter (who'd just finished his shift) to get some. It was after her bedtime, and I wasn't keen on a sugar surge at this point, but nothing I could say would stop him. The packet was delivered to our room and sure enough, our daughter was up well into the wee hours.

Wherever we went, she would announce that her name was Leila and watch people do a double-take. 'But that's a Turkish name!', they'd say in amazement. 'I know! That's because I was made in Istanbul!' came the reply with a twinkle in her eye. That just about entitled her to honorary citizenship status, and she was metaphorically handed the citadel keys on a velvet cushion. Apart from sweets everywhere (which she loved), the Grand Bazaar provided gifts of apple tea (which she didn't, but accepted graciously), sweetmeats, baklava, free bracelets, all just because she'd stop and chat with the merchants. 'Tashakkur a daram' (thank you), she'd pipe, when handed a treat. She was a hit wherever she went.

Leila took the little girls wearing the hijab in her stride. 'Their scarf keeps the sun off their heads, Mummy'. They ran around the place, racing up and down the steps to the Blue Mosque, jumping over the low hedges, buying sesame snacks and generally giving their parents the usual hard time. Sometimes, we'd see little boys dressed in sumptuous Ottoman tunics and sharwal, and wearing a feathered hat. She assumed they were celebrating their birthdays. (We decided not to tell her that they had just been circumcised.)

Leila was thoroughly romanced by the Blue Mosque and Topkapi Palace. She took in the architecture, the Islamic gardens, the jewellery, pottery, ornate costumes, arms on display, and all of this prompted imaginary stories about beautiful queens, valiant kings, as well as their own happy-ever-after children: the princes and princesses."

Susan Wicht

▶▶ Attitudes toward marital status tend to be conservative, so if you're unmarried or a single parent, think about how you'll handle reactions to your status and discuss it with your children, too.

▶▶ To avoid showing underwear, get your children to sit with their legs together or to one side when sitting on the floor; also check that they don't point their feet at anyone nearby – this is considered an insult.

▶▶ Ask your children not to point with fingers (use the whole hand instead), and don't pat children on the head; in many places, the former is considered to be a lewd gesture and the latter disrespectful.

▶▶ When visiting homes, the areas outside may be family graveyards, so don't let the children run around without asking first.

Clothing

▶▶ The standard advice of keeping legs and arms covered extends to children: go for trousers or longish skirts for girls, and if your boys wear shorts, they should be long enough to cover the knees.

▶▶ As tattoos can be taboo, leave body stickers for the children behind.

Eating

▶▶ Get your children to wash their hands before a meal, even if they aren't dirty, and to only use the right hand to eat; the left is considered unclean.

▶▶ In most households, everyone – children included – is expected to finish every last scrap of food, so to avoid offending anyone, allow your children to accept only small amounts to begin with. It's fine to ask for food to be put back in the pot if it remains untouched, but any food or drink that's been handled or fiddled with can't be used by anyone else. Partly because of this, parents often finish whatever their children can't eat before serving their own meal.

▶▶ Some food items, particularly bread and dates, have special cultural and/or religious significance, so don't let the children play with these, and make sure they eat what they take.

Greetings

▶▶ While men and boys might not extend a hand to greet women or girls, or even make eye contact (it can be considered a sign of disrespect), small children are often expected to kiss and be kissed by men and women alike – so prime your kids if you think they'll object.

Segregation of the sexes

▶▶ In the Arabian Gulf Arab states, segregation of the sexes is a part of daily life, so don't assume that you can go everywhere together as a family. You will be able to eat out together, but expect separate hours for women in parks, swimming pools and Turkish baths; women are usually able to take young children of both sexes with them.

▶▶ In general, boys are given more leeway to be curious and run around than girls, which can be a headache if your tomboy daughter understandably wants to go everywhere that her brother is allowed – either stick to places where all your children can be themselves, or compensate girls when they're left out.

NORTH AMERICA

Canada, Greenland, St Pierre and Miquelon, USA (including Hawaii)

With its first-class infrastructure and 24–7 service hours for everything from restaurants to pharmacies, **North America** is a particularly easy place for travels with your family. Facilities specifically for children are excellent, but even if you don't plan on going to theme parks and the like, you can expect plenty to keep kids happy – in fact, prepare to spend a fair bit of time tearing them away from carousels, balloons and toyshops, and to return home loaded up with more toys than when you arrived. There are also numerous publications and guides aimed at parents, with ideas of things to do and detailed information on logistics.

Most children will find plenty of references to help them feel at home here; after all, this is the land of Cowboys and Indians and Dr Seuss's *The Cat in the Hat*, as well as comics and cartoons from Mickey Mouse, Casper and the Flintstones all the way up to Archie and all the superheroes.

LOGISTICS

Child's car seats

▶▶ Car rental companies will provide child car seats on request, but bear in mind that the regulations for using them vary from state to state within the USA – check ⓦwww.nhtsa.dot.gov for a breakdown.

▶▶ When taking internal flights, some airlines insist on using FDA-approved seats, so if you're bringing a seat from home, check if it'll be OK.

Child discounts

▶▶ Pre-school children get discounted fares or go for free on most public transport, and the same applies to attractions, although if you have several young children, you may find that just one child gets the discount.

Food

▶▶ Bear in mind that when eating out in the USA, portions can be large enough to feed the entire family, so be prudent when ordering.

Supplies

▶▶ Availability of baby or infant food and nappies/diapers in Canada and the USA is as good as it gets, and there's plenty of choice elsewhere in the region; you'll only need to take start-up supplies from home.

Toilets

▶▶ From city centres to small towns, public toilets are widespread, making for easy road trips with children.

FROM NEW YORK TO SANTA FE

"We lived in the States for eighteen months, starting with a baby and ending with a toddler. During that time we travelled around as much as we could afford to, and it gave us the chance to become familiar with the culture, which I found surprisingly different from England. I thought I knew what America would be like, having seen plenty of it on television over the years, but I hadn't a clue. I also worked out that there are several different versions of America: rural, urban, New England, California . . .

How much fun you have with a child in the States depends a good deal on where you go. New York itself is like London ('You, with the pushchair! You're in the way! Die, scum, die!'), but in upstate New York I felt comfortable enough to ask a total stranger to please wipe the snotty nose of the infant in the carrier on my back. And he did ('Gee, sure! Hey honey, let me see that nose!'); mind you, it was a very hippy, right-on bit of upstate New York. Struggling out of the bank, with the same tot in a pushchair, another man leapt to our assistance, holding the door wide. 'Thanks!', I said. 'Say, well, I guess it really does take a village!', he exclaimed, clearly expecting me to know the rest of the quote ' . . . to raise a child'.

It's not just where you go, either, it's who you meet. Travelling in the southwest, we pitched camp for a few days at a fairly basic campsite near Santa Fe. Soon after we arrived, we watched a huge RV reversing into the spot next door, dwarfing our little tent. We expected the usual couple of perky 'seniors'. But no – out popped a youngish chap with an elderly dog, both of them very amiable. 'Say, honey', he said to the tot, 'do you wanna pet the doggie?'. Later that day his boyfriend, huge and butch and head to toe in leathers, turned up on a Harley. He opened the luggage carrier on the back of the bike and carefully extracted . . . an arrangement of lilies. The tot, sadly, was far too young to be awestruck by this as I was.

She was much more impressed by our neighbour the other side. He had set up there for the summer, offering massages as a way of making money. He mellowed towards her instantly, and a few days later, when we were about to go and were busily packing, he (having already fed us breakfast) brought out his bubble kit to keep her entertained. Huge bubbles, two or three feet across, glistened and shimmered amongst the dry trees and the parched ground. It kept her blissfully entranced as we heaved everything into the car and prepared for another epic drive.

Everything about America is huge. The malls are huge. The portions are huge. The distances are huge – and it's these things that are the real challenge with a small child. It doesn't look too far on the map from upstate New York to Boston, but I think it took us about five hours. Crossing the vast distances of the Navajo Nation, we kept the tot occasionally quiet with bribes of beef jerky, but even so, she howled her way across a lot of desert. Before we took the rental car back, her father spent quite a while picking shards of spat-out jerky off the upholstery."

Rebecca Blackmore

CUSTOMS, ETIQUETTE AND CULTURAL INSIGHTS

General etiquette

▶▶ In Canada, thanks to the "Anywhere, Anytime" campaign, you can breastfeed openly in most places. Elsewhere, just follow your instincts or ask before feeding, perhaps taking your cue from local women.

Clothing

▶▶ Relaxed dress codes are part of the charm of travel in North America – your children can stay in shorts and sneakers the whole time if they want.

Greetings

▶▶ How children greet others is pretty much up to them, as people tend to be very informal; nevertheless, a Maam, Sir or equivalents will always go down well.

SOUTH AND CENTRAL AMERICA

Argentina, Belize, Bolivia, Brazil, Chile, Colombia, Costa Rica, Ecuador, El Salvador, the Falkland Islands, French Guiana, Guatemala, Guyana, Honduras, Mexico, Nicaragua, Panama, Paraguay, Peru, Surinam, Uruguay, Venezuela

With wide open spaces, sprawling ranches, llamas and colourful markets, **South and Central America** offer plenty to keep both children and adults absorbed, and it's easy to do things together without making a special effort to find activities geared just for the children. Getting off the beaten track is particularly tempting here given the spectacular and varied scenery, but you do need to check security advice before heading into the hinterland, as safe areas within a country or even a neighbourhood can border others that represent a high risk for outsiders.

If you're travelling without your child's other parent, you may need to carry parental consent papers (see p.42–3) in some countries; this is particularly relevant where adoption by expatriates is common (such as in Colombia), but also within Brazil, where such papers may be examined when crossing state borders; check with your destination's local embassy before you leave home.

LOGISTICS

Child discounts

▶▶ Reduced rates on public transport and at attractions vary, but in general, pre-school children will go free or get discounts if the site or bus/train is government-run.

Food

▶▶ Children won't have problems with the food here (although they might not take kindly to the idea of eating guinea pig or *cuy*); there'll be plenty of grilled meats, corn pancakes, manioc or plantain chips and fresh fruit juices, and hot chocolate which – particularly in cold mountain weather – is worth sampling. Vegetarians can have a hard time, as even the typical bean dishes – *frijoles* – tend to have meat in them.

▶▶ Other than in Mexico, where some food and even tamarind and mango-based sweets can be loaded with chillies, food tends to be plainly seasoned and arrives with optional chilli sauces (*aji*); take care as some of these are easily confused with ketchup.

▶▶ If you want no-fuss, fast service when it comes to eating out, there are plenty of international chain restaurants as well as self-service *comida a kilo* places, where dishes are laid out in a buffet and you pay by weight.

Supplies

▶▶ You'll get baby food, infant formula and nappies/diapers in most cities and

TRAVELLERS' TALES

CHILE WITH THE CHILDREN

"My husband's family comes from Chile, mine is from Madrid. We started travelling to Chile soon after we first met, and have been doing so ever since – it's now the children's second home.

We usually start each trip with some time with the family, and then rent a car and go exploring on our own. There are a few contrasts which strike us each time we arrive, like the night sky – the children love the fact that the stars are the other way around. The moon is different, too: in Spanish, we have a phrase about the growing (cresciente) and waning (descresciente) moon, which helps us to remember that it looks like a "C" when it's waning and a "D" when it's growing – but of course, it's all the other way around in Chile. There is also the particular formality and polished manners of the Chileans; I used to have to remind the children to practise their manners, but now they instinctively know how to fit in.

Our time with my in-laws (for me at least) is not without problems, but actually represents welcome comfort. They live on large sprawling grounds nestled in very beautiful countryside – perfect for letting the children loose.

If you go, do prepare your children for the insects; some are HUGE. Amaya, our younger daughter, used to have no trouble picking up large beetles and moths. She even managed to play with the hairy Chilean spiders called araña pollito ('little chicken spider') which look like tarantulas – Chilean children keep these as pets. Nowadays, however, she has transformed from tomboy into the little lady, and is more likely to scream at the sight of them instead.

I always save some time for the craft shops; you get the old traditional stuff as well as inspiring work by new artists; and these shops know how to cater for parents, with parrots or other animals to keep children busy. I usually pick up some wooden games and puzzles made out of a local wood called madera de raulí – they make great presents for children at home.

In terms of food, the spices are simple which works well for children. Our favourites include pastel de choclo, a minced beef dish topped with a layer of ground sweet corn, similar to shepherd's pie. Then there are humitas, ground corn (and sometimes a few herbs) steamed within the corn leaf. Sandwiches of mini-steaks laced with salads are other favourites. And when it comes to sweets, try milhojas de manjar, flaky pastry layered with toffee-like condensed milk called manjar – it's delicious."

Beatriz Alvarez-Castillo

large towns, but availability is sporadic in rural areas, so take what you need with you.

Toilets

▶▶ Most are of the Western type, but there are few public facilities, and you'll have to pay to use those that exist; there's sometimes a charge for toilet paper too, so take your own.

CUSTOMS, ETIQUETTE AND CULTURAL INSIGHTS

General etiquette

▶▶ When visiting ancient ruins, bear in mind that people may consider them hallowed grounds, so take care not to let your children run around or be too noisy.

Clothing

▶▶ On special occasions and on Sundays, little girls may be dressed up like princesses, with a dusting of makeup and their hair styled into ringlets; it's a good idea to bring along some fancy outfits for the kids to help them fit in.

▶▶ If you're going to the beach, outright nudity should be avoided; even on beaches famous for beautiful bodies and skimpy swimsuits, local children tend to get carefully dressed and undressed behind towels, or arrive in their swimsuits and dry off before leaving to avoid changing in public.

Greetings

▶▶ Expect a little old-world formality here, and prime your children to use "Don" and "Doña", or "Señor" and "Señora" when addressing adults. Conversely, prepare them to expect more than the usual amount of hugs and kisses, even from new acquaintances.

WESTERN EUROPE

Andorra, Austria, Azores, Balearic Islands, Belgium, Canary Islands, Denmark, Faroe Islands, Finland, France, Germany, Gibraltar, Greece, Iceland, Ireland, Italy, Liechtenstein, Luxembourg, Madeira, Malta, Monaco, Netherlands, Norway, Portugal, San Marino, Sardinia, Sicily, Spain, Sweden, Switzerland, United Kingdom

Europe has to be one of the easiest destinations to travel with your children – the excellent infrastructure and relatively short distances mean you'll rarely be far from transport or food. Furthermore, you won't need to work too hard to seek out entertainment specifically designed for children – even the smallest village will have a playground, and there are plenty of publications that detail events for children, from dedicated magazines like *Kids Out* in London to listings in daily newspapers. Wherever you go, though, bear in mind that in some countries (such as the Netherlands and Switzerland), schools may be closed all day or in the afternoon on Wednesdays, which means that attractions popular with children tend to be packed. In Spain, meanwhile, you can take advantage of the siesta, usually 2–5pm, when shops and attractions close – fall into the rhythm and get your children to take afternoon naps so that they can enjoy later nights out.

Europe is the source of a great deal of children's **literature**, and it's great to be able to read the Asterix and Tintin books or the classic fairytales to your kids in the places in which they're set. They might also get a kick out of the fact that kings and queens still exist here – and live in real castles. And as Europe is the home of so many **foods** that tend to be children's favourites – pasta, pizza, chips, ice-cream, chocolate – you can also bank on finding plenty for them to tuck into.

LOGISTICS

Child's car seats
▶▶ Major car rental companies will provide seats on request, and cars will invariably have seatbelts in the back.

Child discounts
▶▶ Reductions for families are standard on public transport, although you might need to have photographs and ID in order to buy discount cards. You can also expect reductions or free entry at national monuments and museums.

Eating out
▶▶ Pubs and places predominantly oriented to drinking alcohol usually have restrictions for children – they might not be allowed in at all, and if they are, they may have to stick to special areas or clear out by early evening. However many countries – Spain, Greece and Italy, for example – are particularly renowned for making children welcome in restaurants, even for late-night dining.

Supplies
▶▶ Infant formula, baby food and nappies/diapers are widely available, both in the cities and smaller villages or towns.

Swimming gear
▶▶ Boys (and men) may be refused entry to public pools unless they wear close-fitting trunks; this is particularly common in France. Similarly, long hair might have to be tucked into a swimming hat.

Toilets

▶▶ Public toilets are generally widespread, though you often have to pay to use them – make sure you carry a stock of small change.

CUSTOMS, ETIQUETTE AND CULTURAL INSIGHTS

General etiquette

▶▶ Sweden was the first of the Nordic countries to make it illegal to hit children, and has been joined by Finland, Denmark and Norway – so don't smack your children here.

Clothing

▶▶ Attitudes to clothing are wildly different across Europe. People in some countries tend to be conservative, and expect children to be modestly dressed, with underwear and bellies well out of sight. Elsewhere, particularly along the Mediterranean coast or in Nordic countries, you might run into lots of topless bathing or even nudist beaches.

Greetings

▶▶ Greetings mostly consist of combinations of handshakes or cheek-kisses; in some places one peck is enough, but in France, Switzerland and Holland, it goes up to two, three and four respectively – children will be excused the ritual if they really don't want to join in.

▶▶ Ask children to use the usual greetings with the formal term for elders: "Monsieur" or "Madame" in French; "Señor" or "Señora" in Spanish, and so on.

TRAVELLERS' TALES

DUTCH CRUISING

"When our son Callum was 6 months old, my partner Ian and I spent our summer holiday cruising the waterways of the southern Netherlands, directly across the Channel from our boat's mooring on England's east coast. Looking back, we were sailing novices, really, and the fact that the North Sea lay between us and our destination probably should have put us off. But it didn't.

Impatient to get away, we set off after a week of heavy gales, and endured a day and a half of grey, swollen seas as a result. For much of the trip I was trapped down below with the baby, secure but with no fresh air or horizon to view, and with the boat pitching like a wild rocking horse. Sure enough, I was sick as a dog, but the baby was unperturbed by the lurching movements and smiled and gurgled all the way. Setting eyes on the Dutch coastline at sunrise, with the sea flat calm and a stunning red sky, the world seemed quite a different place.

The next four weeks were spent learning how to get through all shapes and sizes of locks, exploring pretty little hamlets, visiting local festivals and buying fresh market produce in the ports. When a breeze was in the air, we would cover some miles, but most of time – with a baby on board – we were content just to do short hops and spend most of our time on land. We found a wonderful three-wheeler buggy in a surf shop one day (just before they became fashionable and expensive), and then nothing could stop us.

Moorings for the night were pretty and tidy market towns that felt relaxed and easy to be in. One of the best parts was being moored alongside other families and sharing sailing stories over a beer. There's a special bond between sailors that makes friendships quick and easy to forge, especially when there are children around. One evening we discovered how some Dutch sailors ensure that they enjoy a full holiday experience despite having young children. We were moored alongside a barge occupied by a couple with their tiny baby; when night fell, they got their best clothes on, climbed on shore and swanned off to dinner in a restaurant overlooking the water. We looked at each other with concern, but later they showed us their hi-tech baby monitor, which would apparently pick up their baby's cries within a one-mile radius, allowing them a relaxed night out. After many a boat-bound night, we were full of envy, but I'm still not sure if I would have trusted the gadget enough to do the same."

Juliet Heller

CHAPTER 4. AROUND THE WORLD

UK & Ireland

Britain
Devon & Cornwall
Dublin **D**
Edinburgh **D**
England
Ireland
The Lake District
London
London **D**
London Mini Guide
Scotland
Scottish Highlands
 & Islands
Wales

Europe

Algarve **D**
Amsterdam
Amsterdam **D**
Andalucía
Athens **D**
Austria
Baltic States
Barcelona
Barcelona **D**
Belgium &
 Luxembourg
Berlin
Brittany & Normandy
Bruges **D**
Brussels
Budapest
Bulgaria
Copenhagen
Corfu
Corsica
Costa Brava **D**
Crete
Croatia
Cyprus
Czech & Slovak
 Republics
Denmark
Dodecanese & East
 Aegean Islands
Dordogne & The Lot
Europe
Florence & Siena
Florence **D**
France
Germany
Gran Canaria **D**
Greece
Greek Islands

Hungary
Ibiza & Formentera **D**
Iceland
Ionian Islands
Italy
The Italian Lakes
Languedoc &
 Roussillon
Lanzarote &
 Fuerteventura **D**
Lisbon **D**
The Loire Valley
Madeira **D**
Madrid **D**
Mallorca **D**
Mallorca & Menorca
Malta & Gozo **D**
Menorca
Moscow
The Netherlands
Norway
Paris
Paris **D**
Paris Mini Guide
Poland
Portugal
Prague
Prague **D**
Provence
 & the Côte D'Azur
Pyrenees
Romania
Rome
Rome **D**
Sardinia
Scandinavia
Sicily
Slovenia
Spain
St Petersburg
Sweden
Switzerland
Tenerife &
 La Gomera **D**
Turkey
Tuscany & Umbria
Venice & The Veneto
Venice **D**
Vienna

Asia

Bali & Lombok
Bangkok
Beijing

Cambodia
China
Goa
Hong Kong & Macau
Hong Kong
 & Macau **D**
India
Indonesia
Japan
Kerala
Laos
Malaysia, Singapore
 & Brunei
Nepal
The Philippines
Rajasthan, Dehli
 & Agra
Singapore
Singapore **D**
South India
Southeast Asia
Sri Lanka
Taiwan
Thailand
Thailand's Beaches
 & Islands
Tokyo
Vietnam

Australasia

Australia
Melbourne
New Zealand
Sydney

North America

Alaska
Baja California
Boston
California
Canada
Chicago
Colorado
Florida
The Grand Canyon
Hawaii
Honolulu **D**
Las Vegas **D**
Los Angeles
Maui **D**
Miami & South Florida
Montréal
New England
New Orleans **D**
New York City

New York City **D**
New York City Mini
 Guide
Orlando & Walt
 Disney World® **D**
Pacific Northwest
San Francisco
San Francisco **D**
Seattle
Southwest USA
Toronto
USA
Vancouver
Washington DC
Washington DC **D**
Yellowstone & The
 Grand Tetons
Yosemite

Caribbean
& Latin America

Antigua & Barbuda **D**
Argentina
Bahamas
Barbados **D**
Belize
Bolivia
Brazil
Cancún & Cozumel **D**
Caribbean
Central America
Chile
Costa Rica
Cuba
Dominican Republic
Dominican Republic **D**
Ecuador
Guatemala
Jamaica
Mexico
Peru
St Lucia **D**
South America
Trinidad & Tobago
Yúcatan

Africa & Middle East

Cape Town & the
 Garden Route
Dubai **D**
Egypt
Gambia
Jordan

D: Rough Guide
DIRECTIONS for
short breaks

Available from all good bookstores

ROUGH GUIDES

Complete Listing

ROUGH
GUIDES

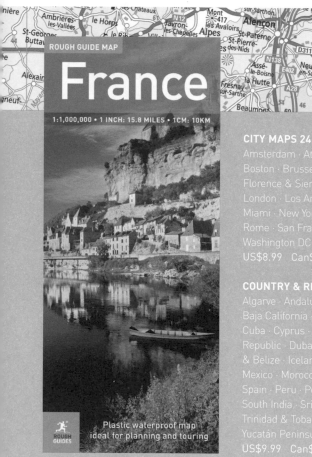

SMALL PRINT & INDEX 5

A Rough Guide to Rough Guides

Published in 1982, the first Rough Guide – to Greece – was a student scheme that became a publishing phenomenon. Mark Ellingham, a recent graduate in English from Bristol University, had been travelling in Greece the previous summer and couldn't find the right guidebook. With a small group of friends he wrote his own guide, combining a highly contemporary, journalistic style with a thoroughly practical approach to travellers' needs.

The immediate success of the book spawned a series that rapidly covered dozens of destinations. And, in addition to impecunious backpackers, Rough Guides soon acquired a much broader and older readership that relished the guides' wit and inquisitiveness as much as their enthusiastic, critical approach and value-for-money ethos.

These days, Rough Guides include recommendations from shoestring to luxury and cover more than 200 destinations around the globe, including almost every country in the Americas and Europe, more than half of Africa and most of Asia and Australasia. Our ever-growing team of authors and photographers is spread all over the world, particularly in Europe, the USA and Australia.

In the early 1990s, Rough Guides branched out of travel, with the publication of Rough Guides to World Music, Classical Music and the Internet. All three have become benchmark titles in their fields, spearheading the publication of a wide range of books under the Rough Guide name.

Including the travel series, Rough Guides now number more than 350 titles, covering: phrasebooks, waterproof maps, music guides from Opera to Heavy Metal, reference works as diverse as Conspiracy Theories and Shakespeare, and popular culture books from iPods to Poker. Rough Guides also produce a series of more than 120 World Music CDs in partnership with World Music Network.

Visit www.roughguides.com to see our latest publications.

Rough Guide travel images are available for commercial licensing at www.roughguidespictures.com

Rough Guide credits

Text editor: Polly Thomas
Design and layout: Diana Jarvis
Picture editor: Sarah Cummins, Jj Luck
Production: Vicky Baldwin
Proofreader: Elaine Pollard, Stewart Wild, Róisín Cameron
Cover design: Chloë Roberts
Editorial: **London** Kate Berens, Claire Saunders, Ruth Blackmore, Alison Murchie, Karoline Densley, Andy Turner, Keith Drew, Edward Aves, Nikki Birrell, Alice Park, Sarah Eno, Lucy White, Jo Kirby, James Smart, Natasha Foges, Róisín Cameron, Emma Traynor, Emma Gibbs, James Rice, Kathryn Lane, Joe Staines, Duncan Clark, Peter Buckley, Matthew Milton, Tracy Hopkins, Ruth Tidball; **New York** Andrew Rosenberg, Steven Horak, AnneLise Sorensen, Amy Hegarty, April Isaacs, Ella Steim, Anna Owens, Joseph Petta, Sean Mahoney; **Delhi** Madhavi Singh, Karen D'Souza
Design & Pictures: **London** Scott Stickland, Dan May, Diana Jarvis, Mark Thomas, Jj Luck, Chloë Roberts, Nicole Newman, Sarah Cummins; **Delhi** Umesh Aggarwal, Ajay Verma, Jessica Subramanian, Ankur Guha, Pradeep Thapliyal, Sachin Tanwar, Anita Singh
Production: Rebecca Short, Vicky Baldwin
Cartography: **London** Maxine Repath, Ed Wright, Katie Lloyd-Jones; **Delhi** Jai Prakash Mishra, Rajesh Chhibber, Ashutosh Bharti, Rajesh Mishra, Animesh Pathak, Jasbir Sandhu, Karobi Gogoi, Amod Singh, Alakananda Bhattacharya, Swati Handoo
Online: **New York** Jennifer Gold, Kristin Mingrone; **Delhi** Manik Chauhan, Narender Kumar, Rakesh Kumar, Amit Kumar, Amit Verma, Rahul Kumar, Ganesh Sharma, Debojit Borah
Marketing & Publicity: **London** Liz Statham, Niki Hanmer, Louise Maher, Jess Carter, Vanessa Godden, Vivienne Watton, Anna Paynton, Rachel Sprackett; **New York** Geoff Colquitt, Megan Kennedy, Katy Ball; **Delhi** Reem Khokhar
Manager India: Punita Singh
Series Editor: Mark Ellingham
Reference Director: Andrew Lockett
Publishing Coordinator: Helen Phillips
Publishing Director: Martin Dunford
Commercial Manager: Gino Magnotta
Managing Director: John Duhigg

Publishing information

This 1st edition published January 2008 by
Rough Guides Ltd,
80 Strand, London WC2R 0RL
345 Hudson St, 4th Floor,
New York, NY 10014, USA
14 Local Shopping Centre, Panchsheel Park,
New Delhi 110017, India
Distributed by the Penguin Group
Penguin Books Ltd,
80 Strand, London WC2R 0RL
Penguin Group (USA)
375 Hudson Street, NY 10014, USA
Penguin Group (Australia)
250 Camberwell Road, Camberwell,
Victoria 3124, Australia
Penguin Books Canada Ltd,
10 Alcorn Avenue, Toronto, Ontario,
Canada M4V 1E4
Penguin Group (NZ)
67 Apollo Drive, Mairangi Bay, Auckland 1310,
New Zealand

Cover concept by Peter Dyer.
Printed in China
© Rough Guides 2008

224pp includes index
A catalogue record for this book is available from the British Library
ISBN: 978-1-84353-704-5

1   3   5   7   9   8   6   4   2

Help us update

We've gone to a lot of effort to ensure that the 1st edition of **The Rough Guide to Travelling with Babies and young Children** is accurate and up to date. However, things change – places get "discovered", opening hours are notoriously fickle, restaurants and rooms raise prices or lower standards. If you feel we've got it wrong or left something out, we'd like to know, and if you can remember the address, the price, the time, the phone number, so much the better.

We'll credit all contributions, and send a copy of the next edition (or any other Rough Guide if you prefer) for the best letters. Everyone who writes to us and isn't already a subscriber will receive a copy of our full-colour thrice-yearly newsletter. Please mark letters: "**Rough Guide Travelling with Babies and young Children Update**" and send to: Rough Guides, 80 Strand, London WC2R 0RL, or Rough Guides, 345 Hudson St, 4th Floor, New York, NY 10014. Or send an email to **mail@roughguides.com** Have your questions answered and tell others about your trip at
www.roughguides.atinfopop.com

Acknowledgements

The list of people who generously lent their experience to this book makes it a slippery task to thank them all. Many unnamed individuals gave their time graciously, despite being interrupted in their busy jobs; such persons include those working in airline reservations, security, manning airports and stations, and those answering helplines for embassies, insurance firms, consuls and hotels – a few, but not all, are named below.

Dr Richard Dawood, author of Travellers' Health, and Dr Andres de Francisco, of the Global Forum for Health Research, reviewed the health-related material. Ancient friends Rebecca Spencer-Smith, Juliet Heller, Tanya and Lilly Cochrane, Katherine Lowe and Gritta Weil reviewed early drafts and helped in many practical and loving ways. Kristina Mänd and Sharifin Dickie brought their many talents to the "Around the World" section. Juliet Heller, Tanya Cochrane, Jo Ralling and Kiki Goshay helped enormously with their networking skills, opening up their address books in ways that sometimes put them on the line. Gloria Rosso and Susan Maheu – parents of children with special needs – helped with networking with others. Through them, the book has been enriched in many little and not so little ways. Deborah Gilbert of One Parent Families provided access to people and information; through this dialogue, I've come to have enormous appreciation for the challenges that lone parents face.

Additional grandparents, parents and children who contributed directly to the contents are: Atsen Ahua (Nigeria); Ismail Alatise (Nigeria); Beatriz Alvarez-Castillo (Chile/Spain); San Amalan; Shushma Amatya (Nepal); Gillian Anderson; Inez Azevedo (Brazil); Elvira Bacci (Philippines); Mazuwa Banda (Zambia); Rebecca Blackmore (UK); Paulus Bloem (Netherlands); J.D. Bonaya (Kenya); Nina Castillo-Carandang (Philippines); Zeba R. Choudhury; Lilly, Tanya and Tom Cochrane); L.C.; Alicia Cogollos; Sarah Cohen; Louis and Virginia Currat; Evelyn Dabrowski; Fu Da Ming (China); Bernadette Daelmans; Ian Daglish; Juan and Ricardo de Francisco Rasheed; Fardiyah and Hussein Dickie (Austria); Sharifin Dickie (Austria, Israel, South Africa); Paul Dittmer; Tanith Dixon (Australia); Nezha Drissi (Morocco); Charles Dunant; Peter Duncan; Tracy Edwards; Sarah Edwards and students from the Campus des Nations, International Schools of Geneva; Hugo Edwards; Kate Fawkes; Maria Fernanda Ferreira (Portugal); Lorna and Ruby Fray (Uganda); Jane Fuss; Debs Gilbert; Nancy Gautier; Sabina Groenweg; Andy Hall; Niki Hanmer; Alan and Matthew Heason; Juliet Heller (Netherlands); Alexandra and Susan Jeffords; Irene Kaliba (Uganda); Frank Kay; Paul Keenan (the Family Fund); Patricia Kehoe (Australia); Liesbeth Keulemans (Indonesia); Lisa Kerrigan; S.K. (Nepal); Annabel, Claire and Monty Kilpatrick; Jasmine Kline; Leueen Laing (Zimbabwe); Simon Laing (China and the USA); Mary Anne Lansang (Philippines); Agnes Leotsakos (Greece); Katherine Lowe; Kumiko Machida (Japan); M.M.; Suzanne Maheu; Halfdan Mahler; Kristina Mänd (CIS countries/Baltic States, various European countries); Ljubov Mänd (Caucasus); Elizabeth Mason; Tim McNally; Naureen Mullick; Nguyen Thi Bao Tam (Vietnam); Peter Morris; Fahmi Mursaleen (Gulf States); Pater Mwaba (Zambia); Jamie Oliver; Julia Ormond; Anna Rankin; Jean-Charles Puippe; Ishtiaq Rahman; Jahanara and Sabrina Rasheed (Bangladesh); Melissa Reardon (USA, Portugal, Germany, Italy); Paul Ress; Jan Reynders (Netherlands); Dinah Robertson; Felicity Rolland; Gloria Rosso; Francois Rouf; Roxana Salam (Yemen); Nishana Schneider (South African Airlines); Banu Singh; Felicity Rolland; Sanchita Sinha Roy (Seychelles); Gloria Serpa-Kolbe (Colombia); Rebecca Spencer-Smith; Becca Stanford (USA, Sri Lanka); John Stanford (Royal Association for Disability and Rehabilitation); Monica Stoll (Brazil); Hilary Stock; Ben Stringer; Lisa Stringer; Simone Sultana (South Africa); Bob Taylor (Thailand); Charlotte Tidball; Rafael Ugaldi (Cuba); Sharuna Verghis (Malaysia); Duncan Vernon; Miriam Vicentini (Brazil); Susan Wicht (Turkey); Ryan Williams (Jamaica); Wendy and Patric Zito. Officials from the Embassies of Algeria, Bhutan, Brazil, Cuba, Dominican Republic, Honduras, Kenya, Morocco, Nigeria, Trinidad and Tobago, Saudi Arabia, United Arab Emirates and Vietnam helped with information on their countries.

Martyn Page at Dorling Kindersley first spotted the potential of the project; he helped place my file at the right desk and provided invaluable advice. Martin Dunford, Publishing Director at Rough Guides, took the project on – serendipity was on my side as he had recently become a father and was deliberating a long-haul trip to New York when I got in touch. I owe him much, including his support for various ideas that inevitably put extra demands on the team. Kate Berens helped me muddle through the early stages and inspired confidence through her professionalism. I also credit Kate for linking me up with Polly Thomas, the Senior Editor at Rough Guides. Polly not only knows her craft inside out, but has an uncanny way of knowing where you are going when you are least able to define it for yourself. She never rubbished work which sorely deserved it, but kept the project moving through a subtle process of well-timed words of encouragement, by example, and what appeared to be a bit of telepathy as well; waiting for her edits and discussions was something I came to look forward to. Vivienne Watton also appeared just at the right moment when I needed help with celebrities; Nikki Hanmer, Head of Marketing, had a baby right on cue in the middle of the project; and the superb design team, led by Diana Jarvis, did an incredible job to make the book look the way it does.

Finally, while thanking one's family is standard, no-one should be in any doubt that without the inspiration, love and support of my rock-steady companion Andres, our fantastic sons Juan and Ricardo, and my own intrepid parents Lydia and Kaiser, this book would simply never have come about.

Photo credits

INDEX

D

E

F

G

H

I

J

L

INDEX

U

V

W

EAGLE VALLEY LIBRARY DISTRICT
P.O. BOX 240   600 BROADWAY
EAGLE, CO 81631   (970) 328-8800